Surf for your life

MICK FANNING

Tim Baker

EBURY
PRESS

An Ebury Press book
Published by Random House Australia Pty Ltd
Level 3, 100 Pacific Highway, North Sydney NSW 2060
www.randomhouse.com.au

First published by Ebury Press in 2009
This edition published in 2011

Addresses for companies within the Random House Group can be found at
www.randomhouse.com.au/offices

National Library of Australia
Cataloguing-in-Publication Entry

Fanning, Mick.
Surf for your life/Mick Fanning & Tim Baker.

ISBN 978 1 74275 035 4 (pbk.)

Fanning, Mick.
Surfers – Australia – Biography.
Surfing – Australia – History.

Other Authors/Contributors:
Baker, Tim.

797.32092

Cover and internal design by Adam Yazxhi/MAXCO
All cover images by Jon Frank
Typeset by Midland Typesetters, Australia
Printed in Australia by Griffin Press, an accredited ISO AS/NZS 14001:2004
Environmental Management System printer

To Mum and Dad, for creating me;
Rachel, Peter and Edward, for teaching me so many life lessons;
Sean, for direction and guidance;
my best friends, for keeping me grounded;
and Karissa, for being the love of my life.

This book is not a biography. I feel I'm too young and still have many episodes of my life to explore. These are just some of the lessons I have learned so far. They are my experiences, and at no point am I claiming that I am right or wrong – make sure you make your own decisions in life. Books like these are just guidance tools; they are there for you to experiment with to find out what works for you. I hope you enjoy it, and if you learn something or gain some guidance or inspiration then that was the main aim. When Tim and I sat down and decided to do this book, he suggested I try and write it as if I was writing to myself at age sixteen – the knowledge, advice, guidance and experience I would have liked to have had imparted to me as a grommet just embarking on the surfing life. That's what I've tried to do. If this book helps anyone get the most of their surfing, take on new challenges or avoid some of life's pitfalls, then I'll consider it a success. Happy surfing and enjoy the ride.

CONTENTS

INTRODUCTION

'I just want my kids to be happy and free, and surfing does that for them. I want them to have the opportunities to do what they want to do. I'm so grateful to surfing. It's taught my boys so much – a love of the environment – what more could you ask for? It's wonderful . . . It's been the best thing that's ever happened to our family. I had no money and five children – surfing was great for me. If you got them a board and a pair of board shorts, that was all they needed.' Liz Osborne, Mick's mum

'I think if one of us made it, we'd all make it . . . We all thrive on each other's goals.' Dean Morrison, aged 16, on him and his fellow Cooly Kids

'You knock on my daydream door and I say warmly come right in. I'm glad you're here with me again. Then we sit down and have a chat.' Dedication written by Mick on a surfboard commemorating his brother Sean's life

1

'Che Guevara said, "You must be tough but not lose your kindness." I can see that in Fanning. He is kind of a new surfing soul . . . Looking at Fanning, we can see his passion for life. He is not just trying to be a better surfer than the others. He is trying to be a better surfer than himself.' Website message posted to Mick from a fan in Joao Paulo, Brazil

'I was kidding myself for a few years that it was me providing Mick with insights, but I've finally realised he's the one giving me insights. And now he's gone to texting me and emailing me with tips about the team and, even scarier, I'm listening.' Matt Elliott, coach of the Penrith Panthers NRL team

'He's very widely read, but as I said to him last year, he can stop reading self-help books now. I think it's time to write one. And I was pretty serious. He's got more to give than he has to learn.' Phil McNamara, Mick's coach

HOW DOES IT FEEL?

Mick Fanning might only be twenty-eight but he already knows how a lot of stuff feels that most of us never will. How does it feel to lose a brother? Win a world title? Rip your hamstring muscle clean off the bone? Weave through a zippering Superbank barrel for twenty or thirty seconds or paddle over the ledge at places like Pipeline and Teahupo'o? Have scoliosis so bad you can't get off the floor? Address the NSW State of Origin team before a match, bowl to Matty Hayden or have Dave Warner belt you for consecutive sixes at the SCG? Walk into the bar of a Brazilian hotel dressed in a G-string bikini to make your mates laugh, only to find your mates have left, and there is only a puzzled bartender staring blankly at you?

You'll notice that not all these experiences fall neatly on one side of the ledger of good or bad. Mick's journey so far has definitely been a mixed bag, but it is the extremes of that journey that make him so interesting. And it's his readiness to learn from each experience and use it as fuel to drive him on that might provide lessons for the rest of us.

I don't want to pretend Mick is smarter, deeper or more virtuous than he really is. Get him at the wrong time (or the right time, depending on how you like your sports stars) and you'll find him as loud, drunken and uncouth as any NRL boofhead. This is a man, after all, whose signature sandal comes with a built-in bottle opener in the heel; who is the face of a recent Victoria Bitter ad campaign; whose alter ego, Eugene, is known to emerge in the most hideous fashion during rowdy celebrations of contest victories.

But even as a youngster, there was always something a little different about Mick to the average, talented, well-sponsored young surf star in the making. I first interviewed Mick when he was fifteen, along with his mates Joel Parkinson, Dean Morrison and Damon Harvey, known collectively, even then, as the 'Cooly Kids'. I shouted them an all-you-can-eat smorgasbord dinner at Kirra Pizza Hut, to hear about their burgeoning junior careers and the lofty expectations already being piled upon them. Back then, Mick came across as the least confident, the most immature, a little in awe of his more highly fancied peers. 'If I can beat these guys, I'm happy. It's sort of fun. I just want to win something,' he said then.

Even today, twelve years, a world title and many potent doses of life experience later, Mick still exhibits a refreshing lack of ego, a healthy self-deprecating streak, and a loyalty to family and long-time friends that is untouched by the fickle torchlight of fame. 'Down-to-earth' is probably the most common phrase used to describe Mick, or 'unaffected'. This last descriptor, though, is not entirely accurate, because Mick has been deeply affected by what he's been through. Sensitivity to his environment and life's ups and downs is another character trait. But it's his ability to take these things on board and use them to his advantage, to turn poison into power, that really distinguishes him.

By rights, Mick should never even have become a professional surfer, let alone the most successful Australian male surfer of his generation. If you plotted a graph of the likelihood of him ever becoming a world surfing champion, it would have started somewhere down near zero per cent. Born into the western suburbs of Sydney, the fifth and youngest child of British migrants, the original 'ten-pound Poms', with no gene pool of aquatic abilities, there was nothing to indicate the ocean would draw him in. When his parents separated when he was just two, it would have been easy to foresee a life of struggle and disadvantage in outer-suburban oblivion. But a couple of years later an unusual thing occurred. His doting mum, Liz, and her recently estranged husband, John, agreed that their four sons needed to be close to their father, and so they moved north to live with him in the quiet coastal town of

Coffs Harbour, a period Liz now describes as 'the worst time in my life'. Mick's father is an earthmover by trade, a hard-working, no-nonsense man suddenly with sole parenting responsibilities for five young kids. But the Fanning offspring pulled together, took themselves off to the beach, tossed their youngest sibling into the salty brine as if to see if he could float. Mick not only floated, but soon found sport riding atop the gentle rollers off Coff's picturesque beaches and solace for what might have otherwise been a difficult childhood. That probability graph of him becoming a world surfing champion edged gamely upwards in tiny increments, but not for long. After a couple of years by the beach, the children moved back to the western suburbs of Sydney to be with their mum, who could no longer stand the separation. Fortunately for Mick, the saltwater bug had infected his older brothers so acutely that their devoted mum would ferry them all vast distances in her little red Datsun to surf the beaches of the NSW Central and South Coasts on weekends. She'd drop them at the surf in the mornings and pick them up in the afternoons, always confident that no harm would befall them while they played in the ocean.

When Liz's work as a nurse took them north again to Ballina on the NSW North Coast, the graph climbed upwards once more as the surfing addiction took hold. Even so, surfing still came second to soccer in Mick's sporting ambitions. It was only when they moved a short hop further north to the Gold Coast that Mick's surfing prospects really shot up. Meeting boyhood friends and sparring partners Dean Morrison and Joel Parkinson helped shape his pro surfing ambitions and those of his next oldest brother, Sean. The development of Mick's lightning-fast and razor-sharp style leapt ahead in the user-friendly point breaks and beaches of the southern Gold Coast. A string of junior results followed as the three Cooly Kids whipped up their own self-generated tornado of super-competitive, accelerated development.

The tragic death of Mick's much-loved brother Sean in a car accident, when Sean was twenty, could have easily brought it all crashing down. Mick had just turned seventeen, and the two boys had dreamed of travelling on the pro tour together. They had been at the same party only a few minutes before, and Mick had nearly boarded the same vehicle that ploughed into a Norfolk Pine in Boundary Street on the Queensland–New South Wales border with such devastating impact. Mick was walking home from that party when an unmarked police car pulled up and a family friend got out to deliver the cruellest news. Mick was driven home and had to deliver that same awful message to his entire family. The death of Sean and his friend Joel Green rocked the entire twin towns of Tweed Heads and Coolangatta. Mick didn't leave the house for days, barely thought about competing in surfing contests for months.

The local surfing community went into mourning, numbing the pain with a monumental, collective bender. For weeks, you could drive to check the surf in the mornings and see teenage boys passed out in shopfront doorways from the previous evening's savage drinking. No-one would have judged Mick harshly for following the lead of those around him and joining in, but even at seventeen he had different instincts. 'All my mates and everyone were just getting drunk around me. I guess that's how a lot of people grieve. They get drunk,' Mick recalls. 'But I didn't. I just wanted to deal with it in a really clear frame of mind.'

Mick later observed that he felt like he'd grown up ten years in a few weeks in the aftermath. All noted a new steely focus and resolve about Mick, no longer the self-deprecating clown.

The next year, when he was just eighteen, Mick was invited to surf in a specialty pro surfing event, the Konica Skins, along with all the top pro surfers of the day. It was held at Sandon Point, Wollongong, on the NSW South Coast, the same break Liz had dutifully driven her sons to all those years ago. Mick surfed against guys whose posters he'd had stuck on his bedroom wall as a kid – Luke Egan, Occy, Munga Barry – in a sudden-death, winner-take-all format and, against all expectations, emerged victorious. The event was held on what would have been Sean's twenty-first birthday. Mick won exactly $21,000.

From there, it has been a rapid rise to pro surfing glory, always with an almost supernatural air that he is not alone on his journey, that Sean's memory, his spirit even, accompanies and inspires him. Mick speaks of having dreams of Sean every night for a week leading up to his best contest performances, of waking up happy and excited for having seen his brother again. A memorial contest held for Sean and Joel Green each year on the anniversary of their deaths is invariably graced with the presence of whales spouting and slapping their tails out to sea, the occasional dolphin and even a turtle cruising through the line-up. Mick talks matter-of-factly about the appearance of a dolphin during a world-title-deciding heat, or a kookaburra laughing in a tree in his backyard, as his brother's spirit paying him a visit.

In 2001 Mick's career fortunes took another leap when he made the final of the Quiksilver Pro at Snapper Rocks, then a second-tier, World Qualifying Series event. Mick finished second to pro tour pacesetter Taj Burrow, and that graph of his pro surfing career prospects headed skywards once more. Yet, the very next day, like a volatile stock-market report, it plummeted as he was left literally flat on his back and immobile with a nagging spinal condition he'd only just had diagnosed as scoliosis, or curvature of the spine. He'd only surfed through the event with the help of constant chiropractic adjustments and painkillers, and again his surfing future looked in doubt.

He embarked on a dedicated stretching and treatment regime – and the greatest competitive roll of his life. In the sort of domination of the Australian contest circuit not seen since Michael Peterson's other-worldly supremacy in the mid 70s, Mick followed up the second at Snapper with a win at Margaret River in another WQS event. Then, as a wildcard invitee to the world's longest-running pro event at Bells Beach, he again toppled the giants of the day to claim victory. He finished the year in the number-one spot on the WQS and had qualified for the elite World Championship Tour by midyear.

In 2002, his debut season in the WCT, he finished in fifth spot, the best debut by any male surfer apart from nine-time world champion Kelly Slater. He rose to fourth in 2003, his career ascendency apparently set on an unstoppable course to the top.

Then, in 2004, after an uncharacteristically poor start to the season, he embarked on an Indonesian surf charter off the remote west coast of Sumatra, hoping to rekindle his form and enthusiasm.

Instead, he almost destroyed his career. Going for a floater on a five-foot wave, he dropped with the lip, his back foot slipped, and he was pushed literally through his surfboard in the splits, tearing his hamstring off the bone. The footage of the accident is sickening: the wave flings him down like a ragdoll, his body crumpling forward, as if this latest blow was simply too much for even Mick's famous stoicism to bear. A twelve-hour boat ride, three plane flights, a couple of mega-doses of valium and a whole world of pain later, Mick was back in Australia facing lengthy and delicate surgery to try and salvage his career. A metal hook was screwed into his pelvic bone and the torn muscle literally sewn onto the hook. The surgeon lifted his unconscious body off the operating table a few inches by the hook, to test it was securely anchored in the bone. It would take six months for scar tissue to grow over the hook and reattach the muscle more securely. He didn't surf at all for five months. Mick had only been back in the water for three months when he again entered the Quiksilver Pro at Snapper Rocks, simply to see if he could still compete at the elite level. Incredibly, he won the event and finished the season rated number three in the world.

Since then, Mick's rise to surfing greatness has been well-documented – the famous jousts with boyhood friends Dean and Joel, and modern greats Kelly Slater and Andy Irons. The relentless training, the nerveless composure around events, the trademark headphones clamped on before a heat as he enters 'the Zone', his uncanny balance standing on a large inflatable Fitball, eyes pinned to the ocean like lasers scanning the waves for hidden patterns and clues. In the latter stages of 2006 and throughout 2007, he was simply untouchable, staring down challenges from world champs Slater and Irons, and fellow Australians Taj Burrow and Joel Parkinson. The graph of his world title prospects soared as he became an almost unbackable favourite. On a crowded beach in Brazil in October 2007, he returned the men's world surfing title to Australia for the first time in eight years, fulfilling a clear-eyed, recurring vision he'd held in his mind for years.

Now, it is his levels of fitness, dedication and focus that are inspiring his fellow Cooly Kids, as they strive to reach the imposing bar he has set. Yet, in another moment Mick will quietly reflect that there's more to life than surfing contests, reveal some private philanthropic streak – his ambassadorship for World Vision, the family in South Africa he supports – or share his hopes for making a difference to the legions of surfing kids who now idolise him.

Some would say, even with all he has crammed in, Mick is simply too young to be retelling his life story, a work very much in progress, its most telling chapters perhaps still ahead. It was a reservation both Mick and I voiced in the early stages of this book. So don't consider this a biography, as such, but more a manual, or an interim report, on life lessons learnt along the way.

It seems to me Mick has become something of a young master of the kind of stuff that is always trotted out in motivational spiels or life-coaching texts: overcoming adversity, turning negatives into positives, ensuring that what doesn't kill you actually does make you stronger. With a metal hook holding his hamstring muscle in place, a twisted spine that could have left him stooped and crippled, his dead brother's name tattooed on his arm, and a tough upbringing and a fractured family life behind him, it would have been easy to imagine Mick as an embittered victim, numbing life's cruel blows by draining another schooner or wrenching on a bong. To be fit, happy, well-adjusted, staunchly drug-free, gracious and giving to friends and family – even complete strangers – might have been enough of an accomplishment. To have reached the top of his sport with those personal values still intact seems little short of miraculous. When I've been asked to summarise the idea behind this book, the most succinct version I've come up with is: how he's done what he's done, and what he's learnt along the way. For anyone wanting to further their surfing, or even just intent on getting the best out of themselves, I trust there are a few valuable lessons in here.

There is a lot of shallow, false and misguided idolatry of sports stars in this country, based on narrow physical abilities even as their lives wallow in dysfunction. In Mick Fanning, at least, surfing has a champion we can be proud of, who might stand as a role model for rather more than the riding of waves.

LIZ'S STORY, PART 1

It is the great migrant dream, one which has driven human movement across the planet for untold millennia – the search for fresh opportunities and a better life for one's children in some new and unknown land. The Fanning family's implausible migrant's tale is one that has both surpassed their wildest dreams and their worst nightmares, delivering grief and joy, loss and gain in unflinching abundance.

Mick's father, John, grew up in the tiny Irish town of Malin Head, the most northerly, and very nearly the windiest, point of mainland Ireland. He was destined for a simple life as a farmer in the home country when fate intervened. John's mother, Eileen, and youngest brother, Patrick, died of tuberculosis when John was just five. His father, Jack, a gunsmith by trade and a soldier in the Irish army, disappeared soon after. John and his only surviving brother, Francis, were taken in and raised by their aunt and uncle, who already had eight children and an ailing grandmother of their own to care for. Jack Fanning wasn't heard of for many years, until he returned out of the blue and wanted to take Francis with him back to England, where he had been living. The boys' aunt and uncle, who had raised them as their own, insisted that the two brothers could not be separated, and so John went with his father and brother to England against his wishes.

'John was so upset because his heart was in Ireland and he wanted to farm, but he came to England,' remembers Mick's mum, Liz. 'It was a very sad childhood, really. He didn't know his father, his mother died, and he was a lovely young man.'

Liz Osborne grew up in a well-to-do neighbourhood in Warwickshire, near Birmingham, England. Her father was Irish, a submariner in the British Navy. He died from an illness brought on by a long-term exposure to asbestos when Liz was seven.

'He died within six weeks of being diagnosed,' recalls Liz. 'That was very sad and my mother really struggled. I had one older brother – she would have liked more but she never married again. She was a wonderful mother . . . I always tried to be as good as her, but I don't think I ever could be. I've got too fiery a temper. She was just always there. I was an exchange student in Vienna and she had no money, but I was given all these opportunities. I never wasted them but I was always a bit of a black sheep, being the youngest I suppose . . . I became a bit of a rebel. I was given a hard time at school because my mother was a widow, even though my father had fought for the country for twenty-seven years. They gave me a hard time, and they gave my mother a hard time.'

Liz's older brother moved to New Zealand when she was twelve, and five years later, when Liz was doing her nurse's training, her mother announced that she was joining him. 'She was devastated that I said, "I'm not going; I'm having a good time." She went to New Zealand and I stayed on in England,' says Liz.

Liz always felt ostracised by the English, because of her Irish ancestry, and naturally gravitated towards the large Irish community in Birmingham. 'They had a lot of Irish dances, because there were a lot of Irish in Birmingham, and I liked the Irish because they were much more fun than the English . . . I used to go to all the Irish dances. There were different types, the one where all the drinkers went or the Catholic church dances. I went to them all.' She laughs.

And so these two teenagers from disparate worlds, who both lost a parent as young children, who'd had their lives suddenly and irretrievably altered by the relocations of others, were now fending for themselves. When they met at an Irish church hall dance it was perhaps inevitable that they would be drawn together.

'He asked me out quite a lot, but I didn't really want to at that stage,' says Liz. 'He was never drunk and he always dressed nicely; he was a lovely guy. I just didn't really want a relationship at that time. I was only seventeen. I was just able to drive, but my car had broken down so I had to go on the bus to the dance. He asked me if he could take me home, so I said, yes.'

Liz appreciated John's work ethic, independent spirit and good manners, and they soon became a couple. 'He was a plant operator at the big motorways in England . . . He's always been a worker.

He loved his work. I don't think my mother was too impressed by that because I came from a very snobby part of England.'

Within a year the pair were married and soon had a baby girl, Rachel, a week before Liz's nineteenth birthday. 'I was so pleased I had my kids young. It's not the thing to do anymore, but I never regretted it because I was a kid as well, really. We had such fun.'

The other thing the young couple had in common was a dream of a new life in a far-off land. 'That was one of the attractions we had for each other, because one of John's dreams was that he wanted to emigrate; there was a lot of work going on here – big constructions and mining and everything,' says Liz. 'It wasn't much fun in England because there were all the troubles going on between the Irish and the English.'

When John saw a sign offering passage to Australia for ten pounds – part of an Australian government campaign to attract more British migrants – they didn't hesitate. Thus, John, Liz and Rachel became one of the original 'ten-pound Poms'.

'We actually applied to New Zealand first. They'd take me because I was a registered nurse, but they wouldn't take John. So, we came to Australia, and it's the best thing we ever did,' says Liz. 'We flew because John wanted to work as soon as we got here. You could come by ship but, no, we weren't going to spend six weeks lazing around.'

The young family arrived in Perth in 1971 and were moved into a migrant hostel, spartan housing commission accommodation on the outskirts of the world's most isolated capital city. But nothing could dampen Liz's enthusiasm for her adopted home. 'I was thrilled to be in this beautiful city. It was just so beautiful, open – the sky, the light – it was just amazing. And John actually tramped the streets for ten days looking for a job in Perth, and in two weeks we were out of the migrant hostel. Most people stayed there two years. He got a job for $60 a week, and he was most upset – he'd come from earning big money. He couldn't believe it, but apparently that was the going rate.'

Still, John's determination for a better life for his family couldn't be denied. 'Soon we had a lovely flat. I used to Mr Sheen the floors every day – I couldn't believe how beautiful everything was. Where were the poor people? There weren't any. I'd been a community nurse in Birmingham and the poverty there is terrible. These are the housing commission? My god, I thought, these are bigger than the houses I grew up in. It was amazing, just the land of opportunity.'

Liz returned to nursing; her mother came over from New Zealand to help care for Rachel; and John headed north chasing better-paid work in Port Hedland. They began to get ahead financially, but change and upheaval never seemed far away. 'One day John came home and said, "We're going to Sydney." I didn't want to go to Sydney. This is the life. I had a great job, a little girl, a lovely two-bedroom flat. It was just beautiful, and you want to go to Sydney?'

But John had heard of better work opportunities in Australia's largest city and was adamant, and so the family loaded up their Valiant station wagon and, together with another couple, drove three days and 4000 kilometres across the country, on the then unsealed Nullarbor Plain, to Sydney.

'When we were young we didn't know anything about Aboriginal people. People would say, "Oh, they're out there; they'll block the road. Just drive straight through." At night we saw all the fires in the bush. I was terrified of these natives. We didn't know anything . . . We had a lot to learn.'

After three days of driving over dirt roads and sleeping in the car, the outer western suburbs of Sydney didn't impress Liz the same way Perth had. 'We came into Sydney down the bloody Parramatta Road, over the Blue Mountains from Broken Hill, and I looked around and thought, This is just like Birmingham. This is horrible; I don't want to be here.'

John found work straightaway with Irish contractors keen to employ workers from the old country. Water and sewerage were just being connected to the outer suburbs and the Blue Mountains, so work was plentiful. They were advised to settle in the western suburbs, close to the work, so they lived in Cabramatta, then Katoomba. But with her second child on the way, and her husband working long hours, the separation and alien environment began to take a toll. 'That was the start of the downfall of our marriage really, which was very sad because we had been very happy . . . The boys all went to the pub after work, because they were all in this little town called Katoomba, and I never saw him. All the Irish women were there, and they accepted it more. I missed him. A lot of the wives didn't care as long as they got the housekeeping money, but I missed him, because we were very good friends.'

Their second child, Peter, arrived and the family moved around the western suburbs following the work, eventually settling in Penrith, where they had three more boys at three-year intervals – Edward, Sean and Mick.

John started his own business, but economic recession only increased the strain on the family. 'There was a big recession in 1982, a big construction downturn, and that really put a lot of pressure on John,' says Liz. 'He had to go to North Queensland. I had no money – people helped me out . . . That separation didn't do our marriage any good because I thought it was easier to be without him than to be with him. So, that was the end of that, really. In some ways he was very gracious, because he just left . . . He didn't harass me; he just left and came back to see the kids . . . The kids were happy because they didn't have any conflict.'

Even so, when Mick was still an infant, Liz drove north to Mackay to see if she could reconcile with her husband. Their efforts to salvage the marriage failed, but the trip proved fateful for other reasons.

'I drove from Sydney to Mackay to meet John, because he was up in North Queensland, to see if we could reconcile, and I came past [the New South Wales North Coast]. I'd never been here before, past Byron Bay and Ballina, and I thought, My God, this is so beautiful. And my father was born in Ballina in Ireland, same spelling. And I thought to myself, I'm going to live here one day.'

Liz and the children returned to the western suburbs of Sydney, but a seed had been planted.

When John moved to Coffs Harbour on the New South Wales mid-North Coast soon after, his eldest son, Peter, then 13, insisted he wanted to live with his father. 'Old things come back. John said, "I'm not taking one – I'm taking them all," just like his father, just like he learnt when he was a kid,' recalls Liz. 'It was really difficult . . . I thought it was the right thing to do, but Mick was so little, and Sean was so little, a real mummy's boy. Mick was tiny – he was four – but what could I do? I thought this was the thing to do, but it wasn't.'

The children moved north to live with their father, but his long work hours meant he was barely home. Money was tight and a hired housekeeper was overwhelmed trying to care for the children on her own. 'I went up there every month and cried all the way home. It was the worst time in my life,' says Liz. 'I thought it was good for the kids. That's when they learnt to surf. They had a good life; it was safe and small enough that they couldn't get into any mischief . . . They were happy there in their own way, because they had each other. The housekeeper, Chris, she was a good woman and really looked after them . . . but it all fell apart. At least they had that opportunity to live with their father, which I thought was the right thing to do.'

The arrangement lasted two years but ultimately proved unsustainable. The younger boys moved back to the western suburbs with their mum, while Rachel went to university to study child psychology and Peter went to agricultural college.

'He was a good father . . . He was an absent father, but he was loving and hugged and kissed and loved his kids in that way. It was very hard for him,' says Liz.

Back in western Sydney, Edward, the eldest of the three boys still at home, wasn't about to give up his surfing because of mere distance.

'Edward would ask me to drive him to the station at four o'clock in the morning. He'd get on the train and go into Central, get on a ferry and go to Manly, or get on another train and go to Wollongong, Sandon Point. And I let him do that at twelve. I can't believe I let him do that. Or I would drive them down from Campbelltown to Sandon Point, or they would all go on the train.'

The beach became a focal point for the family, one that would sustain them through many hardships. The image of the devoted mum in her little red Datsun with the killer sound system, chugging down the Bulli Pass with her three sons, music blaring and surfboards piled high on the roof, is one sure to elicit smiles from any of us who ever badgered our own mums for rides to the beach.

'I had a Datsun SS. It was a souped-up thing with this amazing sound system. I had to have something with a fairly good engine to get up to Coffs Harbour every weekend. We used to go to Sandon Point with this car, surfboards on the top, listening to the Animals, Eric Burdon singing "Sky Pilot", and all those classics. And everyone would be singing at the top of their voices. They love that music because it just brings back those happy days. All down that South Coast they used to surf.'

Alternatively, they'd venture up to Terrigal, on the New South Wales Central Coast, renting caravans for weekends by the beach. 'Every weekend we were doing something special, always to do with surfing,' says Liz. 'When we split, even though I had boyfriends, who were bloody useless really, I made a commitment that my main priority was my children. That was my commitment . . . They made fun of my boyfriends. They sabotaged every relationship I ever had. But the thing I love about my kids is they've always made me laugh. We've been through a lot of stuff together, but they've lightened my life.'

Soon the pull of the coast grew too strong. When Liz was offered a job in Lismore on the New South Wales North Coast, in charge of mental health services, the family was on the move again.

'We had the old red car with the pool table on top and all the surfboards, and all of us inside, including Rachel. It was just an adventure. We were all into adventure, and that was one of the things I was lucky with. I was an adventurer, still young at heart. We had such fun. It was not a problem for me. I've driven to nearly every beach in New South Wales.'

They settled in Ballina, and it was everything Liz had envisaged when she had driven through a few years earlier – the land of milk and honey she and her kids had been longing for. 'That was the happiest time of my life,' says Liz. 'That was the best time in all our lives, living in Ballina.'

It was also where surfing firmly took hold of the Fanning boys. The two youngest, Sean and Mick, learnt to surf in tiny ripples under Ballina Bridge, in the mouth of the Richmond River. The famous Irish hospitality came to the fore when Liz would open her home to the boys' more wayward friends, young runaways living under the bridge where the boys surfed. 'If there was a problem in the family, they would say, "Come and stay with us." The boys would ask me, "My friend's living under Ballina Bridge. He's run away from home. Can he stay with us?"'

Liz was just grateful for the friendships, community and joy surfing offered her boys. 'It's been the best thing that's ever happened to our family. I had no money and five children. Surfing was great for me. If you got them a board and a pair of board shorts, that was all they needed. The best thing I could do was get a nice house near to the beach,' says Liz.

Sport runs deep in the Fanning DNA. 'John's father played hurling for Limerick. My father played soccer for the navy – he was a good soccer player. My brother was a shot-putter and a discus-thrower in the Commonwealth Games, and I was an avid hockey player, so we've always had a lot of sport in our family.'

And those sporting genes were about to express themselves in the waves of the NSW North Coast in spectacular fashion. 'As long as I had the rent and food, the rest went to sporting things, buying surfboards or boogie boards or soccer boots or rugby boots. Peter played for Northern New South Wales in rugby union against Queensland. They've always been really good at sport. Edward was a fantastic surfer . . . Everyone could see Edward's potential. I still think he's the best surfer, he just didn't have the temperament for competition . . . I just wanted them to have fun and enjoy themselves. It cost a lot of money to do contests and, the poor kids, they had second-hand surfboards. Peter wasn't interested in contests, but Edward was. Sean was a boogie board rider, and Mick wasn't that interested. He went along because his brothers did.'

Even so, an extraordinary talent lay dormant in the youngest of the Fanning boys and, nurtured by a doting family, it would soon make its presence felt in ways none of them could have imagined.

chapter 1.
ROLLING WITH THE PUNCHES

A lot of sporting books seem to start with tales of an athletic child-hood protégé always destined for greatness, stunning coaches and older athletes with their extraordinary ability and their glorious, unstoppable rise through junior ranks. This isn't one of those stories. There was nothing about my early childhood in the western suburbs of Sydney to suggest that sport, much less surfing, would provide a path out of a fairly rocky beginning.

My earliest memory is sitting in front of TV watching Roger Ramjet at our family home in Penrith. I must have been tiny, because we moved out of there when I was about two. I was born in Penrith, a long way from the ocean, the youngest of five kids. Mum and Dad split up when I was two, so it must have been a tough time, but I don't remember a whole lot about it. As the youngest, I think I was always shielded from a lot of the conflicts that went on.

A couple of years later, Mum and Dad decided four young boys needed some fatherly influence, so we moved up to Coffs Harbour on the New South Wales mid-North Coast to live with Dad. It was to prove a fateful move. We stayed in Coffs until I was six, and it was there I discovered the ocean. We lived just a block from the beach and the surf became our saviour. I'm not sure if Dad realised what he was taking on with five kids on his own. He worked long hours, so we would take ourselves off to the beach at every opportunity, where I got into bodyboarding and surfing. They were fun times, but it was the last time all five of us kids lived together, because after that my oldest sister went to university. I think we all learnt to pull together and make the best of our situation. We were all born three years apart. My sister Rachel's about twelve years older than me; then my oldest brother, Pete, is nine years older; Ed is six years older and Sean was three.

Apart from the odd beating, it was fun being the youngest, because my older brothers used to take me to the beach and keep an eye on me. I don't remember swimming lessons or anything like that. My brothers just threw me out there on bodyboards and surfboards; it was a matter of sink or swim.

I can still remember my first bodyboard. It was called a Hotshot, and it had an orange top and a black bottom. I graduated to a surfboard when I was five or six. My first board was the old sign of a local board company called Trinity Surfboards. They later changed their name to Piranha. It was a 4'11" thruster, with a fin box so you could change the back fin. We just surfed the little beachbreaks close to home – Macaulays and Diggers – and then we moved into town and were living on top of the hill, near that famous surf shop in Coffs, Coopers, started by the legendary Californian surfer Bob Cooper. The jetty was just down the road and we surfed there from then on.

It must have been hard for Dad, and we had a babysitter named Chris who helped look after us. We never had a lot of money. I remember one morning we had no food in the house except rice and milk, so we had to have rice pudding. We'd take a mouthful and then run to the toilet, spit it out and run back before Chris realised. I've never tried rice pudding again because of that memory.

Chris became really attached to all of us and worked hard for our care. And Dad worked from dawn till dusk, went to the pub for a couple of ales in the afternoon and came home to take over. It couldn't have been easy for anyone.

We lived with Dad at Coffs until I was in Year Two at school. Then we moved down to Bradbury, near Campbelltown back in western Sydney, to live with Mum. It didn't really bother me back then, leaving the beach. But Mum loved the beach and so she'd take us on weekends. My older brothers kept up their surfing despite the distance. We also really got into skateboarding. Not long after we moved to Bradbury they opened up a new skatey bowl close to our place, so it was perfect. My brothers got in a bit of strife because they were 'skegs' (the westies' name for surfers) and the westies would beat them up. We had this huge quarter-pipe, and some guys came and blew it up with firecrackers.

It was a bit of a rough area. I'm sure if I went out there now I'd get beat up, but there weren't too many super-tough seven-year-olds when I was growing up. With three older brothers, I was pretty safe – most of the time. Sometimes my brothers would take me down the street and tell me to fight some kid, just for entertainment. And if I got beaten they were like, don't you cry or *we'll* beat you up. No-one got seriously hurt, just boys being boys, but it hardens you up a bit. Being that young, you just sort of roll with the punches. I was into skating and there were plenty of streets to skate, so I was happy. We rode our skateboards everywhere – they were our main form of transport.

My brothers used to get in trouble all the time. They were always doing something stupid. One time Ed and his mate stole his mate's dad's van to try and learn how to drive and ended up going through a fence. It was just boredom, I think, trying to find ways to amuse ourselves in the suburbs.

Mum was a nurse at Campbelltown Hospital, and on weekends she would drive us up to Terrigal on the Central Coast or down to Wollongong, south of Sydney. I still remember going down Bulli Pass, this massive hill from the escarpment down to the coast, in our tiny red Datsun. Ed was already a really keen, dedicated surfer, and he used to get up really early and catch a train to the beach some mornings. We surfed a bit at Sandon Point, near Wollongong, which I had no idea then would become significant later in life.

HEADING NORTH

It seemed like we were always on the move as kids, but I never minded too much. I was about eight when we moved up to Ballina, on the NSW North Coast. Ed was right into his surfing by then, so he was stoked with the move. Sean and I were more into our skating. Pete was at agricultural college.

We lived in East Ballina, right near the golf course, and it was only a twenty-minute pushie ride to the beach, and that's when we started really getting into surfing. It was great to be back by the beach. Then we ended up moving right next to North Wall, where we would stay for the next four or five years. We surfed North Wall all the time – our place was grommet HQ. Everyone would come and hang at our house, because it was close to the beach and we had this huge garage where everyone left their boards and played pool. Mum would park her car out the front so we could take over the garage; she was really cool with that. All my brothers' mates used to congregate at our place also, so there were kids everywhere, and they all looked after me when I went surfing. We still got all kinds of grommet abuse though: tied to trees by legropes; put in wheelie bins, pulled along the street, then rolled up over the gutters. It sucked at the time, but you look back on it now and it's pretty funny – definitely character building.

I learnt to surf on these tiny reforms under the bridge at Ballina. Sean and I used to surf there all the time. North Wall always seemed to be at least four foot, pretty daunting for a kid, so we'd be shitting ourselves out there. The little waves under the bridge were perfect for us. It was pretty eerie surfing under there as cars whizzed by overhead and we got chased in by sharks a few times. One time during a cyclone swell it was three to four foot there and perfect. We thought it was pumping.

My first-ever heat was at the local boardriders' club, LeBa (Lennox–Ballina) in the under-13s. They held the contest at Boulders, a pretty serious rock ledge just around the corner from Lennox. It was massive, easily six foot. There was me, Odin Green and my brother Sean, and I got last. I think I made a final of the Byron Easter Classic in under-14s, but the two O'Rafferty brothers, Mick and Darren, came up from the mid-North Coast. They were the hot grommets at the time and smoked us. That was probably the first event I performed well in, but I sure wasn't setting the world on fire. I don't think I got through many heats for a long time.

When we were in Ballina I was more into my soccer and cross-country running, to be honest. I loved soccer. I played for the Northern NSW team, and we ended up going down to Sydney and winning the country championships and the NSW titles. I was a left midfielder. They used to call me 'the Dynamo Kid', because I'd never stop running the whole game, just back and forth. We were all in LeBa Boardriders but if a club contest fell on the same day as soccer I wasn't going to LeBa. I just wanted to be a soccer player.

HOW TO GET YOUR FIRST NEW CUSTOM BOARD

The first board I got when we moved to Ballina was one of Danny Wills's old boards, and I had that thing for years. It was a great board, but it was definitely on the way out. I decided I had to get a new board, so I started working on my mum: 'Can I get a new board for Christmas?' But Mum wouldn't buy me a new board until my old one was totally trashed. It was a brown, delaminated thruster, but it only had two fins left. It was so dead. But Mum said, 'I'm not buying you a new board until that one's totally gone.' I was telling Sean about it on the way home, and he went, 'I'll fix that.' He grabbed the thing, picked it up and went WHACK!, breaking it on the ground. I was impressed by his swift and decisive action, but a little concerned about what Mum would say. I got home and went, 'Mum, my board broke. I need a new one.' And she just said, 'All right.' We stuck by that story for years, but we eventually confessed.

And so I got my first new custom board that Christmas. It was called a Surf Blade by a guy called Brian Ingham, from Lennox Head. I was so stoked. My brother gave me some deck grip and a Gorilla Grip sticker to put on it – I thought I was killing it. But karma was about to catch up with me. Christmas Day, first surf, I took off on a wave and went straight over the falls. I went headfirst into the sand, grazed all my face and creased the nose of my board. I was shattered. I went home crying and wouldn't get off the couch all day. Later, my brothers came running in yelling, 'Mick, you've got to come. Tom Curren's surfing out at Speedies, out at Ballina. You've got to come and watch him – he's so good.' But I was still too traumatised by the morning's events. 'Nuh, I'm too ugly,' I whined, because my face was all banged up. So I never got to see Tom Curren surf until years later. But I got the board fixed, and it still went pretty good. My boyish good looks, however, have never fully recovered.

GROMMET HEAVEN

Everything changed when I was twelve and we moved north again to the southern Gold Coast. We went to sign me up at the Palm Beach soccer club, and it must have been the wrong day. No-one was there, so we just thought we'd come back the next week. But I never made it back. After that, we went surfing at Duranbah, because Sean was meant to meet up with Danny Tukino and Scotty Peacock from Quiksilver to see if they would sponsor him. I was surfing with Sean when Danny introduced himself. I said, 'Ah, are you looking for Sean, my brother?' They didn't realise I was Sean's brother, but they'd noticed me surfing and we ended up both getting sponsored. They gave me a box of new clothes, and I was so stoked I wore them to school for weeks.

That was the turning point. I flagged soccer on the weekends and only played at school. That was it: I was sponsored and surfing took over. The waves were way more user-friendly for a kid on the Gold Coast. The surf always seemed to be massive at Ballina, and I was always getting worked, so it was just more fun surfing on the Goldy. Grommet heaven. We lived at Currumbin at first and surfed at Palm Beach. On the weekends we'd head down to Duranbah. When we moved to the Goldy, I was really scared of D-bah. The first time we went there it was about four foot, and I was sitting in the car going, 'I'm so not going out there.' But then we ended up moving to D-bah and it became my backyard. I loved the place.

Dean Morrison was the man back then. He had Billabong stickers all over his boards, riding Mt Woodgee surfboards. He was only about twelve but he had such a mature style – all his turns were so solid. He really inspired me. I didn't meet Joel Parkinson until a couple of years later, down at Narrabeen during the Pro Junior when we were all doing the Cadet Cup (for under-fifteens). Then Joel ended up moving from the Sunshine Coast down to the Gold Coast, and we became our own little posse.

KIRRA BOARDRIDERS

If you were a surfer in Coolangatta, you either surfed for Snapper or Kirra. We joined Kirra because local surf coach Eddie Valladares suggested it to Sean. I just tagged along when he went to his first club contest. I wasn't even going to join, but I ended up going in the contest too and having fun. They're a funny bunch at Kirra. That was when Po Cross was the president, this big bearded longboarder. We'd have meetings in the back of the Patch, a local bar, and I used to ask Mum if I could have a soft drink while all the older guys were getting on the beers. It was always funny watching the older guys try and run these chaotic meetings.

My first surf trip away from home was with Kirra Boardriders down to the Quiksilver Surf League at Cronulla in Sydney. We drove down in the team bus and it was mayhem the whole way. I was only thirteen and hanging out with guys who were anywhere between eighteen and twenty-five, and back in those days they were a bunch of maniacs. As soon as I got on the bus, they were all wrenching bongs. It was radical, so different to what it's like today. I had no-one looking after me except my brothers, and we stayed at the Sharks footy club in Cronulla. In the clubhouse all the showers were open, and I was so embarrassed. I was tiny and had no pubes, and I remember asking the guy who let us in, 'Is there a private shower somewhere I can use?' I didn't want to get naked in front of everyone, so I didn't shower all weekend. On the last night he went, 'I've got a little present for you. There's a private shower down there.' YES!

We terrorised that bloody footy club. There were no separate rooms, just one big open room full of mattresses on the floor. There was a beer fridge and so, of course, the older boys broke into it and drank the thing dry. Sean, me and one of our mates broke into the freezer, and it was full of ice-creams. *Yee-hah!* We'd hit the mother load. I lived on ice-creams the whole time. The Kirra club did all right, considering our diet. I think we lost in the semis. I surfed my heat and did pretty good, so all the Kirra guys decided to celebrate by burying me in the sand. Next thing I know I'm buried up to my neck, with a steamer full of sand. They left me entombed for about an hour. It was a nice introduction to the organised lunacy of club surfing, and I loved it.

The next year we did two more trips like that, the first one to Avoca on the Central Coast for Surf League again. Tommy Peterson was our coach, the brother of the legendary 70s surfer Michael Peterson and a bit of a maniac in his own right, so that set the tone for the trip from the start. Tommy is a really eccentric character. Everyone thinks of him as this stoned old local, but when you get talking to him he is actually really switched-on. He remembers everything – even things that happened forty years ago – like it was yesterday. But sometimes it's hard to take him seriously. I remember a Kirra club meeting at the Patch, and Tom must have had a big weekend because he was falling in and out of sleep. He wound up sleeping under a bunch of chairs that we were sitting on. He would have these random outbursts and everyone would fall into fits of laughter. 'Where's the popcorn?' he would yell. 'I'm at the movies with no popcorn!' That was one of my earliest experiences of Tom, and he always cracks me up. He did have a couple of wild ideas, but he also made a lot of sense from time to time, amazingly enough.

The other trip he took us on was also to Avoca for the Gath Junior Surf Teams event. It was sponsored by Gath Helmets, one of the first surf-specific helmets on the market, and so when you went out for your heat you had to wear one. I was still tiny and they wouldn't fit my head. It was rattling around up there like an ice-cream bucket. The event was for under-twenties, and we were totally un-supervised, apart from Tommy, so it was another pretty raucous trip.

RIGHT PLACE, RIGHT TIME

The other big thing that happened for me around this time was getting on Darren Handley's boards. When I first moved to the Goldy I met a shaper called Darryl Bulger, and I rode his boards for a couple of years, and then I asked Darren if he'd sponsor me. We were both in Kirra Boardriders, and he was the hot young shaper at the time. I'd never ridden one of his boards before, but Jay Phillips was riding them and I thought he was an unbelievable surfer – so I knew the boards worked. I was about fourteen, just being a smart-arse, and one day out of the blue I asked Darren, 'Can I have sponsorship?' And for some strange reason he said yes. I couldn't believe it. I was stoked. Everyone was either riding Darren or Murray Bourton's boards. Darren had just stopped working for Murray and gone out on his own, so it was good timing for both of us.

We were also lucky to have a lot of great local surfers to look up to at the time. As well as Jay, there was Shane Bevan, Will Lewis,

Jason Gale, Neal Purchase Junior and Margo, just to name a few. Occy was coming back too, and Luke Egan had just moved up to the Gold Coast from Newcastle. There were so many good guys surfing D-bah all the time. It was like that beach was the focus of the whole Gold Coast, and you couldn't ask for a better grounding as a grommet. All those guys helped our development. They were all part of my older brother Ed's generation, so I got to know a lot of them. It was pretty cool, and we were very lucky.

SCHOOL SURFING

I actually managed to attend a fair bit of school through all this, at Palm Beach–Currumbin High. If I didn't go to school, Sean would ring up Mum and tell her, even if *he* was at home. I used to go to school just so I didn't get in trouble, but I also enjoyed it. I was all right at maths. I didn't really like English and science, but I did okay. Then in Year Nine they started a sports excellence program, but they weren't going to include surfing. We surfers were outraged, so we all got together and went into the office, saw the principal and told him, 'You've got to include surfing.'

Surfing still had a pretty bad image, as far as the country's educators were concerned, and Mr Bondfield was pretty old school. 'Surfing's not a sport,' he scoffed. 'You can't make a career out of it.' We patiently explained that, in fact, surfing was a legitimate professional sport these days with sponsorships and a pro tour. Somehow we convinced him to include surfing, which opened up a lot of time to surf during school hours. It was perfect. Monday mornings you didn't have to get to school until eleven, and you got to go home early to go surfing some afternoons.

I was already working with a coach, Phil McNamara, and we got him in to head the school surfing program. That's another thing we were really lucky with – there were some great coaches and mentors around us. I was working with Phil, and Dean was working with Eddie Valladares. Dean also had [1978 world champion] Rabbit Bartholomew as a mentor. I just clicked with Phil when he coached us for Gold Coast and state titles. We worked a lot on my technique. As a kid I had shit going everywhere, waving my arms round like a lunatic, so we worked a lot on my technique. I also worked with a guy named Russell Lewis before that, who was really good. But I could understand what Phil was doing, and his work ethic is similar to how I approach things, so it was a good fit.

THE COOLY KIDS

Joel and Dean were the ones who made me work so hard, because I had to try and keep up. Everyone thought that Dean, as Rabbit's protégé, would be a world champion one day, even when he was twelve. Joel was just as good as Dean, but before I met him I had this image of him as really cool and stuck-up, with his new Oakley sunglasses and all his sponsors. But when I met him he was nothing like that – he was really funny and had me laughing straightaway, and we all became friends. There was a whole bunch of us surfing and hanging out, going through school together – Dean, Joel, Damon Harvey, my brother Sean, Adam West, Sam Porter, Shagga and his older brother Damo, Sparrow, Tony Cohen. There were heaps of us.

Shagga's parents had just got a video camera, and we all decided to make a movie. So we wrote out this little script, and it was frickin' hilarious. We didn't have a title, but we were recording over this old VHS tape, and the label on the tape was 'The Magic Show'. So that's what we called it. It was one of those old cameras where you put the whole VHS tape in. The idea of the movie was that we were all living at D-bah and we pretty much dominated the place. Sean was this new guy who moved up, and he wouldn't talk to anyone, so we all beat him up before he even got to the beach. And then we saw him surf and he ripped, so we let him in our group. It was really stupid and our acting was terrible, but it was good fun. Taylor Steele had nothing to worry about.

We were lucky having Shagga there keen to video us surfing. It was always a shock to see yourself on video for the first time. I barely recognised myself. *Who is that manic, skinny blond kid waving his arms all over the shop?* I thought derisively, before I realised that skinny blond kid was me. It was classic. That's where kids today have it good, because video cameras are so much more accessible, and it seems like everyone has someone videoing their sessions – mum or dad or a mate. It makes it a lot easier to refine your style. You don't want to lose your own individual flair and get caught up trying to imitate anyone, but it definitely makes it easier to work out your rough edges.

At the time, Joel was sponsored by the wax company AR4, and Sean and Westy turned the AR into a CK with textas. That's when they came up with Cooly Kids. And they could only figure out how to turn the 4 into a 7, so we were CK7, even though there were more than seven of us. We made our own poster up and called ourselves CK7. This was around the time Taylor Steele started making his movies with Kelly Slater, Rob Machado and that whole crew, like *Momentum* and *Focus*, so we were going to create our own little *Momentum* generation. We called ourselves 'Poorper Productions', because none of us had any money.

We all went through hard times, but I think that's what kept us all pretty close. Some people might look at us today and think we have this jet-setting lifestyle, but that was definitely not the case when we were growing up. We all came from broken families, none of our parents had much money – that's just the way it was. Before I got sponsored I always wore hand-me-down clothes. There were weeks when we literally had no money. It would be Monday and Mum didn't get paid until Thursday. She'd say, 'We've got to ring your dad and get some money, otherwise you're not going to eat until Thursday.'

And there were times Mum had to go and borrow money from friends, which I think she found really hard. It was hard for us too because, being the two youngest, Sean and I didn't really have the relationship with Dad that the older kids did. It seemed like we were only ringing him up for money most of the time, and looking back that really sucked.

Mum used to buy these big jumbo packets of two-minute noodles and, if times were tight, we'd have bacon-and-egg noodles for breakfast, lunch and dinner. Fortunately, I actually liked bacon-and-egg noodles. There were times Mum wouldn't even have enough money to get to work, and she'd have to stay overnight near the Gold Coast Hospital. But Mum always gave us everything. She always figured out a way to make sure we were in a nice house and happy with what we were doing. She always believed that if you had somewhere nice to live, close to the beach, then it was easy to be happy. Even if you had to scrounge to make ends meet, you'd manage.

And it was a similar deal with a lot of our friends. I remember Joel was the leftover king always scoffing everyone else's scraps. But that began to change when we started getting sponsored. All of a sudden we were getting free stuff and even a little bit of money, just for going surfing. It seemed unbelievable.

THE SUMMER SNAPPER GOT ITS BANK BACK

Meeting Joel and Dean was a big thing for me. They were always going to be pro surfers and that was it. There was nothing else in their sights, no plan B, no fallback position, and they weren't too keen on turning up at school because their destiny was already set. I was just this little kid, and I didn't think about being a pro surfer. It was really gradual for me. I was just tagging along and doing what they were doing. We were surfing in Gold Coast and Queensland titles together, duking it out in the finals. It was always Dean first, Joel second, me third and Damon Harvey fourth. Dean and Joel would make it through the normal rounds, while Damon and I had to go through the repechages to make the final. Those two used to knock us out all the time.

Then I made the Queensland team to go to the Aussie titles, and that was a big deal. I ended up getting a third. Things really started to click for me during 1996–97. It was the summer that Snapper got its bank back, and the waves there were just phenomenal, breaking for hundreds of metres from Snapper all the way through Rainbow Bay to Greenmount. This was long before the sand pumping had created the so-called Superbank, but the waves were just as good, maybe better. I would surf all day, every day. I was fifteen, surfing perfect waves with a gang of mates. I really started thinking, *Yeah, this is the life*.

We were living on the hill at D-bah and surfing there and Snapper and Kirra all the time. I was getting free clothes and wetsuits and surfboards. I was even getting a few hundred bucks a year off Quikkie, so I had a bit of cash to go down the shops with. I thought I was killing it. Life for a grommet couldn't get much better.

chapter 2.
GROWING UP FAST

Coolangatta has always been a full-on surf town. As grommets, we had only the vaguest idea of the Gold Coast's rich surfing history and the great lineage of characters that was our heritage. We knew Rabbit Bartholomew, or 'Bugs' as he was known, because he was around. But MP (70s surf legend Michael Peterson) was just a myth, this shadowy legend who you almost never actually sighted. PT (1976 world champion Peter Townend) was in America pursuing his career in the US surf industry. So we didn't get that whole vibe until I got a little bit older. The heavy guys out at D-bah were guys like Bruce Lee, Po Cross, Scammell and Dick Bartlett, and we were deadset scared of them. At Kirra there was Ray Manakaris, who we called Ray Rip-your-arms-off. It used to be pretty heavy back in those days. There were always fights at D-bah. Bodyboarders weren't allowed past Lovers at the north end of the beach. If they ventured too far south, they got sent back. If they backchatted, they got beaten up.

There were guys just a few years older than us who we thought were the best surfers in the world. Jay Phillips was pretty incredible, super-fast and radical with all the new moves. Will Lewis was amazing, with the most perfect technique you could imagine. But, since that first generation of Gold Coast champions in the 70s, like Rabbit and PT and MP, a lot of Gold Coast surfers seemed to be content just to stay home and enjoy everything the Gold Coast surfing lifestyle had to offer. And who could blame them?

The Gold Coast is known for its theme parks: Movieworld, Dreamworld, Wet'n'Wild. Coolangatta is like Surfworld. There are some of the world's best point breaks – Snapper, Greenmount, Kirra and, just up the road a bit, Burleigh Heads – all barrelling for hundreds of metres over sand bottoms in warm water. If the swell is small there are the peaks and ramps of Duranbah to go crazy on. There are surf clubs right on the beach selling cold beer and cheap meals. The beaches are covered in girls from all over the world. And twinkling away in the distance are the bright lights of Surfers Paradise just luring the unwary to come out and play.

It's an easy place to get sucked into the waves and the whole Gold Coast party scene. You see it with kids these days too, and it happened with some of our generation. It's too hard to go off exploring the world because you're too scared of missing something at home, whether it's the next swell or the next party. It's a bit like that with the Hawaiian guys too. They can just stay home and surf and have fun because the waves are so good. You get pumping waves all day, and then you can go out and go crazy in Surfers all night. You just don't want the party to stop. When I was seventeen and eighteen, I was going out to parties and getting drunk more than was good for me. Surfing was the thing that gave us a reason to get out of bed – rather than going to bed – when the sun was just coming up.

Joel and Dean and I never really talked about it, but those guys always had bigger ambitions than just being the best surfer out at D-bah. I got swept along in their wake. It all happened so fast that we never had a chance to get stuck at home. During that time when kids get into the party scene – eighteen, nineteen – we went from the Junior Series straight onto the World Qualifying Series. It saved us, in a sense. Dean was always the one who was really dedicated, and that set a benchmark. We were lucky that we were all in the right place at the right time to push each other, and there were opportunities for us to pursue our surfing. But we also put in a lot of hard work. I think sometimes people look at us and think it was pretty easy, that the path was all laid out for us. From a young age we were lucky enough to get sponsors to pay for our trips to contests and give us free stuff. But we had to go and do it ourselves, and I think that's where a lot of our drive came from. Because we couldn't really afford new boards and gear all the time, we were hungry and we earned it by going in comps and getting sponsored.

But most of all, like every surfer before us, we just fell in love with riding waves. I had a few memorable free surfs around this time that really blew my mind and deepened my love of surfing. I remember filming for the Quikkie movie, *Enjoy the Ride* with Matty Gye. Willsy and I went up to Burleigh when there was a junior contest, and the waves were firing. I got the best barrel I'd ever had up until that point, standing in this big emerald-green tunnel with all my senses firing in overdrive. Another time I went up to Burleigh with my mate Beau Campi and got some massive pits. I was riding my 6'3" gun, pulling into what seemed like enormous caverns, eyes popping out of my head. And, of course, there were lots of great sessions out at Kirra when it still broke the way we all remember it. There was one week in '97 when the Billabong Pro was on at Kirra, and D-bah was firing every morning for a week. It was the year Shane Beschen scored his perfect 30-point heat, back when it was best three waves, and we had an amazing week of waves at D-bah. Experiences like that really etch themselves in your memory when you're a grom and make you want them more. You get an incredible amount of energy from the ocean and I think you can kind of absorb that energy and use it to drive you forward.

Having perfect point breaks to practise on definitely helped our development. Before the Superbank was formed by the sand pumping, the last time the bank at Snapper was really good we were just groms, learning how to do all the different turns. Being able to surf such perfect waves at the perfect time in our development, you have so many opportunities to practise a cutback or a snap on the one wave. If it's not feeling right, you can go out there and practise it over and over again, and iron out the bugs.

HAWAII FOR THE FIRST TIME

I went to Hawaii for the first time when I was sixteen. I was still with Quiksilver then, but I think Darren Handley paid for my ticket. It was about $1000, and I had $1000 to live on for a month. I stayed with a bunch of groms in a big white house right over the road from Sunset. There was me, Joel, Dean, Rasta, Heath Walker and a bunch of others in this big house with an empty swimming pool out the front and surfboards absolutely everywhere. Rabbit was trying to look after us all, but he definitely had his hands full. It was really fun and an amazing experience. We slept in these bunk beds, about six to a room, and scared ourselves stupid telling stories about how big the next swell was going to be. We surfed our brains out, went to Foodland, loaded up our trolleys and cooked up a storm each night, or we'd go to the Sunset Diner and smash chicken plates after a session.

My first surf was out at Sunset and it was perfect. Not that big, about eight foot and really nice but I was terrified. You've heard so many stories: the swell jumping ten foot in an hour; the dreaded West Peak mowing down the unwary; near-drownings and heavy locals. It's overwhelming when you're finally there. I was on my 7'0", which was the biggest board I'd ridden in my life. Dean and Joel had been there the year before, and they got there a couple of weeks before me this time, so I thought they were the full North Shore vets. They caught so many waves while I floated out on the shoulder. They were like the wise old watermen, telling me where to paddle out and calling me into waves. I finally got myself pumped to go one and went straight over the falls on the peak at Sunset and kinked my neck. That was my Hawaiian initiation.

That same trip, Brendan 'Margo' Margieson asked me to caddy for him at Sunset. It was massive, closing out in the channel, and I was like, *Are you kidding me?* If Margo got through he could have qualified for the tour, but I didn't really care about him. I just hoped I didn't drown, scratching for the horizon as every set approached. He ended up losing the heat, and I was so traumatised by the experience I didn't caddy again for years.

Hawaii can be a pretty scary place, especially if you're a skinny, little, blond, aspiring pro surfer from the other side of the world. Over the last few years it's changed a lot, and the local spots have become a lot more commercial and mainstream. So many companies rent big houses right on the beach for their team riders, and they all attack it en masse. But I used to be so intimidated. We were so scared – more than two of us wouldn't go surfing at a time so it didn't look like we were surfing as a crew. If we did, it was like, 'You walk down first and then we'll walk down after you.' Because Bugs was looking after us, he really laid down the law and told us what to do and what not to do. You learnt a lot of respect quickly, and that was a good thing. I think we still carry that respect to this day.

In the surf, I would just keep my head down and not say too much. I remember one time Hawaiian strongman Johnny Boy Gomes paddled out at Rocky Point. I was so scared, and then I accidentally dropped in on him. I didn't even realise until it was too late. The next wave, I was sitting there trembling with fear and he went, 'GO GROMMET!' There was someone already on the wave, but I thought, *Gosh, I better go*. And so I dropped in on someone else. It was terrifying. I felt like a startled dog in the middle of a highway trying to dodge cars.

It took me a while to get into Hawaii, and it was hard to imagine I'd ever feel comfortable there. I remember praying out in the water when I'd wipe-out or get caught inside. 'Please, God, don't let me die!' I was totally intimidated by Pipe that first year – it was just so shallow and crowded, with no room for error. I think I only surfed it once.

Deano seemed so at home over there by comparison. He used to pass himself off as a local kid, because he's got Maori ancestry. It was hilarious. He would sit there and not say anything, and everyone would just assume he was a local, with the dark skin and the Polynesian features. Sometimes he'd actually call himself into waves, under his breath, in this Hawaiian accent: 'GO DEANO!' And he'd actually get waves. Dean and Damon were surfing Pipe a lot that year, and Joel and I would go to all different places: Sunset, Rocky Point, Log Cabins. We were surfing everywhere, trying to push each other. It was a great experience and let us know very quickly what tiny minnows we were in the wider surfing world – and how little a Gold Coast junior title meant when you got to Hawaii. But we had an amazing time and really drank in the whole experience.

My advice for anyone going to Hawaii for the first time is to watch yourself, be polite to everyone and show respect. Make sure you are super-fit, because you are going to have to deal with situations way heavier than you've probably confronted at home. A good Hawaiian quiver for a first-timer of average build would be a 7'3" for Sunset, a 6'9" for Pipe and Off the Wall and a 6'3" for Rockies. Mind your manners, don't drop in, pick your waves and paddle hard. Every surfer needs to go to Hawaii at least once in their life. It will change the way you look at surfing, and the heaviest day at your local beach probably won't seem quite so daunting.

THE LEAPFROG EFFECT

When we were young, Dean was the best surfer out of all of us, and then Joel sort of leapfrogged him when we were about sixteen. Then I went and won a couple of junior events, and then Dean came back and won a couple, and then Joel came back. We kept leapfrogging each other all through our junior career. When Justin Gane was making his first few movies, like *Pulse* and *Unleashed*, we all wanted to have a section in them and were trying to surf hard to get the best clips. So we were all pushing each other. That leapfrog effect has just kept going and going.

There were a few times when the competitiveness tested our friendships. One time Damon thought Dean pulled his legrope in a heat, and they didn't talk for a year. There was another incident where Joel, Dean and I were in a quarterfinal of a pro junior at Winkipop, next to Bells Beach in Victoria. Dean was beating all of us. Joel was in second and I was third, but I didn't need a big score to overtake Joel. There wasn't much time left and this little wave came through; Dean was on the inside and I was next to him. Joel was way down the point. Dean paddled for it, looked where I was and said, 'Oh, you go.' Joel blew up. As I was surfing the wave I could hear Joel losing it: 'Fuck you, Dean, you fucking arsehole.' Joel carried on about it all night. But, as it turned out, I was in the same position again in the next heat, only Dean was in second. I was in third and in need of another wave. Dean was on the inside again, but this time he sat on me and wouldn't let me get a wave – that's just the way it goes. It's competition, and I think you should just leave that out in the water. We've all learnt that over time. Obviously, you get disappointed. But if someone beats me, especially if it's man-on-man and you have the priority system to settle any disputes, it's pretty hard to get pissed off. Unless they do something really, really bad, it's all within the rules. Just deal with it and try to leave it out in the water – the better person won on the day. Learn from your mistakes and move on.

HANGING AT THE FACTORY

I really got into my equipment early on and spent a lot of time at the factory, waiting for my boards to be finished, asking lots of questions and generally making a nuisance of myself. Darren Handley used to tell everybody that their boards would be ready Tuesday, but he didn't tell you *which* Tuesday. So I'd wait and watch Darren shape for ages, enjoying seeing the refined shape of a new board emerge from the foam blank as he ran the planer over it. If there was no surf, that's where I'd hang, waiting for my next board, telling people to hurry up, like the cheeky little grom that I was. I'd even watch them fix dings. I must have asked Darren a million questions. Or, mainly, just one question a million times: 'Why are you doing that?' I still do it today. And Darren would explain patiently, If you put this in there, it will work this way. Darren would write different little things on the stringer about what he'd done. It gave me something to look for in the feel of a board. And as a result I developed a pretty good knowledge of surfboard design. Darren would throw me a curveball every now and again. He'd tell me he'd done something different to my boards but not what, and I'd have to try and figure it out. Or I'd ask him how he thought a board was going to go, and then I'd tell him what I felt and compare notes. We put a lot of time into getting the boards right.

The first board that felt really special was the red and yellow one I was riding on the cover of that CK7 movie we made. I had a few with that spray, but the first of those was my first magic board. It really helped kick my surfing up a notch.

TAKING CARE OF BUSINESS

I didn't really think of surfing as my career until I got my first contract from Rip Curl. They threw a lot of money at me for how old I was, and I was shocked. It was 1998 and I hadn't even competed in any WQS events at that point, just pro juniors, state, Gold Coast and Aussie titles, and I'd made a few finals. But between us, Joel, Dean and I had received a fair bit of publicity as the Cooly Kids, and Rip Curl had enough faith in me to make a serious offer.

I'd just come home from school one day when I got a phone call out of the blue.

'Is this Mick?' a voice asked.

'Yeah,' I replied.

'It's Mick Ray from Rip Curl.'

I was thinking, *Wow, what's he ringing me for?*

'We'd like to get you on the team. I'll just get straight to the point. We want to offer you $30,000 a year.'

I was dumbstruck. 'You're kidding me, right? Have you seen me surf?' I was freaking out. I thought, *This can't be for real. It must be someone playing a prank.*

He asked, 'Is your mum around?'

I said, 'No, she doesn't get home until later.'

He said, 'Okay, I'll ring back then.' I was thinking, *Oh yeah, whatever*. There's no way he's going to ring back. I went surfing out at D-bah, and I didn't tell any of my mates.

Sure enough, Mum got home and he phoned back. They had a serious chat about it. I was only sixteen, and thirty grand a year seemed like all the money in the world. It was more than half my mum's salary working full-time in a responsible job where human lives were on the line. It didn't make sense. All these rumours started going around about how much I'd been offered, and I was scared to tell Sean – it was a lot more than he was getting paid. People would come up and say, I heard you've been offered this much money. And I'd try and play it all down.

I wanted to do the right thing by Quiksilver, because they'd always been good to me. I told them Rip Curl had offered me this money, and it seemed pretty stupid not to take it. Andrew Murphy was the Quiksilver team manager at the time, and he said, 'Give me a week or so.' But they could only offer half of what Rip Curl had. So a week or two later Gary Dunne, the Rip Curl team manager, came up and I signed the deal – I was with Rip Curl. My income went up about ten times in one go. They were pretty wild times.

I was never too sure why they were so keen to sign me. But it turned out it all started from my first trip to Bells the year before when the founder of Rip Curl, Doug 'Claw' Warbrick, was watching me surf. He could apparently see something in my youthful, gangly style that he liked. Claw had been following my progress closely since then but I didn't even know who he was at the time.

At first I felt like I had to live up to something. I thought, *If you get paid all this money you've got to be real good.* It wasn't long after that when I had to go down to Bells with the rest of the Rip Curl team. It was weird because I was the new guy, and I thought this deal of mine was pretty big news and I'd get the royal treatment. But it seemed like it wasn't such a big deal to anyone else – I was just another grom on the team. There were a lot of good young guys on their team at the time – Zane Harrison, Nathan Hedge, Chris Davidson, Darren O'Rafferty, Mikala Jones – so I had to try pretty hard just to keep up.

Mum, naturally, started handling the business side of things. I was still a minor, so she had to sign the contracts anyway. I'd never even owned a credit card. I didn't know what to do with all this money; it was lucky Mum was there for me.

As soon as I signed with Rip Curl I went through the most radical growth spurt where I felt like I couldn't even surf. I was freaking out, thinking, *I'm getting paid all this money and I can't even make a heat. I'm one of those has-beens already, a never-will-be.* It took me a couple of months to deal with that change. I grew three or four inches in six months. I felt like my mind knew how to do a certain manoeuvre, but my body wouldn't react. I was out of sync. I was skinny and had no power, and I felt like a gangly mess. Everyone else had grown into their bodies, but I was still growing.

It's just a part of growing up, and I've seen heaps of kids go through it. I was talking to top junior surfer Owen Wright about it recently. He shot up so quickly and was doing the exact same thing:

freaking out and feeling like he couldn't surf. I just said, 'Don't worry about it – you'll get used to it.' Now he's surfing better than ever. The worst part is you don't know what's going on because you've never been through anything like that before. I expected to be achieving certain goals now that I was a sponsored surfer, but in a way it was a good, grounding experience. It brought me back down to earth and made me look at my surfing from the bottom up again. My short-boards went from 5'6" to 5'10" or 5'11" in the space of six months, so it was a big adjustment.

ON THE SEARCH

My first trip to a non-English speaking country was to Indonesia for the world grommet titles in Bali in 1998. Joel had been there before, and we shared a room. I'd just turned seventeen, and we were living the dream – travelling and surfing and getting paid for it, but it hadn't become too serious yet. If we didn't have to compete the next day, we were out on the town living it up as young blokes in Bali tend to do. We were staying right there on the beach at Kuta in the thick of it. The coaches told us we weren't allowed to hire scooters, and I was shit-scared of driving one anyway, but Joel got one and we went everywhere on that thing. All the partying didn't seem to hurt Joel's performance too much – he ended up winning the contest. We had a pretty big night after he won and woke up the next morning still drunk, acting like idiots. I'd brought over a big box of Weet-Bix, because I didn't know if I'd like the food, and Joel had brought a bottle of duty-free rum. I was eating dry Weet-Bix that morning. We didn't have any bottled water and my mouth was dry, so I was washing it down with sips of rum. And then we went off for a surf. It was out of control.

We came home, and I was only back for a couple of days before I was off on a trip to the Maldives. It was my first-ever boat trip, with a photographer and a bunch of other young pro surfers, to get photos for a magazine article. There was Nick Leslie, Mark Spillane, photographer Andrew Shield and a couple of others. It was a classic trip, because we were on this little sketchy boat. Somehow we'd heard there weren't even any blankets onboard, so we stole those flimsy airline blankets, but we hardly needed them. There was no air conditioning; it was so hot we all slept up on the deck. There weren't even enough beds for everyone anyway. Rain squalls would come through every night, and we'd have to roll down the awnings on the side of the boat and try huddle into the middle of the deck to keep dry. There were six of us on this tiny boat for a week, and I thought that's what all these boat trips were like. We sure started at the bottom. We were eating okay – rice and chicken and chilli and eggs – and the waves were fun, without being mind-blowing, so we didn't care. We were just grommets, stoked to be on a trip. There was a big wide world opening up for me, and I liked what I'd seen and was keen for more. But when I came back from that trip everything changed.

LOSING SEAN

Sean and I were probably like a lot of brothers. We weren't angels and there were times when we'd fight, but ten minutes later it would all be forgotten. We had a really good relationship. He was one of those people who was a natural-born leader. He was always the head of the group, even if he was one of the smallest. If he wanted to do something, then everyone was pumped on doing it. He was a super-nice guy, but when he turned nasty, holy shit, it was full-on. He always looked out for me and I really looked up to him. One time I went to this under-eighteen nightclub in Coolangatta and, when I walked out, Deano and I were surrounded by this bunch of guys going, 'We're going to fuck you up.' Just because they felt like a fight. Deano sort of slinked off, and I was there by myself. I was lucky one of my friends came and said, 'No-one's touching him unless you go through me first.' And so they backed off. But then they followed me home and still wanted to fight. Sean and his best mate, Adam West, turned up and took these guys on just because they didn't want to see me get bashed. So he was a bit of a hero to me, and we did everything together.

Everything was going really well in our lives at the time. I was enjoying my first few travel experiences and this little taste of the life of a professional surfer. I knew that's what I wanted to do. Sean had just returned home from Japan, doing some WQS events over there, and he was amped about competing in the rest of the WQS, but he didn't have all that much money. I was making more money than he was at the time, so I lent him some to go over. I was actually planning on paying for him to go to Hawaii at the end of the year because he'd never been. And then we were going to do the WQS together the following year.

When I came back from that first trip to Bali and then the Maldives, I'd missed about a month of school. It was pretty hard going back. I'd been having such a great time, been on such an adventure, discovering the world, it was hard to sit in a classroom. Rip Curl wanted me to stay in school; my shaper, Darren Handley, was telling me to stay in school – everyone wanted me to. And then, when I went to school, the teachers told me I couldn't miss another day all year because I'd already been gone so much. I just looked at them and said, 'See ya.' I was done. A lot of my mates had already left school anyway, so that was it. A week or two later, Sean passed away. It would have been really hard going back to school after that.

After Sean died I didn't want to go anywhere. I had a real fear that something else might happen while I was away. I was really enjoying travelling up to that stage, but suddenly I just wanted to stay home. I looked at life so differently. I felt like I had to be responsible for the family, in a strange way, and be close to them all the time. I felt like I grew up ten years in a few weeks.

Around the time of his death, Mum would get really worried about us, and she'd always say, 'If you're not coming home, ring me.' She never used to be like that before. We'd all been at this party for the birthday of two friends. There was a band playing in a garage in an industrial area, so we could make as much noise as we liked and no-one cared. It was a really fun party. Sean and his friend Joel Green were being really funny. They'd found some electrical tape, started wrapping it around each other's heads like footy players and tried to tackle each other. They were the kind of guys who always made everyone laugh.

When it came time to leave, one of their girlfriends drove because they'd been drinking. They offered me a lift home, but I decided to walk, partly because I was staying at my mate Beau's place. A little while later I was walking with my mates when this car pulled up. I thought it was the cops, but we weren't drinking or doing anything wrong, so I didn't take much notice. And then two family friends got out of the car and just said, 'Mick, get in the car.' I was thinking, *Has someone I know been busted for drugs or DUI or something stupid like that?* I got in and there were two cops in the front seat. It was an unmarked police car, and they told me that Sean and Joel had just died in an accident. I totally freaked out. Their car had hit a gutter and ploughed into a tree just down the road from our house. The two girls were fine, but the boys, laying down in the back of the station wagon, had both been thrown out of the car and killed. It was unbelievable that I could have been talking to them just a few minutes before – and then all of a sudden they were gone.

The police took me home, and I had to tell everyone in my family. I ran in, woke Mum and told her. And then I rang Dad. Luckily my two brothers were there that night as well. My sister was in London at the time, and I had to ring and tell her too. It was pretty wild, being seventeen and having to break such news to everyone in the family.

Afterwards, I wasn't allowed to go down to the crash site. I was trying to sneak out, because I wanted to go and see the tree they'd hit, but no-one would let me until the car had been removed. I didn't surf either. I just sat in my room. I stayed there for four days. Everyone knew I hadn't been out of the house, and when I finally went surfing, all my mates appeared out of nowhere and paddled out with me. Every single one of my mates was there. D-bah wasn't crowded until we paddled out, and then suddenly there were so many of us.

It was epic. Everyone was screaming and hooting. I was still so over-whelmed by the whole thing. I didn't do a turn the whole surf. I just cruised straight along the wave, feeling the familiar comfort of the wind and seaspray in my face, and the pulse of the wave under my feet. It felt wild to surf again.

It's just really made me appreciate life more. I had known people who died before that – and I was really rattled by it – but when it hit so close to home it was so different. I began thinking about what I really wanted: *I want to be a pro surfer, and that's what I'm going to do.* Sean and I were going to do the pro tour together; that was our dream. So when I did make the tour, it made it that much more special to win an event or do well somewhere.

A friend of ours, Peter Kirkhouse, a surf filmmaker from Victoria, said to me after Sean died, 'Take on his energy and use it.' I didn't really think about it at the time but, when I think back, it really has carried with me. A lot of the time I feel like he's with me when I travel and compete. Sometimes, I'll dream about him every night for a week and get super-psyched. The dreams I have of him are so vivid and so real, it gets me stoked to see him again. Sometimes I feel like I'm with him. I just wake up happy that I've seen him again.

NO EXCUSES, NO REGRETS

Sean was really driven to succeed as a pro surfer. He was always writing to sponsors and training and doing this and that, and he surfed great. He wasn't the most flamboyant guy in the water, but he was really smooth and got results. And he used to really drill that into me. He taught me a lot, and I think that's where my work ethic came from. He was always encouraging. When I got sponsored by Rip Curl I didn't know how he'd react. But when I eventually told him of my better deal, he was nothing but stoked. I thought, *Wow, that is so cool, such a good attitude to have.* There was no jealousy or anything. He was genuinely happy for me. He still stole my wetsuits though. I remember coming home one time and I didn't have any left.

We had a pretty healthy rivalry going. I was almost scared to beat him in a contest because I knew I'd get bashed. In the Kirra club contests it was usually him and me fighting it out in the juniors, and he would hassle the shit out of me. I guess that's what older brothers do.

Sean and Joel were the funny guys, always writing off. Everyone who knew them always wanted to know what they were doing, because that was where the fun and laughter would be. That's why it hit so many people so hard. They had loads of good friends.

Afterwards, all my mates and everyone I knew were getting drunk around me every day. I guess that's how a lot of people grieve. They get drunk. But I didn't. I just wanted to deal with it in a clear frame of mind. I didn't enter too many surf contests after that for a while either. I had one event a month later. A friend of ours, Ado Wiseman, came and picked me up and took me to a contest at Coffs Harbour. It was actually good to get out and get on with life. I won the juniors and was pretty stoked. I won a trip to G-land, a surf camp in Indonesia, but I never even used it.

I did a couple more events towards the end of the year. But it wasn't until the next year that I started again and really decided what I was going to do – I was going to compete full-on, no mucking around. That's when I set my work ethic: if you're going to do something, do it properly. I still carry that idea with me today, and I think Sean had a lot to do with that. But also, ever since I was a little kid, I hated losing. I always want to do the best I could, no matter what it was. I don't want to be left sitting there thinking, *I could have done this* or *I could have done that*. If I do exactly what I should be doing at that time, then I've got no excuses, no regrets.

LIZ'S STORY, PART 2

Liz has always been happy to support her sons' surfing ambitions, even when it wasn't seen as a legitimate or respectable career path.

'People used to knock me, but I want them to have the opportunity to follow their dreams. I want all my boys to follow their dreams,' says Liz. 'Freedom and happiness in life are the most important things.'

Each brother did slightly better in surfing, as sponsorship opportunities and the junior contest scene grew. 'Poor old Edward went on the junior tour on the dole,' says Liz. 'Sean supported himself on a Newstart Allowance and did all sorts of jobs to get on the tour. He always did his own deals with sponsors. I never paid any attention to all this negotiation he was doing. He was amazingly independent, and Mick would have learnt a lot from him. Sean was the businessman, and I'm sure if he was alive today he would be Mick's manager. Maybe not doing the work I do, such as finances, but he would have been the negotiator. Sean and I would have worked together. We would have been a formidable team.'

It was Sean who led the surfing contingent to lobby the principal at Palm Beach–Currumbin High School to have surfing included in its sports excellence program. 'Sean was the instigator of the elite sports program for surfing, with backup from the others. Sean was the one who went in to the principal and said, "We have lots of talent here. We want you to have an elite sports program for surfing." Sean was just so charismatic – everyone wanted to be his friend. They hero-worshipped him, all his friends.'

Life was good for the Fannings on the Gold Coast, it seemed finally the fates had delivered the family some peace and stability. 'Everything was going amazingly great. They were very privileged to be going down to the [Quiksilver] camps at Lennox with Danny Wills and Tommy Carroll and Andrew Murphy.'

But while all the boys were talented on a surfboard, it soon became apparent that Mick had something special. As a mother, Liz found the looming success of her youngest son, and the prospect of how the older boys would deal with it, challenging.

'That was a very hard time for me too because you never want to see your youngest overtake the others, and I could see that happening. Even though Sean had got good results, I knew Mick would probably overtake him, and I didn't know what I would do. How would I support Sean through this and how would Sean feel?' Liz pauses, gulps, her eyes welling with tears. 'And then he *died . . . And I think I could have supported him all right if I could have him back.'*

The family lived in a unit on Hill Street, Tweed Heads, overlooking a notorious intersection where accidents were common. 'I used to look down onto that intersection. Six months before, I was sitting on the balcony and I heard this crash – there were always bloody accidents down there,' says Liz. 'I said, "I just want to go down there, because I want to make sure it's not Sean." It's funny how you get these premonitions.'

Six months later, that intersection claimed her son's life and that of his friend, Joel Green. 'The night Sean died we had a photographer staying with us who did a lot of work with Mick, Peter Kirkhouse. He was asleep in one of the back rooms. When we heard the news, and Mick did give me the news, I thought Sean had been stabbed. I never even thought he would be in a car because the party was just up the road. So I suddenly realised that this guy was asleep, so I left him till about four in the morning, and I went in and told him: "You'll never believe this but Sean's been killed." And he actually said to me, "I want you to go out at sunrise and see the new day, because you need to do that." And he said to Mick, "Take Sean's spirit in and keep it with you, because now he's yours." So, this guy who I've never seen again, he said that to me and he said that to Mick, and that really did something beautiful for us, because I did go out and stand on the top of D-bah and see the sunrise. Nothing's changed really – it's just that Sean's not here anymore.'

Those welling tears can be held back no longer.

Peter Kirkhouse had only met Liz a few days before when he suddenly found himself in the middle of the family's tragedy.

He'd been filming Mick surfing for his sponsor, Rip Curl, and had just enjoyed a day of fun waves with Mick and Sean at nearby South Stradbroke Island. 'You could really tell how close he was to his brother. We'd just had a really good day together, a really fun day surfing Straddy, good little beachies, and his brother was ripping,' remembers PK.

Peter drove the boys to the party that night and came home early. 'I actually heard the accident and fell back asleep. Then there was a knock on my door a couple of hours later.'

Until the rest of the family arrived, Peter was the only one Liz and Mick had for support. 'I remember taking him up on to D-bah Hill and saying, "Your brother's spirit is there, grab it." I could just feel his presence. I've always been a little bit spiritual.' When the rest of the family arrived, PK quietly slipped out the back door and caught a flight home to Victoria.

Out of the tragedy, in the midst of their grief, at least some kind of healing occurred as the family came together. 'Peter, Edward and John had really not seen much of each other but, for some reason, they were together that night. It was unbelievable,' says Liz. 'They were together for the first time in months, and so they just got in the car and came up. Mick stayed in his room for days. One night, John and I were home and Mick came out absolutely so distressed. One of the most beautiful things was that John and I were there for him. John and I were able, as mother and father, to comfort Mick. As much as everyone loved Sean so much, *they were like two little peas in a pod. Sean was his absolute hero, and he lost that.'*

The grieving process was long, torturous and very communal. *'People expected us as a family to rescue them from their grief. I haven't got one thing of Sean's. Because we had an open house and everybody came, I gave things to his friends because I felt for them.'*

When Mick finally emerged from his room, it was the ocean he headed to first for solace. *'It was so sad for Mick. After about a week he came out of his room, and the boys went surfing and they all cheered him,'* says Liz.

PK had no other contact with the family until years later, when he found himself at the bar alongside Mick at the end of the 2006 Rip Curl Pro at Bells Beach. As a rowdy mob celebrated Kelly Slater's latest victory, the pair shared a quiet moment.

'He just commented on it, how he still remembers what I said and how it helped him at the time,' says PK. *'It did mean a lot to me when he said that.'*

MICK'S TIPS – HOW TO SURF BETTER

Everyone wants to surf better, but it's probably one of the hardest sports to learn and improve at. It's not that easy to try something over and over again until you get it right, because no two waves are ever the same and you have to paddle back out each time you fall off. It can be a steep learning curve. But there are ways to make it less steep, and a little knowledge and guidance from experienced surfers can really accelerate your progress. Try and find surf partners who surf better than you and are happy to pass on some tips and advice, or find a surf coach or surf school suitable to your ability.

BEGINNERS

The best kind of wave for an absolute beginner is a little rolling whitewash. Dumpers do exactly what their name suggests: they dump. So avoid waves that are breaking fast and hard. Look for the whitewash that rolls for as long as possible, so that it gives you more time to get settled, then try to get to your feet.

After you find the right wave, the next most important thing is to find the right board. When you're first starting off the most important thing is getting a board that's really stable. You see a lot of beginners trying to ride boards that are way too short. You're not going to be turning your first few surfs, so just find the biggest, most stable board possible - wide, long, thick. Those soft beginner boards are also good because they can't hurt you. Big tandem boards like they hire out to the tourists in Waikiki are great because they provide such a stable platform.

The best way to get started is to practise on the beach. You want to lie about two feet back from the nose, because beginners tend to push forward with their chest. If you are too far forward, you'll push the nose of the board underwater and nosedive. Even draw a line in the wax where your eyes are when you lie in the right spot. Practise lying on your board on the beach and pushing up to your feet. The first thing you need to work out is if your stance is natural or goofy - if you stand with your left foot forward you are natural, and if you have your right foot forward you are goofy. Some people will already know from skateboarding. If you're not sure, try standing up with your feet together and leaning forward so you're almost falling over - whichever foot you instinctively move forward to balance yourself is your leading foot. But don't think about it too much - it's just whatever feels right.

For people who have never surfed before, try pushing up to one foot and one knee, then stabilise yourself with your hands on the rails of the board. Push up again to both feet from there. I find that works best when you actually get on a wave. Your natural tendency is to rush and get up as fast as you can, but you need to slow it down and relax. Just take your time. If you get up on one knee, wait until you get your balance before you push up again, almost like a clean and jerk in weightlifting – two stages. Later on, you can smooth this out into one fluid movement.

You want to find an experienced surfer to take you out in the water for the first time, whether it's a friend or a professional surf coach. They'll know where to paddle out and how to avoid rips and other surfers. They'll help you through the waves with your board and push you into your first few rides. I love taking people surfing for the first time because they get so stoked, so don't be shy about asking an experienced surfer for help.

There are a lot of surf schools and coaches out there of varying quality. The guys who are ex-pro surfers who now coach probably have the most experience and expertise to share, or at least find a coach who is an accomplished surfer themselves. You wouldn't get ski lessons from someone who could hardly ski.

INTERMEDIATE

One of the key things to remember in surfing is, where you look is where you end up. It's like when you're learning to drive – they say that people usually run into something because they are looking at it and freaking out about hitting it. They follow their line of sight without even realising it. It's the same way on a wave. You'll see those classic bottom-turn shots of guys like Kelly, and you can see he is looking exactly at the spot at the top of the wave that he wants to hit, like he has that precise section of the lip in the crosshairs. That's when you surf your best, when you keep targeting the places on the wave you want to hit.

The surfers I like to watch are the people who link everything together with no down spots. I like to see them use the whole wave with a lot of variety – big turns and big airs all mixed together. I really like to watch rail surfing too. Sometimes I see kids who are just learning trying airs straightaway and never learning how to use their rail. You have to have a mix of everything if you want to do well these days.

When I was growing up I had a little sheet that I stuck on my door with the different days of the week. Each day I would write how I wanted to surf and what I wanted to try on that day. For example:

Monday – snaps.
Tuesday – cutbacks.
Wednesday – airs.
Thursday – tail-slides.
Friday – big turns.
Saturday and Sunday – link it all together.

I found this was a really fun way to learn these different kinds of manoeuvres in whatever conditions were on offer. I had days when it wasn't good for airs, but I would still try. I am still trying to learn to land them now!

I still set little goals for what I want to achieve in a surf session. I find when I have a goal I improve a lot more than if I'm just fluffing around all the time.

ADVANCED

I really like to watch other surfers who I admire and try and figure out how they do big airs, or ride barrels, or perform manoeuvres that are a cut above the rest. I also like to watch young guys doing all the new stuff. Although I will probably never do a rodeo flip or anything like that, I am still amazed at what they are doing.

When I was a kid, I used to watch surf videos day and night, especially before surfs. I would see something that impressed me and go out and try to imitate it if I could. Learning the *feeling* of that manoeuvre is the important thing, so your body gets used to the necessary movements involved. The biggest help when trying to take your surfing to the next level is watching lots of footage of yourself surfing and then other more accomplished surfers you'd like to surf like. For instance, I might film my cutback, then watch Taylor Knox's cutback and analyse the way he holds the turn all the way from the top of the wave to the bottom and all the way round to smash the lip behind him. He holds such a good line with the pressure on. I'll study where he holds his arms and where he starts the turn. Those sorts of video comparisons are a big help. I did some analysis on the Red Bull trip in the Mentawais where I could overlay footage of the different surfers and compare their manoeuvres. That was really helpful because you can pick up all the subtle differences in technique. Sofia Mulanovich and Sally Fitzgibbon were studying their tube riding and seeing how they could just angle their foot a little bit more. Small adjustments like that can make a huge difference.

It can be really hard to make all these little adjustments when you are actually out surfing because it all happens so quickly, but through repetition you can do it.

I'm always learning new things - you never stop learning. I sit there and analyse things all the time. If I am going to Tahiti or Pipe, I'll watch footage of Bruce, Andy and Jamie O'Brien, and the way they ride the barrel. Then I'll get out there and try to follow that pattern I've embedded in my mind, without completely mimicking their style. I know goofy-footer Shaun Cansdell used to watch footage of natural-footers in a mirror to reverse the image. You can see it in his style: his forehand surfing is like a lot of natural-footers, because he watches guys like Kelly and Taylor in reverse and takes little parts of their surfing.

It's good to get feedback from a trusted coach or friends. I watch so many different surfers and talk to so many different people about surfing, but you've got to pick and choose which bits of feedback ring true for you. You can ignore or accept any advice. If you're not feeling it, you're not going to do it. Don't be afraid to learn from unexpected sources. Some people are too proud or stuck in their ways to change, but everyone's different and everyone works in different ways. It's like everything else - boards, training, competing - keep experimenting with different things and find what works for you.

When trying something new, go out and do it how you think it should be done, with a clear vision of it in your mind. If you fall off, don't worry. Paddle back out and try again. But before you do, think about where you made the mistake and remember that feeling just before you fell off. Then visualise how you could make the manoeuvre next time and act accordingly. Try something new – that's how you learn.

chapter 3.
WELCOME TO THE WORLD

From that point on, things seemed to happen really quickly. In the space of three years I went from making finals of pro junior events to qualifying for the WCT. I started getting a fair bit of attention in the media too, and there was a lot of hype about the Cooly Kids bursting onto the world scene, but I didn't take much notice. I just wanted to go surfing.

I didn't have a stellar junior career, like some guys. I'd had a third in the juniors in the Aussie Titles. And Dean and I won the schoolboy teams title once. Probably the highlight for me in the juniors was when I won the original pro junior at Narrabeen in 1999. That was the most prestigious junior event in the country, with a lot of great surfers among the past winners: Occy, Tom Carroll, Joel Engel, Luke Egan. It was hard to fathom that my name was on the trophy alongside all these guys. Then we went down to Victoria for the Jetty Surf Pro Junior, and I ended up winning that one too. Two pro junior wins back-to-back was a big thing for me, especially because they were the two richest junior events at the time. But after those two wins I lost the plot and didn't do so well in the overall junior series.

Later that same year I was invited to a specialty event at Sandon Point, Wollongong, called the Konica Skins, alongside all the top pro surfers of the day. I was only seventeen and, looking at the heats, they seemed so gnarly with guys like Occy, Luke Egan, Munga Barry and so many guys I'd grown up admiring. I thought, *This is going to be heavy*. But there was something in the air that day, and I got on a roll. It was the place I used to surf with my brothers when Mum drove us down the South Coast all those years ago. My mum was there, along with two of my really good mates. It was held on Sean's twenty-first birthday, and it was pretty weird because I won twenty-one grand that day. I didn't even know until the end of the event how I'd gone overall. When they said, 'You've won', I went, *'What?'* It was an incredible day. I wasn't even old enough to get into the RSL club for the party that night, but luckily I had a fake ID and managed to get in with all my mates.

A couple of months later, Joel Parkinson won the Jeffreys Bay WCT event, the Billabong Pro in South Africa, as a wildcard. I was sitting down in Durban and having a beer with Joel after he won J-Bay, and we were both asking, 'How is this happening?' We still felt like a couple of kids and, between us, we'd just taken down some of the biggest names in surfing. It was hard to believe that we were suddenly competing against all these guys we'd looked up to as grommets.

In 2000, I joined the WQS. I wasn't really planning on doing it full-time, but I went down to Newcastle for the event there and had to start from the first round because I had no seeding. I didn't expect to do anything but, again, I just kept getting through heats. Before I knew it, I was into the last day, made the final and ended up winning the event. I decided right then, 'Yeah, I'm going to do the 'QS this year.'

That same year, I also had a memorable trip with the Rip Curl team to the Mentawai Islands in Indonesia, and the waves just blew my mind. We scored perfect Macaronis, four to six foot and as good as it gets, with just a few pro bodyboarders in the water. The next day was going to be bigger, with perfect winds for Lance's Rights, so we headed across. At first light, it was big and stormy, but impossible to tell exactly how big because there was no-one out. It was a radical storm, and we watched in disbelief as a waterspout formed out to sea and went straight past our boat, through the line-up and onto land. You could see leaves flying into the air and trees shaking as this thing dispersed over the island. The skipper manoeuvred the boat inside the reef so we could get a better look at the line-up, but we still couldn't tell how big it was, so I figured I'd better paddle out and have a closer look. It was easily eight foot, a little bit onshore, and I was absolutely shitting myself. Gabe Kling came out too and we snuck into a couple; then Chris Davidson paddled out. Travis Lynch and Nathan Hedge had stitches in their heads from the previous day surfing Macca's, so they were watching from the boat. Pretty soon, the wind swung offshore and the line-up was transformed into perfect, barrelling rights, with just three of us out. Eventually, a bunch of American guys turned up – Chris Ward, Dino Andino, Kaipo Jaquias – and we all got shacked off our heads. It was a five-day trip and we scored big-time with perfect waves every day. That Mentawai trip made a big impression. I've taken every chance to go back since and have rarely been disappointed.

I enjoyed the travel and competing right from the start. There was one stage in France when I got really homesick. I was staying on my own; I didn't know anything about the country and didn't speak the language. I was walking to the contest, not really having a clue where I was going, feeling pretty lost and alone, and just felt like packing my bags and going home. But I stuck it out and soon got into the travel groove. I came really close to qualifying that first year – I think I was two heats away from making the WCT. It was a little disappointing because the guys that I was travelling with in 2000, Joel Parkinson and Nathan Hedge, both qualified. So I thought, *Okay, what do I do now?* It definitely helped light the fire under my arse to get on tour.

In hindsight, I'm glad I didn't qualify that first year because I would have gone into that next year thinking, *Oh, this is easy*. I wanted to come out firing in 2001 and have a really good run of events early. And I did, but not quite the way I'd expected.

BACK TO THE WALL

The human spine is a remarkable piece of engineering – all those little vertebrae fitting together to create the central column of your entire body and nervous system. It's pretty much the worst part of the body to have trouble with; if your spine's tweaked then nothing works properly.

I always knew I had a weird back, and that it was getting weirder over time, but I'd never seen a chiropractor or anyone about it. Photos of me surfing Kirra showed my back almost bending at right angles, and I knew something was up. Then it started giving me a bit of trouble. I was on a Rip Curl trip to Samoa, and we were all training because there wasn't a lot of surf. My back started getting a bit sore. Over the next couple of days it just got worse and worse until all my back muscles seized up and I could hardly move. It was so painful. When I got home I tried everything – acupuncture, massage, this and that – but nothing was helping. I had the Quiksilver Pro coming up at Snapper, which was a WQS event back then, and knew I had to try something.

I'd always thought chiropractors were for whingers, and I thought I was pretty hard. But during that Quiksilver Pro I was desperate. I heard there was a chiropractor at the contest, so I went and saw him. His name was Chris Prosser, and it was a good thing I found him. I couldn't even surf at that point. Chris helped me get through that event, with a lot of stretching and adjustments and plenty of painkillers, and I managed to place second to Taj Burrow in the final. Chris got me into a routine of stretching before every heat – I've always been pretty flexible, but that just took it to another level. Being a WQS contest, it was a long event. I think I surfed pretty much every heat against Taj, going back and forth, winning heats or coming second. Taj was really at the top of his game, so that was good for my confidence. But I was having to take two Nurofen for the pain every time I surfed, even free surfing. I'd have to go home and stretch my back out after every session and I had to really plan my surfs.

I couldn't just go whenever I felt like it. I put all my trust in Chris, because he'd seen the condition so many times before, especially among surfers. He knew exactly what I needed to do. I was going to the doctor's surgery for X-rays and getting treated by Chris all through that event, and it seemed to work. In the process, he taught me a lot about managing my back.

The actual condition I have is called scoliosis, which comes from the Greek word for 'crooked'. It's basically curvature of the spine, which can get progressively worse over time, causing pain, limiting mobility and often requiring surgery. I think it's a hereditary condition, but it's made worse by activities like surfing, which puts a lot of strain on the spine and can cause imbalances in musculature. Chris raised the possibility of surgery to correct it, but he said he thought I could correct it myself if I was prepared to work on it conscientiously. That was all the motivation I needed. I've had friends with scoliosis; they've had the surgery and it's a heavy procedure that involves bone grafts or the insertion of metal plates to straighten the spine. That idea didn't exactly thrill me. So I'm glad I was able to deal with it myself, non-invasively. I was always confident I could get on top of it. The most important thing is strengthening your core so that it takes the brunt of supporting your body. The spine is just like a pole – if it isn't strong, it will just bend in the middle.

I also found temporary pain relief from a rather unlikely source, the anti-inflammatory drug Naprogesic that's mainly used for period pain. Chris recommended it, and I can remember feeling a bit embarrassed going to the chemist and asking for a packet. The woman behind the counter started laughing. 'Have you got period pain?' she asked.

Even with all the treatment, the day after the event I couldn't even move. I was meant to be leaving for a surf trip, but I was so stiff and sore I literally could not even get off the floor. I kept seeing Chris a few times a week after that, and he gave me all these different exercises and stretches to strengthen my core. My mate Ado Wisemen gave me a yoga book he'd been using, and I got right into that. I'd been telling Ado how bad my back was, and he was saying I should come and try yoga. I wasn't too keen at first, but as soon as I tried it my back felt so much better. I had this one yoga sequence I used to do religiously every morning when I got out of bed, before every surf and before I went to bed at night. I was doing it four or five times a day, and that helped a lot.

The best core-strength exercise I've found is leg raisers. You lie flat on your back and suck your core down towards the ground so your lower back is flat on the floor. You lift one leg at a time, bent at first, but as you get better you gradually straighten your legs out. I was doing sixty to one hundred of these a day. I still do those them from time to time. I'll get a blood-pressure cuff (those inflatable bands doctors use to take your blood pressure), place it under the arch of my lower back, pump it up and do the leg raisers that way.

It took a good couple of months of hard work and treatment to get my back right. The amazing thing was, while all this was going on and my whole career hung in the balance, I got on the biggest roll of my competitive life. I went over to Margaret River and won a WQS event there; then I got a wildcard into the WCT Rip Curl Pro at

Bells Beach and won that. At the time I couldn't believe it. It was all I could do just to get myself fit and able to surf each heat. But I understand now why I did so well. I had a focal point that wasn't surfing, one that was taking my mind off worrying about the contests. That's also how I discovered the benefits of getting into a routine around contests. Before every heat I had this little stretching routine that I'd do that worked well for both my back and mind. That potential setback became a strength. I also started taking more notice of what I ate and how that affected me. That was just the first step in what I now know about fitness and nutrition. My back condition proved a great lesson: what seems like an obstacle can actually move you in the right direction.

I know a lot of surfers get back problems, because of the arched paddling position and the strain surfing puts on your spine. I have people come up to me and ask if I needed surgery to fix the scoliosis, and I say, 'No, you've just got to put in the hard work.' It's better than going under the knife.

Despite all this, or maybe because of it, I felt my surfing was getting stronger each time I paddled out. I was concentrating on back strength and being more conscious of how I used my body. That seemed to make all the difference. I still have to be conscious of my back or it can flare up. If I don't train right, it can really throw it out, so it's one of those things you've got to keep on top of.

Before I developed my back regiment, I'd always been pretty inconsistent with my results, and I'd never really understood why. But in hindsight, I could see what I was doing before the events where I did well. There was a real pattern to it. I then figured out the routine that worked best for me and stuck to it. Having to focus on my back and stretching routine before I surfed actually cleared my mind of a lot of the mental chatter that can get in the way of doing your best.

When you get on a roll like that, you feel clear-minded. All you're thinking about is the next wave, or what you need to do to get ready for each heat. You go into yourself and don't even notice distractions around you. That's why you seem to have more energy too, because you're not expending energy on unnecessary things. Everything you do seems to be the right thing, because you're feeling it, not over-thinking it. Sometimes you actually learn more when you lose, because it's usually pretty easy to see what you've done wrong. It's not so easy or obvious to learn from your victories. A lot of people don't actually analyse what they've done *right*. But it was a really valuable lesson for me.

Winning Bells as a wildcard was incredible, but totally different to winning an event once you're on the WCT. As a wildcard, it's a one-off event – there's no pressure. If I'd lost in the first round, oh well, that's just what wildcards do. I surfed against guys like Luke Egan, Taylor Knox and Danny Wills, who were deadset heroes of mine as a kid, and I thought I was going to get absolutely flogged. But it's not until you actually get on tour that you realise how daunting it can be surfing against wildcards. They're hungry and under no pressure – they just go for it. They don't care. As a full-time WCT surfer you're fighting for your ratings points, your place on tour and your pride, in a sense, because no-one wants to get beaten by a wildcard.

I had a bit of a mixed event, to be honest. The heat with Louie Egan was actually tied, but I had the higher wave score so I got through on a countback. My best heat was against Peterson Rosa from Brazil in the fourth round. Peterson knocked me out the year before in the same round, so it was daunting. He's one guy who knew how to get under my skin. I really like him, and he's not the prettiest surfer in the world, but for some reason he'd always frickin' get me for a good few years. But this time the waves were pumping, and I scored my highest heat total and got through. I then had a quarterfinal with Taylor Knox, who was pretty much my favourite surfer in the world. It was a morning heat, and the waves were perfect. I said to him, 'Far out, how good are the waves?' And he said, 'I know, there's no way you could have a bad heat.' And we both went out there and sucked, couldn't do anything right, and had to eat our words. I just scraped through.

The final with Danny Wills was probably the single heat I've learnt the most from in my whole career. I paddled out and went, 'Good luck, Willsy.' I was just stoked to be there, in perfect waves, with one of my heroes. And he didn't even look at me. He knew what he wanted. I thought, *Oh, shit. Far out – he means business.* I watched him a lot in the final. Still to this day, out of all the guys on tour, he was the most intimidating for me – definitely. I was stoked that I got to compete against him, let alone win. He was so calculating with everything he did. But winning the event was unbelievable and gave me a huge confidence boost for the rest of the year, like I finally believed I really deserved to be there.

THE LENNOX SESSIONS

In early July 2001, the entire east coast of Australia was hit with one of the best easterly swells in living memory. Everywhere from Noosa to Ulladulla was pumping. The tour was in Jeffreys Bay, so none of the WCT surfers were home, but I was lucky enough be in the thick of it. The points here weren't that good because the wind was nor'-west, sideshore on the points, but Tweed Bar, the sandbar outside the Tweed River mouth, was excellent that morning. I had a surf out there early. When I came in, I was thinking, *Somewhere must be perfect right now*. And for some reason I just decided to drive down to Lennox Head in northern New South Wales. I jumped in the car with my mates Shagga and Guts. We got there and it was just freight-training down the point. I went, 'WHAAAAAAAATTTTT!' It was low tide in the morning, so the swell was just pushing with the tide, and we scored incredible waves all afternoon. We went back down there the next day and it was like J-Bay – strong offshores, the spray whipping off the tops of the waves. I was hardly out of the water all day. We surfed Lennox in the morning, went and got some food, then surfed this left near Ballina. I only got a couple of waves, but they were pretty sick. Then we went back to Lennox, and it was *still* firing. There are a lot of really good local surfers round that area, and I thought I was going to have to wait my turn and pick up scraps. But every time I paddled for a wave they just went, 'Go, go, go.' They're probably the two most perfect days I've ever surfed on the east coast. I've never seen it like that before or since. The swell was just so consistent and clean and from the perfect direction.

I had one of those sessions where you can't do a thing wrong. You're so pumped on the waves that everything you do just sticks. I wasn't doing anything crazy – I was more just trying to find the barrel – but it felt so good drawing really long lines, setting things up, not having to try and fit manoeuvres in like in a heat. After the roll I'd been on at the start of the year, it really felt like things were going my way. I was riding a 6'6" Wade Tokoro the first day, and it felt insane. The next day I rode a 6'1" channel bottom that DH made me, because the waves were so perfect.

QUALIFYING

After that start to the season, I qualified for the WCT about halfway through the year. By the time we got to France, the pressure of qualifying was gone. I slackened off a bit and was ready to have some fun. We had a house in Hossegor that was crammed full of a lot of my best mates – Joel, Dean, Hedgey, Aaron Waters – because none of them had booked any accommodation. And we had ridiculous fun. Joel was on a roll, too, and won two six-star WQS events, so we were all loving life.

I lost a bit of that intensity through the middle of the season, and I didn't really get it back until Hawaii at the year's end.

It was really important to me to do well in Hawaii. I was coming second on the WQS ratings to Taj, but it wasn't even about results and ratings – I wanted to prove to myself that I could surf those waves. And it was big that year. Haleiwa was huge for the contest, and I slipped into that mode where everything seemed really clear. I ended up getting second to Andy Irons at Haleiwa, and I made the quarters at Pipe and Sunset, so it was a really good Hawaiian season for me. I surprised myself at Pipe, and that gave me a lot of confidence going into my first year on the WCT.

When you go to Hawaii and you've had a bit of publicity, everyone's like, 'Oh yeah, this kid has done this or that – but can he cut it over here?' You've got to prove yourself all over again in Hawaii, and you don't get any respect from the locals until you've done something there. Fortunately, I started getting a few waves at Off the Wall, and the Haleiwa event felt like a mental breakthrough for me, as much as anything. Big Haleiwa is as scary as anything I'd seen, and I was petrified, but everything just felt right when I got in the water.

It was the first year I got a big quiver of boards from Wade Tokoro, and working with a Hawaiian shaper definitely helped too. I remember getting ready for my first heat at Haleiwa, and I was like, 'God, it's so big out there.' And Wade just said, 'Don't worry. Sit off this little spot and it will keep you out of harm's way, but you can still paddle into the sets.' It's so important to have good line-up spots in Hawaii that let you orient yourself out in the water. It could be a little marker on land, like a tree or a house or a mountain, that helps you position yourself. It's almost like having the key to the spot, and then you can work it out. I've sat on the same spot there ever since.

Sunset is a whole different kettle of fish, though. Every year I paddle out at Sunset, I think, *Oh yeah, this is the spot I sat on last year*. But it seems to keep changing. The next thing you know, a big west seat will rear up and mow you down. I don't think you ever really master that place.

I haven't had too many really bad wipe-outs in Hawaii, touch wood. That year, I had a pretty heavy one at Backdoor, and I thought I was going to get really worked. But instead of pushing me down into the reef, it dragged me in towards shore. It was like I was riding the wave underwater and I could feel the reef racing past me, inches away from my face. I remember thinking, *If I hit the reef, I am going to lose my head.* All of a sudden, I felt my hips get stuck on this one bit of reef. Luckily I was wearing a spring suit, but it still cut me through the rubber. I'll always remember that one.

I was lucky, too, that I got to know a few of the locals early on. Me, Beau Emerton, Andy Irons and Ian Walsh all shared a house that our sponsor, Red Bull, rented right on the beach at Off the Wall. I got to know Andy and his brother, Bruce, pretty well, and then I met all their boys from Kauai – Kaiborg and Kala and all those guys. They are some of the heaviest guys over there, but you get to go to their parties and meet everyone, and it all seems a bit less intimidating. It's changed a lot since the old 'Bustin' Down the Door' days, and the Australians and Hawaiians get on really well these days. Back in the day, a lot of the Hawaiians didn't really leave their shores very much, whereas now they all go to Bali and Tahiti and Australia, and a lot of the time everyone's travelling together, becoming friends. A lot of the guys are doing the tour, staying at each other's houses and helping each other out.

I can totally understand the localism that exists in Hawaii, because for those six weeks of the year the whole world's on their doorstep. The local surfers are there to get their wave, get cover shots and photos, do well in the events and make careers. It's like when the whole world comes to Coolangatta, all I want to do is surf my home break. I think the crowd control and all that kind of stuff in Hawaii is definitely needed, otherwise things get chaotic. On a big wave at Pipeline, if someone falls out of the roof on you, it can kill you. You see how many people have died there, even without other people dropping in on their waves. A certain amount of localism's a good thing to keep everyone honest.

MICK'S TIPS – KNOW YOUR SURFBOARD

Understanding your surfboard is the most important thing any surfer can do. Getting your boards right requires so much work, and the hardest thing is to explain to your shaper exactly what you like. So having a good relationship with your shaper is the first step. When I was young, I was always asking DH about why boards do this and that. Sometimes I think he wanted to just kick me out of the factory so he could get some work done. The average punter might not notice, but no two boards ever go the same, not even if they are made to exactly the same specifications. There is just too much manual labour that goes into a custom board, from blowing the blank, getting a machine to cut it, the shaper shaping it, the glasser glassing it, finning the board, filler coat, sanding, sand finish or gloss. Any of these things can go right or wrong. And when they all come together, that's when you get your magic board. In saying that, though, every person surfs differently and feels different things. So what works for me probably isn't the best thing for you. That is why there are so many shapers in the world, because they can work their magic differently for different people.

Even when you find the magic board, that board might last for a year, maximum, because every surfer is evolving as they go through life. I don't ride the boards I did in 2007 now because I have evolved my surfing in a different direction. Over the years I have worked with a few people to get a better understanding of the things that work for me. I can give advice on how things should work for others, but I can't feel what others feel.

Today, I work with two people as much as I can: Darren Handley and Wade Tokoro. Of all the shapers I have used over the years, these two guys consistently give me the best results. DH makes the best shortboards in the world for me at the moment. We have a really good understanding of each other and have almost created our own language when talking about boards.

BOTTOM CURVES

I can ride the curve that we have created over the past fourteen years in all conditions. It's a smooth, gradual curve with a slight flip in the back 3 to 6 inches of the tail. This gives me plenty of drive but allows me to turn tight to the curl of the wave. Growing up I would use single concaves and nothing else. This gave me plenty of speed in small waves. Over the past few years, as I have grown stronger, I felt I needed something in the fins that would help with direction changes without sucking to the face of the wave. So with the deep, single concave we had, we added some double concave through the back 12 inches of the tail. This breaks up the water and makes changing direction a little more free-flowing.

TAILS

Ninety-nine per cent of the time I ride rounded square-tails. This tail seems to be the all-rounder for me. I used to ride round-tails a lot as a kid, because I liked the feeling of drawing out a turn. But now it's rounded squares. It feels similar to a round-tail with the long, gradual curve back to the tip, but it still lets go when needed. Plus, I like to push hard and it stays on top of the water, so I don't bog a rail. I have this problem when riding pintails as shortboards – I feel I bog a lot when doing hacks and cutbacks. The turning axis becomes smaller with a pin because of the reduced width in the tail. Pintails are great for tube-riding and bigger boards. Swallowtails are boards I just cannot ride. I find they lose touch with the wave when transitioning from axis to axis, and I don't like that feeling.

RAILS

I like what you could call a low boxy rail, which might sound contradictory. Boxy rails are full and round and very forgiving. They very rarely catch, but they are extremely hard to bury. Low rails are the exact opposite of the boxy rail. If you round a sharp kitchen knife at the tip, you'd get the profile of a low rail. They are, literally, knifey and very unforgiving, but extremely easy to put on a rail. They are great for clean waves and when going fast. They make your board feel thin and sensitive. A medium rail is somewhere in between low and boxy, and is what you'll see on most stock boards or for guys who enjoy their surfing with little fuss.

A low boxy rail is a melding of the two concepts – boxy at the curve of the rail and really soft, but still a lot thinner than the middle of your board. This rail gives you the non-catching sensation and smoothness through turns, but still allows you to bury the rail with ease. It's a tricky rail to ride for most surfers, but I've found it gives the best results for high performance.

FINS

Fins can alter any board dramatically. Fins can change a board from bad to amazing, if you know what you are looking for. I could go on for days about fins because there are so many out there. For me, glassed-on fins are the best. They feel so much smoother and more responsive. But don't get me wrong, a lot of the fin systems around today are incredible and allow you to experiment with different fin shapes. If I was searching for a new style of fin, I would use an interchangeable fin system to try various models out on the one board. That way, you know the fin is responsible for any variation in the way the board surfs. When I find a new fin I like, I take it to the fin-maker and ask them to duplicate the fin for me as glass-ons.

Then there are the number of fins you use on a board. Obviously the thruster, or three-fin, is the one that gives the best results in a wide range of conditions. It has drive, speed and turning capabilities that no other set-up has. What Simon Anderson did when he came up with the thruster in 1981 – the year I was born, by the way – was the biggest breakthrough ever in surfing. As I use thrusters day in and day out, I often love to get on different equipment and enjoy the different styles of surfing that you can do on these boards.

SINGLE-FIN STYLE

I love riding single fins. They have so many great qualities that I really enjoy in surfing. They can feel slow but, ridden correctly, you can have so much fun. They teach you to ride a wave for what it is. It's hard to generate speed on a single-fin, because you don't have the side fins to push against through turns, so being in the right spot on the wave is crucial. They will teach you how to draw nice lines, too. But the thing I like most about them is how they carve. You have to be on rail and you have to guide them through the turn with the right amount of pressure. Push too hard and you'll spin out, push too soft and you'll lose your rail pressure. They also hold really nice lines through the barrel.

I just like the way people ride different boards and draw really nice lines. One of my favourite surf photos is of a guy named Wayne Williams at Angourie, NSW, on an old single-fin. It's a black-and-white shot from some old surfing magazine that I had framed by my bed for years as a grom. That photo, how he's on rail on that sort of board, really inspired me. Every time I ride a single-fin, I want to see if I can do the same turn. I know I never will, but it's fun to try. I get amped on things like that.

TWIN-FIN FUN

Twinnies are really fun boards. They can generate a lot of speed because they don't have the drag of the third stabilising fin. They are great for little running waves, because they just get up and zip along. You have to be careful turning them because they release so easily. They are great for flowing turns together and make surfing fun when the waves are boring.

QUAD-MANIA

There has been a lot of interest in quads, with Kelly riding them in competition, but I haven't spent much time on them. I find them very similar to twinnies, but maybe a little more stable through turns. They keep their speed well and are great for small waves.

ROCKER

The rocker, or the bottom curve from nose to tail, varies according to the sort of waves you surf. Sometimes you think you have the perfect board, but then you surf a different type of wave and the board won't work.

Flat rockers, with little nose entry and tail lift, are amazing for going fast. They are best in small, mushy waves as they will pick up speed, keep it and fly across dead sections with ease. The downside is they don't fit in the pocket of the wave very well and you might find yourself surfing mainly out on the face of the wave rather than close to the curl.

Medium rockers are probably the most commonly used on shortboards – anywhere from 4½ to 5¾ inches of nose lift and 1½ to 3 inches of tail lift will suit pretty much all conditions, from your local beachies to point breaks. I generally use 5¼ inches of nose lift and 2¼ to 2⅞ of tail lift in a shortboard. This will vary according to exactly what sort of wave you want to use it on. The flatter the wave, the flatter the rocker. The more hollow the wave, the more curved the rocker to fit the contours of the wave.

GUNS

Which brings us to reef breaks. When surfing hollow reef breaks, like Hawaii, Tahiti, Fiji and Indonesia, I find the best shapers for these boards are the Hawaiians. They grow up in these kind of waves and learn what works best in them. Waves like these have so much power that you don't need to get extra speed out of your board. These guys learn to harness the power of the wave and produce boards that turn with relative ease. For me, Wade Tokoro is the best shaper of guns in the world. He makes my boards so they have enough speed but still turn with ease, and this is a fine balancing act. He can make a semi-gun turn like a shortboard and, when surfing waves of consequence, that is exactly what you want. Having confidence in your equipment is such a huge factor in big waves. The last thing you want to think about when coming out of the bottom of an eight to ten footer at Pipe is whether your board is going to turn or stick. One wrong split-second decision on a wave like that can be life threatening.

VARIETY IS THE SPICE OF LIFE

I enjoy riding lots of different boards. It keeps things fresh and exciting. So I recommend jumping on a single or twinny or fish every now and then. Ride it for a few days, then when you jump back on your regular shorty you will have a new respect for how surfboards have evolved. But most of all, enjoy your surfing.

Shapers today often don't like their surfers jumping on other boards. I think this is silly. Build a good relationship with your shaper and be honest with him, but don't be afraid to try other people's boards. I have tried so many different boards – some I've loved and some I've hated. But giving feedback to your shaper is crucial, not only for the shaper to understand how his boards work for you, but for you to understand how boards work. I have ridden boards that have been great in one area but haven't worked well in other aspects. Take that positive and try it with something else. Communicating with your shaper about how a board works depends on the surfer developing a good understanding of design and how he likes a board to feel on a wave. Give that feedback to your shaper and he'll be stoked to try and incorporate that into your next board. He is a craftsman and is always learning too. Don't be afraid to experiment, and always try to find the good and bad in every board.

PICK UP A PLANER

I've actually shaped a couple of boards myself and really enjoy it. One was a round-tail that had so much double concave in it that it would only work when the waves were really sucky, but I thought it was the best board ever. I shaped a single-fin that I still have, and it goes insane. That experience of actually shaping a board myself has really heightened my appreciation of the craft.

I've always enjoyed riding different equipment. You can get stale sometimes, riding the same boards all the time. There was a period when I was riding my 6'0"s for so long I felt stale. I couldn't tell which was a good board or which was a bad board because they all felt exactly the same. So sometimes I like to jump on a single-fin for a day or two and freshen it all up. Some guys say they don't like messing around with different boards because it interferes with riding their normal board in heats, but I've jumped on my single-fin in the middle of events just to get the excitement of jumping back on my normal board. It takes you back to square one.

MY CURRENT SLED

Over the past couple of years DH and I have found a design that really suits me so, despite subtle curve adjustments, my boards haven't changed all that much. I've been riding a 6'1" $\times$ 18$\frac{1}{4}$" $\times$ 2$\frac{3}{16}$" rounded square-tail with single concave into double through the fins. Last year, though, I watched Kelly ride 5'10"s, and he seemed to be surfing better than ever. His equipment looked really lively, and his turns were always on the money. It inspired me to try chopping half an inch off the tail. I noticed the change instantly. It felt like my board fit better in the pocket, and I found that I had more options as I approached the lip. It's amazing with surfboards how such small changes can alter the performance and reinvigorate your surfing. My new all-rounder is 6'½" × 18¼" × 2³⁄₁₆".

DARREN HANDLEY – THE SHAPER

Nothing is left to chance when it comes to Mick's wave-riding equipment. Darren Handley has been shaping Mick's boards since Mick was fourteen. The same sander sands every one of his boards; the same glasser glasses each one. They must come in under 2.3 kg. Each board might have a life span of just 150 waves, and Mick goes through around 100 boards a year. It's a relentless process that might produce a handful of magic boards each year.

Mick might push his surfboards pretty hard, but it's just as important that the boards push back. 'We've got this thing called "push-back",' says Darren. 'Every time he throws his weight into a turn, it needs to push back. If it doesn't, the board's no good and he can feel that in the first bottom turn, the first cutback, the first off the top.'

Mick and Darren have one of the most sophisticated surfboard programs in history, up there with the great Slater–Merrick partnership that yielded nine world titles and some of the great design breakthroughs of the modern era.

'One guy glasses his boards, one guy sands his boards – we don't change anything. Every board's sanded to a weight. If it's not light enough, he won't ride it, so we won't even start it if the blank's not the right weight. It's really high-end stuff we're dealing with,' says Darren. 'They've got to be under 2.3 kg. If they're 2.32, they're too heavy. "Sand more out of it. I don't care," he goes, "I'd rather break it than not surf it."

'He loves a fresh board. He can pick up a board and, if it feels good under his arm, he can wax it up and surf it in a heat. A fresh one's got all the life in it. You surf them too much and they lose a bit of their life after about 150 hard, competitive waves. When they're surfing competitively, I reckon they put an extra eight to ten per cent into their turns.'

Darren's boards are produced at one of the most modern surfboard factories in Australia, BASE, a cooperative of a handful of the best shapers in the country, including the legendary inventor of the three-finned 'thruster', Simon Anderson. The BASE factory, in West Burleigh on the Gold Coast, produces around 300 boards a week, distributed all over the world. Mick's range of signature models are by far their biggest sellers. The entire factory is united in the quest to put the best possible boards under the feet of their most celebrated team rider.

'Every time he's surfing a heat they stop work and come and watch on the computer,' says Darren. 'They really feel it when he loses and when he wins, and they feel it even more when he breaks a board – they take it personally. I come into work and their heads are down: "We made a mistake, Darren. We're sorry. Is Mick okay?" They don't want to let Mick down as well, so the pressure's on.'

Breakages are inevitable when boards are made so light for high performance rather than durability, but all understand the fine increments involved in satisfying Mick's demanding appetite for boards.

'He's probably the best, if not in the top two or three people in the world, to give feedback on surfboards. He gets a lot of boards, but he doesn't just get them and break them. He is actually trying to make the holy grail every year, the magic board,' explains Darren.

It's this kind of long-term collaboration, Darren reckons, that elite surfers need to give themselves the edge in competition. 'You look at history and you look at shapers and surfers' relationships, and they're the ones that have won all the world titles – Kelly and Al [Merrick], Occy and Dahlberg, Andy and Eric Arakawa. They're long-standing relationships . . . They don't have to worry about what boards they're going to get next week or next month. They know there's a supply of the things they've been working on. That's one of the keys, and there's a lot of keys, but that's just one less thing you've got to worry about.'

Darren sees himself as just one member of a team – along with Mick's coach, trainer, chiropractor, sponsors – working to give him the best possible chance of success. 'We're his pit crew. Surfing reminds me of car racing. You've got your driver, and then *you've got your mechanics and all the people around him. All he has to do is jump in the car and drive the thing. That's what I am, the mechanic, and he has all these other people, whether they're changing the tyres or keeping his body in shape to drive the car.'*

Surfing has always been an intensely individual sport, but Mick's collaborative approach to his career, surrounding himself with the best possible people for every form of support he needs, might have set the template for the future, Darren reckons.

'The turning point was 2007 at the Quikkie Pro. We were all sitting around him through every heat in the competitors' area: his wife, his mum, Claw, Griggsy the pit boss, Chris Prosser, Phil and me. So he's surrounded himself with these protectors; he was like a boxer and we were all in his corner. Anything that's needed, boom, we're all running to get it. I think that was one of the things that helped him win it. That's one of the things that Mick's understood. Spend a bit of money, get these people around you, get all that stuff right, and you'll win contests. And if you win enough contests, you'll win world titles.'

chapter 4.
THE DREAM TOUR

Going into that first year on the WCT, I didn't set ridiculous goals. I didn't come out saying I was going to be world champion. I was just looking forward to trying to re-qualify for the tour. I still did quite a few WQS events because I knew I was up against the best surfers in the world and didn't want to leave anything to chance. I think that worked for me; it kept me striving to make the cut. Some guys come on to the WCT thinking they're going to win first year or cruise into the top ten. If you're reading that sort of bullshit in the magazines about yourself, then you start believing it. I think even unconsciously you take a bit of a step back and don't push as hard as you otherwise would, because you think they're going to give it to you. The reality is you've got to go out and fight for it. There's not one guy on tour who will give you a heat. It's their livelihood, too, and no-one's about to roll over for some cocky young rookie.

The WCT is a lot different to the WQS. On the 'QS, the judges see so much of the same thing that when someone like Josh Kerr or

Jordy Smith come out and start boosting huge airs, it's refreshing. The judges are like, 'Oh wow, one big air – I haven't seen that today. Eight points.' But once you're on the 'CT you've got to do big turns, and it's in good waves. A lot of the waves you can't even do airs. It's a totally different ball game. Every guy on that 'CT knows how to win a heat. They're not there by mistake.

I just tried to set realistic goals. I wanted to re-qualify on the WCT, without relying on the WQS safety net, and I didn't want to get any thirty-thirds. It took me a while to get into the right mode. I started off the year with four seventeenths, and I was aiming to go and do the big European leg on the WQS just to play it safe. I was freaking out, thinking, *I'm going to be away from home forever.*

I went to Jeffreys Bay, South Africa, knowing I needed a big result. I'd never been there before, and Joel and Dean were telling me, 'You'll love J-Bay – the place is so cool and the people are so nice.' It felt really special to be a part of the lore and surf this wave that has such a revered place in surfing history. But when I first surfed J-Bay, I was having a shocker. I thought, *This place is overrated.* I guess from growing up with point breaks on the Gold Coast, I thought I'd naturally be able to surf it, but it's a vastly different wave. You've got so much speed; you've got to work out the right place to do the right sort of turn or you lose the wave. One afternoon I just seemed to get my head around it and started having a lot of fun out there. It was like a mix between Lennox and Burleigh. Flying down the line, you've got these big walls and you can draw big, long lines. I started loving it. I was watching footage of everyone surfing it, studying the best surfers' approaches, and then I went out one afternoon and it all came together. I ended up winning the event. We had great waves that year, four to six foot and offshore winds, and I had a pretty tough draw - Damien Hobgood, Kalani Robb, Taj Burrow, Danny Wills and Mick Lowe in the final - so I was pretty pumped to win.

That contest definitely changed the way I approached the WCT. Even though I'd won Bells in 2001 and had good results as a wildcard, it's so different when you're fighting for the points. The stress that goes on behind it all is intense. It's easy to rock up as a wildcard and just think, *I'm here for one event, and I'm that psyched just for this one event.* You don't have to worry about twelve events. That win at J-Bay gave me the confidence to carry on with the rest of the year.

SURFER POLL AND THE RISE OF EUGENE

In 2001, I had my first experience of the US *Surfer* Poll, an awards night voted for by the readers of *Surfer* magazine. I was awarded the Breakthrough Performer of the Year and won a Ford Ranger truck, which I promptly sold. It was pretty wild. I had no idea what the *Surfer* Poll even was, and suddenly I had to fly over to California to front the biggest gathering of surf industry types in the world. I didn't know what was going on, but everyone made such a big deal about it that I figured it was important.

In 2002 I made another big impression at the *Surfer* Poll, but for very different reasons. We'd just finished the Trestles event and all the surfers had started drinking after the contest. Someone put on free Red Bulls and vodka, and that's never going to end well. By the time we got to the awards ceremony we were all pretty primed, and my alter ego, Eugene, emerged. Eugene is my middle name so, whenever I've had a few too many drinks, I try to blame it on this other character, who just happens to look a lot like me. Eugene's become fairly notorious and is a far cry from the dedicated athlete I present to the world most of the time.

It was the first time in about ten years that Kelly hadn't won the *Surfer* Poll for the most popular surfer. Andy Irons had just taken his crown. I'd been hanging out with Andy, so a few of us tackled him as he got up on stage. Apparently this wasn't the done thing at these affairs, and everyone was pretty freaked out. Not that it deterred me. Kelly got up to make this big speech, and I was just in one of those moods so I started calling him Jimmy Slade – the character he played in *Baywatch* a few years earlier. Then I decided it would be a good idea to join him on stage, and you could see Kelly going, *Oh shit, how do I deal with this drunken interloper?* So he came back with, 'Mick, what would happen if I came to your country and I carried on like this?', basically suggesting that it would be a good idea if I simmered down a little. I looked at him and went, 'You'd get laid!' That brought the house down. I guess it was a bit disrespectful to him and the occasion, but I didn't really appreciate that at the time. I just thought it was all in good fun.

There was a story going around that I got thrown out, but that's not strictly true. I was very drunk and making an idiot of myself, so the security guards, whom we know well because they work at all the events, gently suggested it might be time for me to call it a night. I wasn't about to argue but, as I couldn't really walk straight by that point, they gave me a bit of a hand. Everyone was saying, 'Oh, Mick's getting thrown out,' but I was happy to go. So, just for the record, I wasn't thrown out – even though I deserved to be.

I was woken the next morning by Rip Curl co-founder Doug 'Claw' Warbrick, who's basically my boss. 'That was so funny,' he said, and through my foggy consciousness I thought, *Thank God, the boss thinks it was funny*. But then he added, 'We might just play it straight for a few years and let the fuss die down.'

Luckily for me, the Trestles contest has still been running when they've held the *Surfer* Poll for the past few years, so the surfers all have a mellow night and go to bed early. I still have people come up to me and say, 'That was the funniest thing ever,' so I don't think there was any great harm done. But I took Claw's advice and played it pretty straight the next few years.

BLOCKED UP IN PORTUGAL

The rest of the year wasn't without its obstacles, including some literal ones. We had a WCT event in Portugal, at a place called Figueira da Foz, and it was a really long contest. We waited for swell right up until the end of the waiting period, and they ended up cancelling the event. I wasn't too sure about the food in Portugal, and I wasn't conscious of my diet at the time. They had all these little cakes and stuff for breakfast, as the Europeans do, and I wasn't into it. So I started making myself little scrambled-egg rolls for breakfast. And I'd brought my own vegemite, so I had vegemite rolls for lunch. I did that every day for about two weeks. I was drinking coffee in the mornings, so everything was still moving through okay, but then something went wrong somewhere in the internal plumbing. We were driving from Portugal up to France for the next event and, by the time we got there that night, I was racked with pains in my stomach. They grew worse and worse. I was lying in bed, unable to sleep, wondering what was going on. I called Mum, who was at work at the hospital, and she put one of the doctors on the phone. He was asking me questions and instructing me to press different parts of my stomach and tell him if it hurt. And I was saying, 'Yes, it all hurts.' He told me to get to a hospital because it could be appendicitis.

I didn't speak a word of French, but luckily Andy Higgins from Rip Curl did. He took me to hospital, but they didn't really tell him what was going on. I was lying on this bed when they stuck a drip in my arm and said I had to stay overnight. It was so heavy. I was in a room with this guy who sounded like he was dying. He had all these tubes coming out of him, and you could hear his bowel movements gurgling away all night. I was thinking, *Get me out of here*.

I woke up in the morning and they gave me something to drink. I still didn't know what was wrong, but through Andy they explained I was constipated. I went, 'You're kidding me?'

'We're going to keep you in until it's not painful anymore,' they said. So I had to skol this laxative. And then they came back in at lunchtime and gave me another one of these drinks and this other device that was a bit like a bike pump. Andy was still translating, but something was almost lost in the translation.

They said, 'You've got to use this.'

'What is it?' I asked.

'You've got to spray it.'

And I went, 'What? In my mouth?'

'Nah, up your arse.' I was freaking out, hoping Andy had mis-understood – but no. So I skolled the drink and went into the toilet to do the business with the pump. I felt so weird and awkward, but I accomplished the task at hand. The flood gates opened.

That afternoon I was lying in bed, a couple of stone lighter, still next to this guy who was on his death bed. Hedgey and Andy came in and asked, 'How are you feeling?'

I went, 'Get me out of here. I don't care how.' So Andy got the nurse and told her I wanted to go home.

'No,' she said, 'he told me his stomach was still sore at lunchtime.'

'Nah, I'm fine now,' I said. The nurses still wouldn't let me leave, so I ended up ripping all my tubes out, and Hog and Andy busted me free.

GOING HOME

After the European leg, I decided I wanted to visit my ancestral home in Ireland. Parko, Hedgey and Shagga came along. My family come from a place called Malin Head, the most northerly point of mainland Ireland. I saw my godparents, all the cousins and my great-aunt. It was something I'd always wanted to do and was really special. I saw the house my dad grew up in, this tiny little run-down place in a village. There's just one road in and out, a lighthouse, church, school, pub and a few houses – that's about it.

My father's mother died when he was young, and his father just took off, so he and his brother were sort of adopted by their Aunty Mary, my great-aunt. Her son Jimmy is my godfather, so he and dad grew up together like family.

I'd always heard stories about Ireland and my family over there, but I'd never met them before. It's quite close to the border with Northern Ireland, so there were all these military checkpoints when they were growing up. They weren't far from Belfast and all the troubles. Even when we were there you could still see tanks rolling down the streets.

There are waves there, but it's just too cold and windy – not inviting. It's not far from Bundoran, which is where most of the Irish surfers are, but we hadn't gone there to surf. I rang up my godparents, Jimmy and Barbara, and told them I was coming to visit. They were so excited.

On our way there, this car pulled up alongside us while we were doing about 120 kilometres per hour, and the driver started waving at us. We thought, *Gee, people in Ireland are friendly* and waved back. But then he just kept waving, pulled in behind and followed us. *This is a bit weird.* At that moment, my jacket came flying out of my board bag on the roof, so we pulled over to retrieve it. This guy pulled over too. And we all went, 'Shit, what's going to happen here?' I ran after my jacket and left the boys to deal with it.

When I got back they said, 'You idiot – it's your cousin.' So that was my introduction to my Irish family. My cousin, Cahir, was on his way home from work when he spotted the surfboards on the roof and knew it was us. I felt immediately at home. We stopped and had a Guinness on the way, and then he led us into Malin Head to meet the rest of the family. There were lots of kisses and cuddles; they took such good care of us. Barbara cooked the best Irish food. When we left, we went out shopping and filled their whole house with food.

Jimmy told a lot of funny stories about Dad and the mischief they used to get up to, and Barbara told me all about Mum. They drove us around and showed us all the sights. It was a real eye-opener to see how my parents had lived and what my life might have been like if they'd stayed there. They're all farmers and live the simple life, but with that great Irish hospitality and warm-heartedness. Mum and Dad are still like that. Dad can walk into any pub, anywhere, even if he's only been in town a week, and he'll know every person by name – and they'll know him. And Mum's always helping out anyone in need, cooking them a meal or giving them a bed for the night. I think Irish hospitality must pass through the genes.

After that, we headed down to Galway, a university town with great nightlife, to have a big night out. On the way, Joel kept asking me how it felt when I was constipated in France. I said, 'Oh, mate, I don't really want to talk about it.'

And then he said, 'I haven't had a shit for two days.'

Oh no.

So Joel headed off to the chemist to find some laxatives. He was trying to discretely locate them and approach the counter without drawing any attention to himself. Hedgey followed him in and, in the worst Irish accent, said to the lady behind the counter, 'Hey, love, my mate here hasn't taken a shit in two days. Have you got anything to help him out?' Joel went bright red and muttered, 'Thanks a lot, mate.'

The lady was laughing her head off and found what he was looking for. As we were driving along Joel was reading the packet; it said to take them at night and by the next morning you should be okay. 'Stuff that, it's hurting too much,' he said and popped two straightaway. We stopped for lunch at this pub and had a nice Irish stew and a pint of Guinness. Joel took one sip of his beer and a mouthful of stew and went, 'Uh-oh!' and ran to the toilet, while we sat there laughing.

We all finished our lunch and our beer, and he still wasn't back, so we ordered another round of Guinness. Then Hedgey ducked out to the car, got two more of the laxatives and put them in Joel's drink. Because the Guinness is so black, you couldn't see them down the bottom. Joel finally came back with the full-on sweats, and we went, 'Come on, let's get going. Joel, skol up.' So Joel grabbed his Guinness, downed it, and when he got to the bottom there were the remnants of these two tablets. He put the glass down and went, 'What did you guys do?' We all lost it.

We piled in the car, headed on to Galway without further incident, found a hotel and got a room to get ready for our big night out. We all headed down to the bar, but Joel was taking a bit longer than everyone else. He sent me a text saying, 'I'll be down in a couple of minutes. I've got to go again.' We had another beer and he still wasn't down, so I sent him a text: 'Where are you?'

I got a text back: 'It just won't stop.'

So we said we'd go out, find a club and text him the location. Half an hour later he showed up and went, 'You guys are the biggest bunch of pricks.' All night long, everywhere we went, Joel had to keep visiting these seedy nightclub toilets. Galway is an awesome party town, but I don't think it's one of Joel's favourite places.

MISSION ACCOMPLISHED

I did pretty well in the second half of '02. I went on and made a final in Brazil and a final at Pipe, which was a real highlight, and finished fifth in my first year on the WCT. Andy won his first world title and I was staying with him in Hawaii at the time, so it was cool to see up close. It was the first year I stayed with him, and it seemed inevitable that he was going to win. Luke Egan was his closest rival, and he had a lot of work to do to catch him. In the end it was all settled pretty quickly. Andy won the title, won Pipe and the Triple Crown (for the best results in the three prestigious Hawaiian events), which must be just about as good as it gets, especially for a Hawaiian surfer in his home waters. It was great energy to be around and a real lesson to see just how focused and on his game Andy was that year.

Even though I made the top five, I didn't feel like I had the best year. I had three or four solid results, the rest were just ninths and seventeenths, and I was never in contention for the world title. I had wanted to make the top sixteen and not place last in any events. And I wanted to qualify without having to go back to the 'QS. So I was pretty stoked that I realised those goals.

MUM'S THE WORD

Now that I was on the WCT, there was no getting around it – surfing was my career, and in some ways I needed to treat it like a job. But I was still only twenty and had no idea about business or finances or how to do my tax. All of a sudden, I had to see an accountant and keep receipts. I thought, *Can't I just go surfing and let someone else worry about this stuff?* To be honest, I've never cared much about money. When we were young, we didn't have much and still had a lot of fun. You see people who come into a bit of money and become the full Scrooge McDuck, but you can't take your money to your grave. You definitely want to be smart with your money, but it's nice to be able to spread it around a bit, take someone to dinner, whatever, so I've never been one to dwell on my hip pocket.

Luckily for me, Mum was always there to help deal with my finances. I've had heaps of people approach me about being my agent. When Joel signed with an agent, I was thinking maybe I should do the same. I went home one day and said to Mum, 'What do you think about me maybe getting a manager?' I was very close to getting slapped in the head.

She said, 'You don't need a bloody manager. They're all drongos. *Are you kidding me?* I'll teach you how to do your stuff.' Mum was still working full-time, but she started helping me learn how to deal with the business of pro surfing.

Then one day Mum was going for a new job, and she was really stressed out. So I said, 'If you don't get the job, I'll employ you.'

'What do you mean?' she asked.

I said, 'Well, you handle all my stuff anyway – you may as well do it full-time. It would save me paying someone else.'

She came home from this job interview and went, 'Guess what? I've got a new job.'

'Did you get it?'

'No, *you're* employing me.'

And that was it. She's been my manager ever since, and it's been a really good arrangement. It's hard sometimes when you don't want to talk business and you just want your mum. But you always know that she has your best interests at heart; she's not there for the dollar signs. I'm glad it's worked out that way. I could see that work was really affecting her, and I was the only one living at home at the time. I had enough money to support myself, and my brothers were old enough to look after themselves by that stage. So I think it was a good decision. She's worked so hard to support all of us for so many years. And now I try and give her an overseas trip at least once a year, and she loves it.

Mum's really switched on. She's managed huge hospitals – Gold Coast Hospital, Prince Alfred in Brisbane – as a director of nursing. In the end she was pretty high up there in nursing in south-east Queensland. She's got a really smart business head. Sometimes people might underestimate her because she's a woman in the surf industry and not a career sports manager. There have been times when people have tried to take advantage of her – they find out quickly that's not a good idea. I remember the first few times she was dealing with one of my sponsors, who was asking me to do this and this and this.

She just said, 'No, he's not,' and just erupted. We all knew growing up, when she goes off she *really* goes off. She doesn't care who it is. If you're attacking one of her babies, she will annihilate you.

We make a pretty good team when it comes to negotiating with sponsors. She'll sit there and tell me what they're offering. I'll either say yes or no. She'll ask my rationale and then put across her point of view. I'll take that on board, and we'll set a plan and go and ask for what we want. She'll say to the companies, 'What are you offering now?' If it's in the ball park, then she'll keep talking. If it's not, she'll say, 'No – come back tomorrow with something better.'

It's great to have Mum deal with all that kind of stuff. I don't even question her. Guys with managers always have to have someone who checks on their managers – so they're still thinking about the business side of things in a way. But with Mum, I totally trust her. She feels bad taking ten bucks off me.

FANNING THE FIRE

In 2003 I had my most consistent year up to that point. I got a lot of thirds, but that's as far as I'd get. It was cool, I wasn't really a contender for the title or anything, but I finished the year in fourth place – one better than the previous year. I was happy with how I was surfing and learning all the time.

One of the most memorable events for me was Brazil. When we got to our hotel in Florianopolis there was a huge black out. Florianopolis is an island, and a truck had crashed on the bridge to the mainland and caught on fire, which had melted the main power cable. When we checked into our hotel they gave us our room key and a couple of candles. I was sharing a room with Deano, so we went off to dump our stuff. There were candles burning all along the hallways. Deano wanted to take one of his boards over to get a ding fixed by this local, and I tagged along for the walk. I thought we were only going to be gone about five minutes, and I must have left a candle burning on top of the TV. We dropped his board off and this guy then invited us over to his friend's house for lunch. All up, we were gone for a few hours, and when we came back there were all these fire engines outside the hotel. We thought, *I wonder what's going on over there? Some idiot must have left a candle burning.* Then Mick Campbell and Danny Wills came up to us and starting writing Deano off: 'You idiot, you left a candle going in your room.' They were roasting him so bad, because Deano has a bit of form when it comes to fire lighting, and I was going to let him take the rap.

In the end, I confessed: 'Well, actually, I guess it might have been either one of us . . . Nah, actually, it was me.' Mick Lowe thought we were still in the room asleep and had kicked the door in to rescue us, and the whole TV was on fire, black smoke billowing everywhere. Deano's passport was right next to the TV, so that was all charred around the edges, and our boards were totally black. All the wax was melted. We went through our stuff to see what we could salvage, and everything was smoke-ridden and sooty. Fortunately, the owner of the hotel had just paid his insurance the day before, so it was all covered and they gave us a new room.

We tried to clean our boards as best we could, but they still had all this black residue all over them. My first signature video,

Fanning the Fire, had come out not too long before that, so every time I ran down the beach with my black board everyone was laughing at me and calling out, 'Fanning the Fire!'

I didn't have any clothes to wear and borrowed Joel's the whole time. I ended up coming second to Kelly on my blackened board, so it hadn't thrown me off my game too much. Everyone was telling Dean that he'd have to go into the capital, Brasilia, to get an emergency passport, but Brasilia's out in the middle of nowhere. He just said, 'Nah, I'm winging it.' And he pulled it off. He got home on his driver's licence and this charred passport. Only Deano could have pulled it off. He'd get to the immigration counter and pull out this blackened passport that looked like an old pirate's treasure map and make these puppy eyes. They'd look at him and go, 'You're kidding, aren't you?' But they let him through.

SHOWDOWN AT PIPE

Kelly and Andy had the big showdown for the world title at Pipeline in 2003. They took off pretty hard that year – Andy won five events and Kelly won four, so no-one else really had a look-in. The title race was fascinating to watch as it came into those last couple of events. It was like having a ringside seat at a heavyweight title fight.

We were getting ready for the Sunset event, when it was still a WCT stop. Andy had almost given up because Kelly had won the last two events in Brazil and Mundaka. Andy said, 'He's already got it.' I couldn't believe anyone would give up on their dream that easily.

We were going for an early at Sunset one morning and I said, 'What do you mean? It's still in your reach. You've only got to beat him at Sunset and it's still game on.' Sometimes all it takes is one person saying something positive at the right time to completely switch your thinking. You could see he just turned things around and started believing in himself again. Before that he was all laid-back about it, as if he just didn't care.

It's a big thing to really go after a goal, because it sets you up for a lot of disappointment and heartache if things don't work out. But it's better than having regrets that you didn't give it your all. Andy turned back into that super-confident guy. Kelly ended up losing early at Sunset – Andy got second – and it was down to whoever did better at Pipe. It got pretty intense. There were a few words exchanged between them free surfing out at Pipe, which is all good, competitive stuff. And it was good for pro surfing. Everyone was talking about the showdown and how it would play out. After Sunset, Andy knew he was going to win. You could see it in his eyes. Being in Hawaii, with all the local support behind him, it felt like he had the energy working for him.

Then, right before Pipe, Kelly walked into our house one day. It was so funny. I was sitting on the couch watching TV when the door opened, but I couldn't see it from where I was. Everyone went quiet, like in one of those scenes in a Western saloon. Then I saw Kelly and thought, *Oh shit, what's he doing here?* The American photographer Steve Sherman had been hanging out, and he never normally came around, so I don't know if he had something to do with it. Kelly said something about looking for a friend of his.

Andy was looking at him like, *What the fuck are you doing in my house?* Andy didn't say much: 'The guy you're looking for is not here.' After Kelly turned around and walked out, Andy just said, 'What the fuck was that all about?' It was all-time. It was really cool being in the house and seeing it all go down. It gave me a taste of the level of intensity that went into a world title campaign. I don't know if Kelly was just trying to play mind games, but, if he was, it kind of backfired.

Kelly's a tricky guy. I've always got along with him, but there are times when he only talks to you when *he* wants to talk to you. I found when I was going for the world title, when I was at the contest, he wouldn't talk. It didn't bother me. I'd sit there and talk to Andy and Joel and Taj or whoever. Kelly plays mind games occasionally, and there are times when it definitely works in his favour, but that year at Pipe wasn't one of them. Right before they paddled out, Kelly came up and told Andy he loved him. I'm not sure what that was all about, but it didn't change the result: Andy won the contest, the Triple Crown and the title again.

Kelly was rattled for a long time after that – you could see it. He was trying so hard to win, and it was the first time he wasn't the favourite or the golden child. I watched his heats after that, and he would lose his shit when he lost. He was surfing great, but he wasn't surfing no-holds-barred like he usually would. He was trying to manufacture a win and it wasn't working; I think it freaked him out a bit. He didn't win an event for a whole year and half after that, which is a long time for Kelly.

I guess no-one really teaches you how to deal with that kind of loss. As they say, no-one remembers second. I've seen other people go through it, and I've heard Mark Richards talk about when Cheyne Horan lost the world title, or Gary Elkerton. You put so much effort into winning, and you believe in it so much. And then to have your dreams crushed, it's hard to pick yourself up and go again if you don't actually deal with that loss there and then.

Andy and I had become pretty good mates. We hung out a fair bit through my first few years on tour and, because we were both sponsored by Red Bull, stayed together in Hawaii. We still catch up for a beer every now and again, and he's a good guy. The documentary *Blue Horizon* portrayed him as a complete arsehole. I was really surprised by that and how Billabong would let that go through. He's meant to be their number-one guy, and suddenly everyone thinks he's a prick. Sure, for those three years he won the world title, he was a prick when it came to competing, but that's what you've got to do to win a world title. That's just how he rolled. It was the same with Sunny Garcia. They're the sort of guys who surf better when they're angry, and if Andy was losing he'd get pissed off and try that little bit harder. And all of a sudden he's popping two nines out. He's kind of like a McEnroe character – when he competes he tries so hard and he cares so much that he just blows up. It shows how much emotion he puts into it. But sit down and have a beer with him, and he's the coolest guy in the world.

Everyone's different and everyone gets the best out of themselves in different ways. Parko's a guy who surfs best when he's really happy, and he knows that. When Joel starts trying too hard, he loses a tiny bit of his edge, starts to force turns – it just doesn't suit his surfing, which is all about flow and throwing it up wherever and staying loose.

The bottom line is you've got to find what works for you. That's where the rookies come unstuck a lot of the time. They're trying to figure all that out, and they've got to figure it out in a hurry or they'll be eaten up on tour. It can consume you. But if you look at guys like Kelly and Andy, when they're away from the events they switch off and stop thinking about it completely. I think that's what preserved Kelly for so long and what kept Andy going during his three world titles. They know how to flick the switch when they need to go into contest mode and how to switch it off and recharge. It's definitely something I struggled with when I first made the WCT, particularly with the extended waiting periods. Once the event started I'd just want it to run straight through, but it doesn't work that way. You might surf on day one, not surf again until a week later, and be put on stand-by in between. I'd be up and down like a yo-yo, and by the end of the event I was exhausted. It was a lesson I was going to have to learn myself, in my own time, though I never could have imagined it would be such a tough education.

DOUG 'CLAW' WARBRICK – THE SPONSOR

Sponsors don't normally applaud their athlete's drunken antics in public. But Rip Curl co-founder Doug 'Claw' Warbrick reckons Mick's infamous performance at the 2002 Surfer Poll awards did his career no harm at all. 'It established him in world surfing. I think it did his career good,' says Claw. 'It's not something you'd want to do too often in your career. However, in those complex set of characteristics that is Mick Fanning, there's a couple of wildcard pieces to the puzzle. And he's got this great advantage of the alter ego of Eugene,' Claw observes. 'Because he puts so much pressure and tension on himself, because he sets such high standards, sometimes he's extremely disappointed. He's also very highly wound in the run-up to a contest. Having that Eugene thing is a pressure valve to let off steam and have a bit of fun. He's got that Aussie–Irish larrikin streak – it's a fantastic thing. But what he did there at Surfer Poll, I actually think it was one of his greatest performances. It's probably something that every

Australian surfer wanted to do. He definitely had more drinks than he should have. I think the audience is 1500 there at the Globe Theatre. They're mainly Americans, the core of professional surfing, the pointy-end of media and people that present American surfing as the crowning glory of all surfing. To do that in front of those people, at that point in his career, when he wasn't that well known . . . He couldn't have done that before then, he probably can't do it again – it was just that moment in time. And it was really well received. I think probably five per cent of the audience were completely offended. Some people took a little while to laugh about it. Afterwards, they were going, "That was unbelievable." But the fifty per cent who knew Mick a little better and had seen a bit of Eugene, they were just with him all the way from the first words that came out of his mouth. That was probably what encouraged him . . . That onstage performance at Surfer Poll will be remembered forever. This Eugene character he's got, it will be part of him forever and part of his legend in the future.'

Claw speaks with some authority when he discusses the role of Eugene, as he has experienced Mick's alter ego at quarters that were sometimes rather too close for comfort. 'We've all seen Eugene come out. He's getting too strong, though. I'm worried about some of the headlocks he gets you in. Somewhere or other, when he won something and was rejoicing, he was wrestling on the ground with his mates and throwing them around. He got me in some headlock, threw me on the ground. My neck was crook for about three weeks . . . He's a very powerful young man.'

Claw has a long history of talent identification. A keen

observer of pro surfing contests, he's been earmarking the surfers to best represent his surf label for forty years, from Wayne Lynch to Michael Peterson, Tom Curren to Mick Fanning. Claw is an excitable old surf dog, renowned for bouncing on the spot and clapping his hands with delight when something pleases him. From the grandstands perched over Bells Beach each Easter, he has watched hundreds of aspiring pro surfers chase their dreams. What was it about the skinny blond kid from the Gold Coast that first caught his eye?

'When I first saw him live, that sort of speed and electricity in his surfing definitely struck me, and it struck me that he had a brand of surfing that was unique and could really go somewhere,' says Claw.

Mick was probably the least well known of the so-called Cooly Kids at the time, but Claw liked what he saw in and out of the water. 'He was achieving high levels in two other sports. Middle-distance running, he was at a high level, one of the best in the country or the state for his age. And then the Soccer Federation had identified him, and they thought he could go the distance. He'd be outstanding in any sport but he happens to be a surfer, and he's a surfer in his heart and his mind, and surfing's got that extra appeal. It's not just a purely competitive sport.'

When Claw watched the youngster dominate a junior final against a stacked field at Bells Beach, near Rip Curl's home base in Torquay, his mind was made up. 'I could see something special in the surfing, and then as I got to know him I could see that he had some real special qualities as a human,' he says. 'The more you understood, the more it became apparent to me that he was something very special, a very special person, and could go a long way.'

That faith was repaid many times over as Mick overcame one potential setback after another. 'He's set a whole new standard for competitive surfing for ticking all the boxes: identifying the boxes that need to be ticked and then making sure he ticks them. And then he goes and ticks them over and over. He's a pretty good and keen yoga practitioner. We know he puts a lot of time in the gym. He's got all these little tricks from other areas, and he's put together his own package . . . When he takes on any of those tests against other athletes, he's coming up on just about every one in the absolute elite group, with people who win gold medals in Olympics and so on. Sometimes they're very surprised by how well he goes.'

LIZ'S STORY, PART 3

Being a woman dealing with the upper echelons of the surfing industry can't always be easy. But sponsors who think of Liz as merely 'Mick's mum' and treat her accordingly are likely to be in for a shock.

'It's not that they had a problem with me; it was just that I was a woman and Mick's mum, and they didn't know what to do with me,' says Liz. 'Of course, they all go for a beer, and I don't go for a beer. And I wear a suit and no-one wears a suit in the surfing industry. I'm a professional person. I do have to remind them that I have a Master's and I am capable. I've found it quite hilarious, really. I think it's great.'

Her career in mental health has also prepared Liz well for the challenges of dealing with the pro surfing world. 'Being in the positions I've been in, my clinical area was mental health. I've been in executive director's positions, and it's all about negotiation and team-building, and also managing millions of budget dollars and things like that, so I had a very good understanding of all that. I've always been in mental health and management roles for many years because it was a Monday-to-Friday job. And I've been very, very lucky, being in the right place at the right time.'

Liz sees parallels between her mental health management roles and her role in managing Mick's career. 'In mental health, the patient or the client is the centre of your care, and you have all these people working to care for the person – this is exactly the same,' says Liz, tracing a circle with her finger, then various branches stemming out from the circle. 'Mick is the centre. The athlete's here,' she says, stabbing at the centre of the circle. 'And all these people are here to support him. And I saw my role as being here to coordinate all these people for Mick.'

Though Mick and Liz are understandably coy about discussing specific dollar amounts, it is widely recognised that Mick is one of the highest-paid and wealthiest pro surfers in the world today, which speaks volumes for both Liz's negotiating skills and her financial management.

'I took a different energy to the negotiating process – there was no ego involved,' says Liz. 'Because he's my boy, I want the best for my boy. We've had such longstanding relationships [with Mick's sponsors], so we've all grown up together. It's been great, and I think I have some respect from the surfing industry. I've enjoyed it. It's a man's world, for sure, but everyone's been really nice to me.'

And no-one underestimates her anymore. When newspaper journalist Will Swanton rang Rip Curl team manager Gary

Dunne for a quote about Liz's role, Swanton observed, 'Liz is like a mother hen with her family.'

But Dunne disagreed. 'Nah, mate, she's a bloody lioness.'

'That's how they see me.' Liz laughs. 'DHD [Mick's surfboard shaper, Darren Handley], he shakes in his shoes when he sees me. It's not that I'm nasty – it's just that business is business and blood is thicker than water.'

But she has come into conflict with other sports managers who'd like to take on her high-profile son. 'It has been a fight because they have tried to walk over me. They didn't really understand what they were getting into,' she says. 'A lot of people have come to me through Mick's career and said they want to be Mick's manager: "We could do a much better job than you; we've got all these opportunities."'

The career sports managers were unimpressed when mother and son both insisted they were more than happy with their current arrangement. But they were even less impressed when other pro surfers began seeking out Liz's services. 'I did have conflict with other managers because other surfers wanted to come to me,' she says. Though she doesn't manage any other surfers, she has negotiated contracts on their behalf. 'If they want a contract negotiated, they come and see me. Not everyone's got as much as Mick. Mick's got a multimillion-dollar business here, but a lot of people haven't got that.'

Liz also oversees Mick's investments and has built up an impressive real estate portfolio. Like a real-life game of monopoly, the three Cooly Kids have each bought up large chunks of real estate around Coolangatta and installed many of their closest friends as tenants. For some of their friends, it's the only way they'll keep a foothold close to the beach as rents and real estate prices have soared. In their own way, the Cooly Kids, a product of successive generations of home-grown surfing talent, are providing a kind of safety net for the local surf community that nurtured them. Although the boys all stand to do quite well out of the arrangement themselves.

'My job really was to grow Mick's wealth so that when he retired he would be self-sufficient for the rest of his life, and hopefully that's going to happen,' says Liz. 'In Waves magazine, they said Mick's worth a lot more than he gets paid because he's invested his money very well, so I took that as a compliment.'

The first investment property Mick bought was the two-bedroom unit the family used to occupy in Hill Street. 'Mick owns that unit now. That was the first thing he ever bought. I said, "Wouldn't it be nice if you could get that unit," and I drove past and that unit was for sale.'

Mick built his dream home two doors up from his mum: a modern, sprawling hilltop castle. He's also been used to promote a new apartment building being built on the top of Duranbah Hill, where he will be occupying the penthouse. A large Hawaiian holiday home on the top of the Pupukea hills, with panoramic views of the North Shore, is currently under construction.

With Mick's profile entering the realm of mainstream sporting celebrity, it is unlikely that he will ever be stuck for work. 'It's just grown, really. In the beginning, it was concentrating on competition surfing. That's where all his energies were lying. The surfing world was his bubble. Now he's thinking more long term about corporate sponsorship; he's on television a lot; he's branching out into all that and being asked to do more things – so we're branching out the team.' Now, Mick also employs a part-time media manager, surfing journalist Ronnie Blakey, purely to coordinate his media commitments.

What Mick seems to most appreciate about his mum's role is that, amid the many competing commitments and responsibilities he now shoulders, he knows he can trust the person pulling the levers.

'Mum just deals with all that kind of stuff, I don't even question her at all . . . She does the money side of things and makes sure that I'm happy. She's awesome,' he says.

Liz concurs. 'I do think parents that have that relationship with their kids, they are the best people to do that job for them, because no-one wants what's best for them like their parents. They need that foundation of family.' But Liz is also conscious of the need to not over-manage her son's life, to sometimes just be 'Mum'.

'One thing I'd like to say about being a mum and a manager, it's great that Mick has asked me to do this job, but it's important that I don't intrude in his life. He's free to do what he wants. That's something I'm really conscious of. He wants his mum sometimes, and other times he wants his manager to give professional advice without that emotion there. He knows who does the job for him. I've said, "Mick, you make all your own decisions, but I can help you make informed decisions." I work for Mick. Mick doesn't work for me.'

She also takes a considerably smaller slice of his income than most managers. 'I don't take twenty per cent. When I started doing this and Mick asked me to do this full-time, I said I was a bit scared because nursing has put food on the table. I said, "If you pay me what I got paid as executive director of nursing at Logan Hospital, I'll come and work for you." It wasn't much, really. He said, "No problem," so I got $52,000 a year, and why would I want any more? It's not about making money out of Mick. It's about Mick making money for his future. I get a few perks along the way – a trip here or there. He said, "This will be your bonus for this year. Where would you like to go?" I've been down the Amazon. He's opened so many doors for me. How can I not feel privileged?'

And Liz has found her own place among the world's top surfers when they're away on tour, as a kind of communal mum, providing emotional support, a shoulder to lean on or an ear to listen.

'I found it a bit awkward but Mick wanted me to go to all these places, and I'd mix with these surfers and we'd all have a drink together, especially when they lost,' she says. 'It's just been amazing. I guess they see me as a surrogate mum on tour, and Mick's done that, not me. I haven't put myself forward; he's put me forward, and everyone is very, very special for me.'

MICK'S TIPS – A USER'S GUIDE TO THE DREAM TOUR

GOLD COAST

Obviously, the Goldy is home for me and where I feel most comfortable. I haven't always been super-relaxed competing at home though. My first few years on tour I felt a lot of pressure to perform. Having friends telling you every day that you're going to win the event can mess with your head. Also, starting at home can be hard for a rookie. You know what the waves are like and what you can and can't do on them, and you can limit yourself. It took me a few years to learn how to deal with that. Now the first event at home is by far my favourite event on tour. There's no place like home.

The contest is usually held at Snapper, and everyone seems to surf Snapper differently. Some people like to really open up and draw long lines, and other people like to keep it really tight in the pocket. I like to keep it really tight in the pocket, and I actually look for the double-up waves. They're a lot steeper and you can go straight up and down, whereas someone like Joel looks for the bigger ones with a more open face where he can draw out his turns a lot more. And Deano chases the ones next to the rock most of the time. He likes the ones that grow down the point. There's no right or wrong way, and all three of us have won the event, but a bit of local knowledge sure helps pick the kind of waves you want.

BELLS BEACH

Bells was the first-ever WCT event I went to, other than the Kirra Pro. I was fifteen and Matt Gye convinced Andrew Murphy, the Quiksilver team manager at the time, to take me to Bells. I fell in love with the place immediately. I thought the whole event was planned for the surfers. It definitely helped when I was hanging with the Quik team at the time: Willsy, Cambo, Hoyo, Jake Paterson, Tom Carroll, and I met Kelly Slater for the first time. That event left a lasting impression. Hoyo won the Rip Curl Pro that year (1997) and Occy won the Skins event, a specialty event held just after Easter. That first two weeks at Bells I learnt so much, asking the pros questions. I still use a lot of the things I learnt that first trip – where to sit in the line-up, where to eat and hang out. Plus, it helps that most of my sponsors are based in Torquay. The natural amphitheatre of Bells always excites me, and it feels like what I imagine running out of a tunnel onto a footy field feels like. Plus the elements make the event so much harder to win. Whoever wins Bells deserves it, and no-one can say otherwise. Shane Dorian once said, 'No kook has ever won Bells.' It's true.

You almost have to slow your surfing down a bit for Bells. It doesn't allow you to come straight off the bottom, straight into the lip. You've almost got to guide it off the bottom and pick your section accordingly. It hasn't got a real defined bottom to the wave, it's more of a slope, so it tends to make you open up your turns a lot more. A lot of carving out of the roof, not so much fins through the lip. You can only get two or three turns out the back, and then you've got to start working the inside section. It either shoots off into the close-out end section or you have to cutback and grovel it through. It's hard because you're in a wetsuit and it's cold, and it's almost like the wave dies on you. It takes a lot out of you to surf those sorts of waves. It's mentally tough, because you've got to surf the wave three different ways on the one wave. Out the back you're going fast and doing big open-face carves, and then you almost start doing the Huntington Hop to get through to the inside, and then the shore break's all back-washy. It's really tricky.

TAHITI

Heaven and Hell. The water is incredibly blue, but when it gets big it changes to black. I stay with a family that has become really close to my heart, the Riou family: father, Georges, and his wife, Marika; son, Alain, and daughter, Caroline. Alain is one of my best friends and so funny. When we first went to stay with him he didn't speak much English. After that first year he would come stay with me for a couple of months at a time. He learnt English and now is a big part of my extended family.

In Tahiti, I stay in a little bungalow right on the water. You always know how big it is before you even fully wake up. If there is swell, waves will splash in the front door. It takes five seconds to walk from my room and jump aboard either a jet ski or a boat. From their house at Vairao, or Big Pass, it takes about fifteen minutes to get to Teahupo'o. If the event is on, it's chaos in the channel. Boats of all shapes and sizes, packed with locals and competitors, bang into each other. When you're in position and a wave is coming, you'll know about it. The whole channel, sometimes crammed with 1000 to 1500 people, starts to hoot and holler. Your nerves kick in, your heart climbs to your mouth. If you see one you like, you start to paddle like crazy. Focusing on the drop, all goes quiet in your head. Time slows down to milliseconds, and your concentration level goes through the roof. You grab your rail, hang on and if all goes well you come out to the same screaming crowd. It is amazing the emotions you go through for a twenty-second ride. The scenery is jaw-dropping in itself – lush, green mountains rising out of the blue lagoon. It is one of the most amazing places on earth.

FIJI

Even though it's no longer on the tour at the time of writing, Fiji is one of the favourite events of all the surfers. There's no place like Namotu Island. It only takes five minutes to walk around, like the classic tropical island of your imagination. On arrival, you first meet the amazing locals of the Namotu boatshed, then Scotty and Mandy, the owners. An entire luxury resort somehow fits onto this tiny island.

The atmosphere and local warmth is like no other. Surrounding the island is coral reef that supports a fun right called Swimming Pools, and on the other side of the island is Namotu Lefts. Across a dangerous channel – I'm sure it's full of tiger sharks – is the most perfect shallow barrelling left in the world: Restaurants. Out on the horizon you can just see the feathering whitewater of Cloudbreak. It is heaven for the goofy-footers and extremely tricky for the natural-footers. The two waves where the contest is held, Restaurants and Cloudbreak, are so different, but I just love the challenge of them both. Surfing them all day, then coming in to the hospitality of Namotu Island, it feels like a home away from home. I never want to leave. The celebration at the end of the event is probably the most fun party on tour. It's all good times in Fiji, especially because all the Aussies hang together.

JEFFREYS BAY, SOUTH AFRICA

For some reason, J-Bay feels like the event run by mothers. From the first time I went there, the local Billabong licensee, Cheron Kraak, has made me and all the surfers feel so welcome. She is the unofficial mayoress of J-Bay. And then all the local ladies who work in the houses we rent remind me of being at home with my own mum. Where we stay, Salome and her daughter, Marissa, really look after us. You get this amazing, warm energy from the place. There is a special scent of aloe in the air. J-Bay is not what I imagined before I went there. I thought it would be like Lennox Head or something, a classic point break running down a big headland. But instead it's part of a huge bay, and Supertubes is only one small section of the point.

People say that South Africa is dangerous, but I always feel safe there. J-Bay is a small town on the coast, and the main street runs parallel with the coastline. It's like a normal beach town in Australia with one difference: at the end of the street is the Location. This is where all the blacks and coloureds live. Some parts are shanties and others are basic houses that wouldn't pass a building inspection at home. This is where most of the white residents' maids and domestic staff live, along with others who do cheap labour around the town. I have been there many times to go to my friends' house.

Primrose has been a cleaner at the house where I've stayed since 2005, and we have become great friends. She and her family always seem so happy when we are there. They once organised a special church service for us where the local church-goers came, read scriptures, sang and danced for us. It was very special. One little girl fell in love with my wife, Karissa. The girl didn't know her name but just called Karissa 'pinky'. Karissa was so touched by this young girl. Each year I take Primrose; her sister, Timbaland; and Timbaland's son, Dolla, out for dinner. It's always so funny – all Dolla wants to do is take photos of everyone. They are really great people to hang out with.

J-Bay is one of the fastest waves on the planet. It always takes a couple of surfs to get your timing down. At first I'm always racing down the line, then I realise I haven't turned the whole surf. The trick to J-Bay is to set your top turn up from strong, driving bottom turns. As you come around sections you have a split second to pick a turn and set your feet. The guys I love to watch out there are Occy, Taylor

Knox and Parko. They have this style of surfing down pat, and it's a style of surfing I really respect.

TRESTLES, USA

The USA is big. Everything there is big, from cars to trucks to highways, buildings and billboards – and the biggest up-sized meals in the world. Trestles itself is an exit south of San Clemente, California, on a military base. You can check the wave pretty easily by doing a quick on-ramp/off-ramp drive-by. But to surf the wave is a different story. It's closed off to cars when the competition isn't on, so most people park in San Clemente and either ride, skate or walk the couple of miles in. You would think this would discourage some people from surfing it, and anywhere else it probably would. But it is always really crowded. From pre-dawn you have the early crew, a group of older locals who are there 365 days a year. That's their morning ritual. As they slowly drift in for work, their spots are taken by a mix of young local rippers and a broad cross-section of the surf community. I am used to crowds, but Trestles is different. With a very small peak take-off area, it can sometimes become chaotic. Guys crossing over each other and collisions occur nearly every set wave. But people put up with it because it is such a fun, rippable and easy wave to surf. I think it is probably the most rippable high-performance wave in the world. The only thing Trestles doesn't have is gaping barrels. If you can dream up a move on a wave, chances are Trestles will have the perfect section to do it. It's almost like practising in a skate park. When the comp rolls into Trestles prepare to see some of the best surfing match-ups you'll witness all year.

HOSSEGOR, FRANCE

If you hesitate in France, chances are what you wanted to surf will be gone. The tides are so dramatic it is forever changing. La Gravier can be like Pipeline and just as heavy. It only works on high tide and can break right on the shore, metres from screaming fans. France is a place that can be your best friend or your worst nightmare. My first time there I didn't have a clue about anything. Now I love France – the beaches, the fun, the whole culture. The thing I like most is trying to find the best waves on any given day. The banks and tides change constantly, so you can never go back to the same place expecting to find the same wave you surfed yesterday, or even an hour ago. But the beach breaks get amazing, and they back onto the most amazing forests. It is so green, and I love the fresh mornings, racing through the trees to get to the beach and see what the ocean has in store for you. Get up early, surf and head home for a fresh breakfast – that's the routine I love. Healthy living in a healthy environment.

The beach breaks there have so much power you have to guide what's going on, control the speed. Go too fast and you start spinning out. With the rip bowls you almost sit on your back foot the whole time and pivot. When you surf La Gravier, it's a lot of hunting for corners and pulling in.

MUNDAKA, SPAIN

When you cross the border into Spain, you change climates. You leave behind the sun and sand of France and rug up for the cold.

Mundaka is a small fishing village at the mouth of a river, nestled in a mountainous area of northern Spain just over the French border, and it cops a lot of weather. If you see Mundaka for the first time at high tide, you would laugh at the thought of a perfect left-hand sandbank, but when the tide starts to drop the rivermouth comes to life. People say the wave is like Kirra in a mirror. And when it's on it's true – the barrels are so similar it's wild, truly a wonder of the world. To be honest, I don't spend a lot of time in Mundaka. I usually stay a thirty-minute drive south through a winding mountain road, at a place called Bakio. This is the backup spot when Mundaka is flat. Last time I stayed there on a vineyard two-minutes' drive from the beach, in a little bed-and-breakfast style cottage. We know a family down the road who look after us. Margari and her brother, Txetxu (pronounced 'Che-chu'), treat us like their own children. Txetxu is always behind the bar. Mama, Margari and Txetxu's mother, prepares dinner for us every night, and she is famous throughout the Basque country for her meatballs. They are the nicest people and always shower us with hugs and kisses when we arrive. The first couple of times we were there we couldn't even speak to each other, but we understood that they loved and welcomed us. I always seem to do well there because of their hospitality. Mundaka is definitely somewhere I would recommend to any travelling surfer, and after you get some amazing waves, head to Josie Mari to meet the amazing people.

Mundaka is very similar to a Gold Coast point, I reckon, the way it hits the sand bottom. It's very similar to Snapper when it's running down the point. You learn which ones are good pretty quickly. It can be tricky on your backhand when it's really low tide and fast, small and drainy. You've got to know when to go for your turns and when to pull in.

IMBITUBA, BRAZIL

Brazil is wild. I don't care what anyone says, the energy of the place is like being in a football match, 24/7. I usually stay in Imbituba, which is an hour south of Florianopolis, the nearest major town. Imbituba is an old port and fishing town. The waves vary on different swells. On solid south swells it is a right-rip bowl breaking in between two islands. In north swells, it is a running left. Some people don't enjoy the intensity of Brazil, but I do. I love to people-watch. The way people carry themselves there is like no other place in the world. They are extremely sports-oriented and never stop running around the beach, playing soccer or with a bat and ball. They don't wear much either – the guys get around in Speedo-style swimmers, and the women are all in G-strings and tiny triangles to cover their nipples. When thousands of them are at the beach together, the energy slaps you in the face. Florianopolis is a cool place to visit and is situated on a beautiful island, a bit like North Stradbroke – a fun place to party.

HAWAII

Hawaii is so intense at any time of the surf season, but when the contests are on it is doubly so. I focus on Hawaii a lot. I never really used to enjoy it – I was intimidated by the crowds and the waves, and scared of the locals. I didn't want to annoy anyone and get hit. But meeting all the local crew was a real eye-opener. You learn who's who; you know you can paddle and sit next to someone and he won't slap you just for being there.

It really pays to put in a full Hawaiian season at least once or twice in your life. I remember one local guy telling me, 'Come back in February when the contests are over and you'll meet everyone.' So I did, and it's almost like a different place.

A lot of people go there just because their sponsors make them, and they don't really like the place. But I just enjoy surfing the waves. There aren't many better places to get consistently good, big waves. I've done a couple of late seasons, and spending a bit of extra time in Hawaii has definitely been one of the most important things I've ever done for my surfing.

A lot of people ask which is heavier between Pipe and Teahupo'o, but it's hard to compare because they are very different waves. Teahupo'o stands up and throws so quick you've almost got to be underneath it, whereas Pipe sort of peaks and you can almost get a roll-in on the right ones. The first few years surfing Backdoor I thought everything looked like a close-out. It's tricky figuring out which ones to take off on. Over the years you just learn to pick it. It's like anywhere, you've just got to spend time out there to get comfortable. Pipe starts off big and then drops by about half by the time you come out of the barrel, and you've got to fight your way out a lot more than somewhere like Teahupo'o that is so open. At Pipe you've always got to be on your game and ready for anything. You've got to make sure you're deep enough, but not too deep, to get spat out the end.

THE ART OF TRAVEL

Try to pack light. I'll generally pack four to five pairs of shorts, five shirts, three to four jumpers and a few pairs of jeans. This should get you through most trips without having to wear the same thing twice.

Pack boards with care. I travel with glassed-on fins, so it's very important that I pack my boards well. I can fit six boards in a coffin bag most of the time. Put bubble wrap in between fins and noses – this will hopefully protect them a little more. I pack two boards nose first, and then two boards tail first, and so on, so that the nose of one board rests between the fins of the next. When you have packed all your boards, fill up the rest of the bag with bubble wrap. This adds more protection and stops your boards moving around. It also feels like your board bag is lighter than it really is. I very rarely put anything else in a board bag because of the weight factor. Most airlines will not take any bag over thirty-two kilos, plus the airlines are starting to charge for excess baggage.

Always be prepared to pay for excess baggage. It shouldn't come as a massive shock, but always try to bargain them down with a smile. People that create a scene usually get stuck with the full amount because the airline people think they are dickheads.

When travelling to another country with a different language, always try to learn at least a few words – please, thank you, excuse me, etc. And always try to greet people with a smile.

Try to get to know the locals and let them have their space when paddling for waves. Wait your turn and stay happy. Even if you've done something wrong, it is hard to hit someone with a smile on their face.

When travelling to a poor country and you have clothes or boards that you don't really need, offer them to the locals. If you ever come back, they will look after you. And young kids love stickers if you have any.

Try not to travel in big packs. There is nothing more irritating when you're surfing a place and a ten-pack of people paddle out. And if you are in a big pack, take shifts so others can catch waves too.

Soak in all the culture and ask questions if you're unsure whether something is appropriate or not. Some places have strong beliefs that you probably wouldn't normally think about, like dress codes, gestures and so on.

Driving on the wrong side of the road can be tricky. When first doing it, remember that the driver is always closest to the centre line. If you think you'll have problems, put your watch on the other hand to remind you which side of the road you are meant to be on.

Try the local food with an open mind. You never know, you might really enjoy the taste.

When away, always remember that not too much changes at home, so don't rush back at the first sign of homesickness. Enjoy the travel and stay safe.

chapter 5.
WE CAN REBUILD HIM

Even though I was now living my dream, I was beginning to understand that it came at a cost. I knew going into 2004 that I was in trouble. I'd really lost the passion for my surfing and felt burnt out. I'd hardly been home for more than a month in five years. You'd have ten days, or three weeks maximum, at home at a stretch. I don't want to sound like a whinger, because I know I'm incredibly lucky to do what I do, but it had all happened so fast. I'd never had a chance to really take stock and process what I'd been through. Everything got to be so stressful. You'd get all these people in your ear going, 'If you don't do it this year . . .', or, 'You've got to be world champ this year', 'I've got my money on you this year.' It all started to feel like a lot of pressure.

I was really feeling over the Gold Coast, too, and knew I needed to get away from the party season. The surf had been terrible over summer, and I got drunk for a week straight. I was actually at the Gold Coast races, on the brink of another bender, when I received a phone call from photographer Ted Grambeau, asking if I had Darren O'Rafferty's phone number.

I said, 'Let me check. What do you want Raff's number for?'

'I'm thinking of going to check out this new wave.'

'If Raff doesn't want to go, I might come,' I offered on the spur of the moment.

Ted said, 'Oh, all right, I didn't ask because I thought you'd be busy.'

He was actually leaving the next day, so I jumped in a cab and headed home to pack. I was pretty hung-over in the morning. I didn't know anything about where we were going – and neither did Ted for that matter. Everyone knows where this place is now, but back then it was a complete secret. He just had a few photos of this break, and you couldn't tell how big the waves were because there was no-one on them.

I picked Ted up and we drove up to Brisbane airport. On the way I realised I didn't have any legropes. I thought, *There's no way there's going to be any surf shops where we're going*, so we started figuring out what we could use to make a legrope.

We arrived at this tiny airport on this little Pacific island in the middle of nowhere, and the waves were pumping. So, I went, *Right, what do I do about a legrope?* I got all the laces out of my shoes and tied them together. Then I got Ted's flipper savers and tied them to one end, and that was my legrope. The only other surfers there were four fifty-year-olds from Guam, and I didn't want to just go up and ask them for a leggy. Ted didn't care though, and he just went up and asked. But they just said, 'Nah.' They were real salty sea-dogs and didn't look like they were interested in doing any favours for some young pro surfer with his own photographer in tow. So I paddled out to this sick reef pass at about eight foot, using shoelaces for a leggy.

The first wave came in, and I asked the other guys if they were going to go. They said no, so I swung around, took off and got smashed. Because the shoe laces were so short and had no give in them, my board pulled me back over the falls. I was trying to swim through the back of the wave, and I felt it just grab me, drag me back under and pin me to the reef. I came up going, *Man, if this is how it's going to be every time I fall off, this sucks.* I brought four boards, and that first wave broke one of them, so I was suddenly down to three.

After that first wave, the other guys suddenly remembered they had a spare legrope. They must have seen the wipe-out and felt sorry for me or thought I might drown if they didn't give me one. I couldn't stop thanking them. I surfed for three days straight with these four guys, getting barrelled all day long, and went through all my boards except one. It was all-time. It felt amazing to just head off in search of this mysto wave and score such incredible surf. It makes you wonder how many other undiscovered waves are out there. We'd had no idea what to expect, but it's like the old saying goes: seek and ye shall find. There was a basic surf camp there, but it looked like they hadn't had many guests. It's a pretty fickle wave when there's no major swell. I've heard of people booking for ten days, and they might not even surf. It's one of those places you've just got to go when you see a swell coming. Ted said, 'Keep this quiet.' And I went, 'Okay, I promise I won't tell anyone.'

But pretty soon someone blew the place out and published an article telling exactly how to get there – and it was all on. Now heaps of crew go there. I said to Ted later, 'Did we just ruin that place?' And he said, 'It wasn't our fault. We didn't tell anyone.' But it was a heavy lesson how easily a secret spot can get exposed. I've been back once since, and it was really fun . . . and I made sure I brought plenty of legropes.

DOWN SOUTH WITH DAD

Back home, I knew I didn't want to get stuck in another Gold Coast summer bender, and I knew I needed a change of environment, so I packed up my things and went, 'I'm out of here.' I invited two of my favourite cameramen and really good friends, Shagga and Jon Frank, and we headed down the South Coast of New South Wales. My dad was living there then, and I really wanted to take the time to connect with him and go surfing without any crowds or pressure. We'd be in the water all day, and I really started to enjoy my surfing again. Then we'd have a beer with Dad in the afternoons. I'd have one beer and be so tired from surfing all day that I'd fall asleep. Then we'd wake up at five in the morning, go check the surf and do it all again.

I'd never really spent a lot of time with Dad growing up, not since we were kids in Coffs Harbour. I realised I didn't have many memories of him. I decided I wanted to make the effort to get to know him. It was hard when we were kids, because a lot of the time the only reason we'd speak to him was because we needed money. And that's not a proper relationship. So I took the initiative and went to hang out for a while. He's always moving around with his work. He drives a fifteen-tonner and goes wherever the work is – whether it's main roads or waterworks. My sister and brothers had all spent time with him, and my brothers had even worked with him, so they had a good relationship. But because I was a bit younger it had just never happened. We always kept in touch, and he'd drive up and watch me compete in Newcastle and things like that, but that time on the South Coast was really special. The only other time we'd really talked was when Sean passed away. He'd never been into the surfing thing, but after that he sat down and said, 'I've finally realised that what you're doing with your surfing and the friends you've made through surfing are pretty amazing. I'm really proud of you.' That's really all any son wants to hear from his dad, and it meant a lot to me.

When Ed and Sean were doing the Junior Series, he always said, 'You can't make a living from surfing,' and they were so determined to prove him wrong. But he said to me then, 'I'm so glad I bought you a surfboard for Christmas.' He's seen how much we enjoy it, how much fun we have and where surfing has taken me. He was pretty overwhelmed, and it really helped our relationship.

HAMSTRUNG

I came back from that South Coast trip refreshed, but my heart still wasn't into competing – and it showed. I started the season off with a thirty-third at home, which felt like a disaster. I managed a fifth at Bells and a ninth in Tahiti. But then I copped a seventeenth in Fiji, and all of a sudden I felt like I was on a real downward slide. I didn't know it then, but Fiji would be my last event for nearly a year. I was down around nineteenth on the ratings and I knew what I had to do to turn things around. I'd been getting too far ahead of myself, reading magazines about how I was going to be a contender this year, filling my head with all this crap, thinking it would be easy. I had started believing what everyone else was saying.

Rip Curl had organised an Indonesian boat trip for a bunch of us, and it felt like the perfect opportunity to take some time out, just go surfing and clear my head again. I was really excited about going away. I felt like I was getting things back on track. I was just going to get healthy and strong. I wasn't drinking and felt like it was the best I'd been surfing in ages. Then it all just fell apart in an instant.

We were in the middle of nowhere, on a boat off the west coast of North Sumatra, not far from the epicentre of the tsunami that would devastate the area only six months later. The surf wasn't big, only about four to six foot. I was going along this wave and went up to do a floater, and I was on the roof of the wave when it sort of jacked up. As I came down, I tail-dropped, my back foot came off and I went into the splits. Then the wave landed on me and pushed me further into the splits and almost through my board. My hamstring muscle ripped clean off my pelvic bone. I felt this incredible pain coursing down my leg, like a cramp. Then my whole leg cramped up, and if I tried to move it just got worse. I remember being under-water, thinking, *Oh, I can shake this off and paddle back out*. But as I was trying to kick up, it just got worse and worse. I realised I'd done something really bad. I managed to get back on my board and copped three or four waves on the head. I was then washed into this little keyhole. I screamed and waved for the boat, holding onto my leg, because it was flopping about uselessly. I couldn't even climb onto the tender when it came to pick me up. I think I was in shock. I just had to hang on as the boat towed me over to the big boat, and then I couldn't even climb the stairs. Once they lifted me onboard I was a blubbering mess. The captain could see it was bad and gave me some valium. I'd never had any pill like that before, and you could tell it kicked in straightaway because I stopped crying and started cracking jokes. We still had a ten-hour boat ride in front of us back to the mainland, and by the end of it I was writhing in agony again. Then it was still another three plane trips to get back to Australia. We had to bribe a local guy at the airport in Sibolga to get on a flight to Medan. I then flew from Medan to Singapore. In Singapore I went to see the doctor at the airport and asked him to pump me full of valium again. It was a long trip home. The reef we'd been surfing was actually raised a metre by the earthquake that caused the Boxing Day Tsunami. When I saw the devastation wrought by the disaster, I felt like I had nothing to complain about.

At that stage, I still didn't know what I'd done and figured I'd be right for Jeffreys Bay in a few weeks' time. As soon as I got home I went to see the Brisbane Broncos' team doctor, and they weren't sure how to treat it. Then Chris Prosser put me in touch with specialist Merv Cross in Sydney. I spoke to him on the phone. He knew exactly what I'd done and said, 'Get down here right away.' So I went and saw him and his partner, Dave Wood, and they booked me straight into surgery. Dr Wood passed along the bad news: 'You're out of the water for six months.' I gulped and thought, *Well, I'd better hope I get the injury wildcard.*

I was a bit nervous about the surgery, but I had a lot of confidence in Dr Wood. He'd done more of these operations than anyone. He basically said if I didn't get the surgery I'd never be able to run again.

'Okay, I guess I'm getting the surgery,' I said.

'We can't guarantee that you'll be able to sprint again, even with the surgery.' There was really no way of knowing if I'd ever get back to the level of surfing I'd accomplished. At that point I just thought, *Oh shit. This is serious.*

I remember sitting there in my robe, waiting to go into surgery. I was a bit worried about how it would go, but I was confident I was going to be okay and trying to stay positive. I was thinking, *Let's do this.* I had to fast for twenty-four hours before the operation and, apart from anything else, I wanted to eat again. They put a drip in my arm, and then the nurse got this huge needle full of white liquid, and I asked, 'What's that?'

She said, 'I think you might enjoy this,' as she injected me, and I felt this cold sensation spread up my arm. I looked at her and then, BOOF, I was out cold.

The next thing I remember is waking up in the recovery room. I'd been dreaming that I was out with my mates. I felt hung-over, and I honestly thought I'd woken up from a big night out in Surfers Paradise. Then the pain started kicking in and they gave me some morphine. I was like, *more, more, more.* Once the pain had subsided I felt surprisingly good.

They said the operation could not have gone any better and that, after a full rehabilitation of the leg, I should be able to surf without a problem. The procedure itself is pretty radical. They basically slice open your buttock, peel it back, drill into your hipbone and screw a metal grappling hook into it. To make sure it's strong enough, the doctor said he was lifting me off the operating table with just the grappling hook. Then they literally sew the ligaments from the hamstring muscle onto the hook. That's why you can hardly move for the first six to eight weeks – because the only thing holding the muscle in place is stitching, until the scar tissue grows over it. The hook stays in there for good.

For the first six weeks I just lay on the couch watching TV and movies. Even just slipping on a stair could have ripped the muscle off again, so I had to move around as little as possible. Mum reckons I was terrible to be around for that time – and she's a nurse. After those six weeks, I started drinking a fair bit and feeling like a slob. I was depressed at times. It was hard not knowing when I might surf again and whether I'd still have a career. Eventually I shook it off and realised I had work to do if I was going to get back in the water.

I started learning to walk again, because the leg was really weak. After about three months I got in the pool and walked up and down the lane, and when I started swimming I wasn't allowed to kick. Then I began using an exercise bike and doing a few gentle rotations. It was a really slow process but, in a way, it was really good just to stop. I'd been going so fast for so long, it was nice just to be still for a while. It was hard not being able to surf, but it was flat anyway, one of the worst winters we've ever had for surf, so that made it a bit easier.

I'd just moved into my newly finished house, two doors up from Mum, so it was nice to settle into my own home and get to know it. If I hadn't injured myself, I would have been in and out of the place between trips. I just came home, put my leg up for six weeks and relaxed. I didn't have any appointments. I'd sleep in till eleven in the morning, have a nap during the day and go to bed at eleven at night. And I really got to know all my mates again. Coming home for a few weeks here and there, it's hard to maintain your close friendships. It was cool to hang out and catch up with what's been going on in their lives in a way that wouldn't have been possible normally. My mates were the ones who kept me going during that time. They'd get me out of the house, drive me to get food or see a movie.

I really think everything happens for a reason, and that injury taught me a lot about myself. I learnt a lot about diet and training. In a weird way, it was the most fun year I've had, because I had nothing to think about or worry about apart from my recovery. It was a real blessing in disguise. The doctor was great. We kept in close contact. He gave me as much information as he could, and I told him everything I could about my progress. It was a big learning curve for everyone, but I was always confident I'd get the leg right again.

CHEK TRAINING

My chiropractor, Chris Prosser, introduced me to CHEK (Corrective Holistic Exercise Kinesiology) training, and it was the perfect rehabilitation program for my leg. Paul Chek is a health and fitness expert from California who's developed his own holistic approach to wellbeing. He's worked with the Chicago Bulls basketball team, as well as a lot of other elite athletes. I was working with a local CHEK trainer on the Gold Coast, Jan Carton, who's worked with the Canberra Raiders rugby league team, and she played a huge role in my recovery.

At first, because of my scoliosis, we started by getting my body aligned, straightening me out so that my body was symmetrical. After sitting on the couch for six weeks, it felt good to get the body moving again. CHEK training is gnarly. They concentrate on strengthening your core and then build you up from there. It's evening out the body, keeping a good posture through all your movements. I treated my training like a job, and I was up there five days a week from August to December 2004 during my rehabilitation. Each training session was about two hours – I'd stretch for half an hour and then train for an hour and a half. At first I wasn't allowed to do any squats or anything that would put pressure on my leg. So we concentrated on strengthening my core and the muscles around my spine, and pulling my shoulders back. This was really a continuation of the process I'd begun with Chris Prosser when my back first flared up in 2001, but taken to another level. We did a lot of work with the Fitball – a large, inflatable rubber ball – which is great for balance and core strength. In surfing you are on an unstable surface, so it really helps to train on an unstable surface like the Fitball. Learning to kneel or stand on the Fitball gets your core fired up.

It was tough sweating it out in the gym day after day, but all I was thinking about was trying to get back in the water. I was fighting for my career, and anything was better than just sitting on the couch wondering what the future held. I always thought, *If there is anything at all I can do to help my chances of getting my surfing back on track, then I am prepared to do it.*

At first my hip was really tight and it would get sore after training, so I had to take it slowly. It was a long process, but I knew I had to be patient and not overdo it. Jan also taught me a lot about diet and nutrition, which really helped. CHEK's holistic approach to health and fitness encompasses everything: training, diet, sleep, psychology. At first I was really only interested in the physical training, but then I began to see the benefits of the total approach.

DIET

Jan got me to keep a food diary, so I wrote down everything I ate during the day and then how I felt straight after eating it, half an hour later and two hours later. That way, you can figure out exactly what foods are best for you and how you are affected. I'd recommend this to anyone. It's amazing to think you could go through life without ever understanding what sort of fuel you run best on. We're all unique; everyone responds differently to different foods. Some people work better on a high protein diet and some people work better on mainly carbohydrates. I'm mixed, but I run best on about seventy per cent carbs and thirty per cent protein. So if you imagine a dinner plate like a pie chart, mine should be made up of mainly vegetables and a small serving of protein. I also discovered I don't really work that well on red meat. I used to eat a steak the night before an event and wonder why I felt lethargic the next day, but it was because my body took so long and used so much energy to break down the red meat. I'm much better on fish or chicken, so that is how I usually get my protein now.

Some people are super-conscious of everything they eat, but I think you can take it too far. I don't freak out if I stray from my ideal diet from time to time. It's hard to always find the right foods, especially when you're travelling, but I try my best. When I'm competing, my ideal diet would be porridge or muesli with fruit and yoghurt for breakfast, and maybe scrambled eggs if I'm really hungry, and a freshly squeezed fruit juice. For lunch, I'll have a light meal, like a salad with a little bit of chicken or tuna for protein, or a chicken and salad sandwich. For dinner, I'll usually have vegetables or salad with chicken or fish, and maybe a handful of pasta to get that sustained energy through the day. I drink a lot of water, especially when I'm competing, probably anywhere from four to six litres. I always have a water bottle handy and swig on it through the day.

I used to have a pretty bad diet. I've always loved chocolate, and I still do. I don't think I'll ever give that up. But I used to just eat junk food, KFC or whatever. As soon as I started changing my diet, I was amazed how much better I felt and how much more energy I had.

ALCOHOL

I don't drink alcohol at all when I'm competing, and I very rarely drink during the week or at home. I'll have a drink when I go out to a party, or maybe a glass of wine if we go out to dinner. I'll still have the occasional big night when the contest is over, especially if I have something to celebrate. But I've found when you cut out alcohol altogether, you become really clear-minded and everything seems to work better. Even your thoughts and instincts on a wave are sharper.

Again, everyone's different, and I know a lot of guys who will have two or three beers at the end of the day just to relax and unwind. But it doesn't work for me. I won't even have a beer in the week or two leading up to the event or throughout the contest. I don't like that fuzzy-headed feeling after a big night, and I don't like surfing when I'm hung-over. I always want to be really clear when I'm in the ocean. When I hurt my leg, I made a decision that I wasn't going to waste any more time being clouded when I go surfing. I don't want to have any regrets or excuses if I lose, and I want to give myself the best chance of winning. I remember that feeling of going out a night or two before a heat and then losing, knowing I'd blown it. I hated that feeling. I made up my mind that if I was going to do this, I was going to do it properly. If I won, that was great. If I lost, at least I knew I'd done all I could.

There's definitely a time and place to get loose. It's hard to stay on the straight and narrow all the time, especially with the pressures of travelling and competing. Sometimes it's hard for other people to accept that you don't want to drink. My first few years on the tour, if someone suggested going for a beer, I was like, 'Sure.' So when I started saying no, people asked, 'Where's Eugene? What have you done with Eugene?' But after a while they just stop asking.

THE FIRST SURF BACK

The injury happened in June 2004, and I didn't get back in the water for my first surf until November, a full five months later. I didn't even *touch* the ocean for about two months. The first time I walked down the beach onto the sand and put a toe into water, I felt all this extra energy, this *clean* energy, come over me. I don't think you fully appreciate what you get from surfing and the ocean until it's taken away from you.

I was seeing the doctor a lot, and he was testing the leg to see how strong it was. He said it was all looking good, but I just wanted to know if I could go surfing again. He said no, but I could go body-boarding. So I went bodyboarding for a few weeks, which was pretty funny. All my mates were writing me off, but I didn't care – getting back in the water was amazing. I was seeing Chris Prosser two or three times a week, and towards the end it was all about trying to get myself surfing again as soon as possible.

I can clearly remember my first surf back. I borrowed my friend's mini mal. The surf was only about two foot, but I was shit-ting myself. It actually felt good to have that scared feeling again, because it stopped me being too gung-ho. I was surfing against the wall at Duranbah and I was really worried about how my leg would go, but I caught this little wave, stood up and thought, *I remember this.* I cruised along and kicked out really carefully. My next wave I did a gentle little cutback. I couldn't bottom-turn but I'd just do these little cutties, and each day I surfed after that I kept getting better and better. I was so excited – I wanted to stay out all day – but I knew my leg would get tired, so I had to pull myself back. My leg would be a little stiff and sore afterwards, like after a training session, so I paced myself. But from that day on I was like a grommet again. I was going surfing every morning, no matter what.

I'd get up at 6 am and ride to my mate's house on top of Duranbah Hill and borrow his mini mal. I was frothing. My mates would want me to come out at night. 'No way,' I'd say. 'I'm not going out. I'm getting up for the early.'

And they'd say, 'But the waves are terrible.'

'Are you kidding me? I haven't been surfing for five months. I'm out there.'

Each day I'd improve a little bit more. It was like learning to surf all over again. One day I'd do a little cutty; the next day I'd go for a little foam climb. Then one day I got my first proper barrel. It was about three foot and I was terrified. I thought the lip was going to land on my head, push me into the splits and wreck my leg all over again. It was always in the back of my mind to look after my leg.

I had to apply for the injury wildcard to get back on to the WCT, because, of course, my rating had fallen while I was off tour. I was confident I'd get the wildcard, but it was still a bit nerve-racking. I had to turn up to the surfers' meeting in Hawaii in December and plead my case. The criteria is based on how close you were to qualifying, your results in the past and how severe your injury was, so I knew I had a pretty good case. Still, there are forty-five sets of eyes staring at me, deciding whether I deserved to continue my career or not. It was heavy. Everyone was telling me I'd be fine, I'd get the wildcard, but I didn't know for sure until they made their decision. Once I knew I was back in, I had to turn my focus to that first event and see whether I could even compete at the professional level again. Pipe was really good for the contest. It was torture just watching it and not being able to compete. But it got me so excited to get back in the mix. I went for a few surfs in small waves, at V-land and Off the Wall, just on my single fin. I took it really easy.

Once I realised I could surf again, I always believed I'd be able to get myself back to where I was before the injury, but I never put any huge expectations on myself. I didn't start riding a short-board again until January 2005, and even then my leg would still get a little bit sore and tight after surfing. It wasn't until mid-January that the pain went away and I felt like I could start pushing it. I remember surfing Snapper. It had been really fun through summer, and I decided I was going to give it a bit of a go and see how it felt. My first wave it didn't hurt at all, so I kept pushing it. Even so, there were some tentative moments, but I think as a result I became super-conscious of my technique and doing every turn properly.

MICK, MYSELF AND EUGENE

As soon as my leg was right I knew exactly where I wanted to go to really test it out. I went straight back to Hawaii in February, just to go surfing prior to the first event, and everything felt really good. With all the training I'd been doing and my improved diet, I felt stronger and fitter than I'd ever been. And I had a new appreciation for just how lucky I was to even go for a surf. Every time I paddled in from the water I had a smile on my face. I surfed every day in Hawaii and all over the place – V-land, Sunset, Off the Wall. I didn't surf anything huge, but I had a few decent wipe-outs – and it even felt good just to get smashed. Normally I would have been rattled, but I was coming up pissing myself laughing, happy to be back in the water.

My surfing felt a lot stronger from all the core work I'd been doing. I felt like I could hold a carve for a lot longer. And my energy levels were way better than they used to be. I used to get really fatigued, but now I felt like I could surf all day and paddle for kilometres, and get up the next day and do it all again without a worry.

It was probably the best trip I've ever had in Hawaii. I was there with Jon Frank, and we stayed with Pancho Sullivan and his wife, and they'd just had a little baby girl, Kirra. They live over the back of the North Shore in Pupukea Valley, so it was really quiet and mellow. Pancho would get up early every morning with his little girl, so we were up early too. We'd just sneak in and out. Our main goal was to surf Pipe every morning. From there, we'd surf all over the place. We had really good Backdoor and Off the Wall, and I surfed Haleiwa a lot. Pancho was great to have there to gauge what sort of level I was at, because he's one of my favourite surfers in Hawaii. He carves harder than anyone, and I was never going to match him with my little chicken legs, but it was a good benchmark to aim for. We'd surf all day then cruise back to the house; it was so peaceful. You wouldn't know what was going on in the world out there.

I was still a bit timid with my leg, but I was lucky because when we first got there Backdoor was small and fun, so I had a good warm-up. By the end we had some solid swell and I was surfing six to eight foot Haleiwa with no-one around. It was insane. It was the perfect time to get into the waves over there.

Frank and I were working on the film *Mick, Myself and Eugene* while we were there, and he's so much fun to work with. Right at the start he told me, 'I'll probably miss your best waves, so you better get a lot of them.' I went, 'Oh, okay, no worries.' That's just Frank - he's actually one of the best in the business. I really clicked with him. Some filmmakers stress out and you've got to be out there all day to get the shot, but with Frank, if it happens it happens. If it doesn't, so be it. He doesn't try and force things, so that's really cool. He's so good in the water, and he's got this weird way of looking at things, a different angle. He thinks he's a poet, and he's always coming up with little poems. And he's a ladies' man - just ask him. He falls in love about six times a day. He's a shocker. But then, who am I to talk?

WHEN LOVE COMES TO TOWN

When I first got injured I started going out a fair bit, and that's when Fisherman's Wharf, or 'Fishoes', up at Southport was really pumping on a Sunday afternoon. I used to head up there with my mate Andy, or, as we call him, Fuckface. It was at Fishoes that I first saw Karissa, and I was taken with her right away. I thought, *What is the dumbest pick-up line I could ever try?* So, I stopped her and went, 'You've got the most amazing eyelashes.' We had a bit of a chat and then went our separate ways. The next time we saw each other she was out celebrating her friend's twenty-first birthday, and I just happened to know her friend.

'Remember my eyelashes?' she asked. We hung out some more. I bought her a drink and she asked me along to this other club. There was a huge line to get in.

The bouncer took one look at her and said, 'You're in.'

'I'm with her,' I said.

'No, you're not.' She was already through the door when she turned around and went, 'See ya.' *Damn*, I thought, *I didn't even get her phone number*.

I had a couple of young Hawaiian guys staying with me, Kekoa Bacalso and Gavin Gillette. They were out here for some of the pro junior events and were always pestering me to go out. So, I decided to take them to Fishoes. I wasn't drinking by then – I was dead sober – but they were loose and I was laughing at them. They started talking to these two girls. And then I saw Karissa walk by and we got talking. She'd had a few drinks, and I offered to give her a lift home but she declined. So I asked her if she wanted to come over for dinner the next night. She asked, 'What are you cooking?' I told her a roast, and I think that lured her in.

So the next day she came over, not knowing I was a professional surfer or anything. She must have thought I was a dole bludger, because she pulled up outside my house and rang me: 'I'm at the address, but I don't know if this is the right place.'

'Yeah, that's it,' I said. So she came in and saw the house. Because it was all brand-new and pretty big, she probably thought I was house-sitting. I must have cooked a decent roast, because that was it, she pretty much never left.

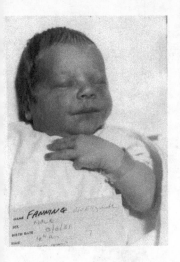

Above left: Just born and stoked to be alive. *Above right*: Family photo in front of our house in Penrith. Rachel is holding me, while Sean, Edward and Peter are nicely lined up in front of Mum. *Bottom left*: Sean and me. I look cool; Sean looks like a gangster. I think we are about five and eight here. *Bottom right*: I found a bunch of my sister's clothes in a box. Here's my catwalk parade in a ballet tutu.

Above: My early sporting photos, the first as a state rep for cross-country and the second as a member of the Northern Rivers soccer team. *Below*: One of the last photos of Mum with all of her kids. (*From left to right*) Peter, me, Rachel, Mum, Sean and Edward.

Above: Sean and me in front of his green Mini, visiting Dad in Port Macquarie for Christmas. I think Sean had bad scoliosis by the looks of this photo, but we never knew.

Right: Fancy dress for a Kirra Club presso. I think this was the closest Sean got to growing a real mo.

Above: Franky getting all *GQ* on me, trying to take an arty portrait.
Below: Swimming with stingrays in Moorea – scary but fun. (Photos: Jon Frank)

Above: Coming over a foamball in Hawaii. *Below*: Larry Layback in Moorea. Love the backdrop, so picturesque. (Photos: Jon Frank)

Above: The flying boat! My friend Georges Riou and me taking off. (Photo: Jon Frank)
Below: My first trip to P-Pass, Caroline Islands. Life was great with only four others out. (Photo: Ted Grambeau)

Above: The wave that ripped my hamstring clean off the bone, miles from anywhere off the coast of Sumatra, Indonesia. (Images courtesy Rip Curl/Jon Frank)
Below: This is about two hours after the injury. I think the drugs may have kicked in because I don't look too concerned. (Photo: Ted Grambeau)

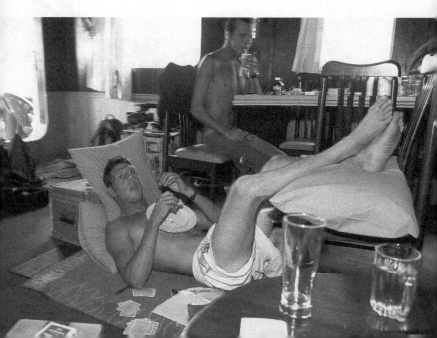

Above: Fighting fit again on the tornado ball.
Below: My trainer, Jan Carton, making sure
my spine is straight and the right muscles are
working while targeting paddling strength.
(Photos: Ted Grambeau) *Insets*: My back before
and after scoliosis rehab.

Above left: The young Kirra boys with welcoming signs. (Photo: Ted Grambeau)
Above right: I finally did it – World Champion 2007. (Photo: Jon Frank)
Below: Getting carried in at my surprise world title party with 300 friends who have always supported me. (Photo: Ted Grambeau) *Bottom*: Mum crowd-surfing to Grinspoon with everyone going nuts. (Photo: Ted Grambeau)

Above: Fins-free at Bells, 2008. *Below*: Driving through a pit at Off the Wall, 2008. (Photos: Ted Grambeau)

Left: Lactate threshold training in the Mentawais on the Red Bull trip. (Photo courtesy Red Bull)
Below: Visualising before a heat at Bells under the famous Bells Beach cliffs. (Photo: Jon Frank)

Opposite: Surfing Small Pass in Tahiti, so different to Teahupo'o.
Above: Trying to go as fast as possible through one at Teahupo'o.
(Photos: Jon Frank)

A snap at J-Bay. (Photo: Matt Kelson)

Above: Young Dolla inspecting my face. I really like this shot. *Below*: With Dolla and Primrose in front of Dolla's house in the Location. (Photo: Matt Kelson)

Above: The most special day of my life, marrying the girl of my dreams.
(Photo: Simon Williams) *Below*: Held aloft by my best mates – Parko and Deano.
A huge sporting gesture by Joel. (Photo: ASP/Cestari)

The Quiksilver Pro was on at Snapper not long after we met, and she was telling a friend of hers, 'I'm seeing this guy who's in the contest. I don't know how he'll go. Do you think he'll do any good?' And then her friend told her who I was. It was pretty funny, she didn't know a thing about it. Kekoa's on the WCT now, and he still says, 'I can't believe I was there when you met your wife.'

WELCOME BACK

In the lead-up to my first event back I was feeling a bit nervous, so I went and saw a sports psychologist while I was doing the rehab work. Phil Jauncey has done a lot of work with the Brisbane Lions AFL team and the Olympic diving team, and he was able to answer a lot of questions for me. Earlier on in my career I'd seen Steve White, and he was really good at helping me find trigger points to get me in the mood to surf a heat. I haven't been to a sports psychologist since, but it was cool to have those guys' help at the time. I've also learnt a lot from other people along the way about sports psychology. Ultimately, though, people can tell you all kinds of different things, but you've got to be the one to go out and do it for yourself. It's a matter of synthesising all the things you take in and finding out what works for you. I've still got a lot of the books and material those guys gave me, and I'll go back and read it every now and again just to refresh.

By the time the Quiksilver Pro came around at Snapper, I was feeling really good within myself. But I still didn't know how I was surfing compared to everyone else and how I'd compete. I surfed a few practice heats with Joel and actually beat him a couple of times. That was the first time I thought, *Wow, maybe I'm getting back close to where I was.* I just wanted to prove to myself that I could surf at that level again.

I was super-focused going into that event. I had a heat with Sunny Garcia in round three, and you always know a heat with Sunny is going to be full-on. The waves weren't epic, but as I kicked out of a wave I found myself paddling back out next to him, and he said, 'Welcome back.' Sunny is usually such a ferocious competitor, so having him say that made me feel like I really was back. I had an amazing event. I won all my heats pretty clearly, apart from a close quarterfinal with Andy Irons. The waves were small for the final against Chris Ward, but by then I really felt like I was on a roll and nothing could stop me. It's hard to describe the feeling when I won. I'd gone into the event just hoping I'd still be competitive, so to win my first event back after nine months – and five months out of the water – felt incredible. I think it was relief more than anything, knowing that I'd made it back on par with the best in the world. A huge weight fell from my shoulders. All the hard work had paid off in that one moment.

PARTY TIME

With that win, all three of us Cooly Kids – Joel, Dean and I – had each taken a turn at winning the season opener Quiksilver Pro. It's always a massive celebration when one of the local boys wins the contest. The local crew take over the Snapper car park, lug whole lounge suites and wheelie bins full of ice and beer down to the beach to watch the final day's action. More family and friends are crammed on the balcony of the Rainbow Bay Surf Club with panoramic views of the line-up. It's an amazing environment to compete in. Everyone's there from our first heat to our last. When one of the boys wins, everyone erupts. Those nights are really good fun. The celebration then moves from the car park to one of the pubs in town. I don't really remember my own parties, but Dean and Joel's have been epic nights.

We used to go to the Calypso Tavern in Coolangatta for the post-contest party, because that was the pub everyone went to when we were a bit younger. They were always really stoked to have us, even though we were pretty loose, and they'd have us behind the bar pouring drinks. We've had house parties at Dean and Joel's places in the past, and pool parties the next day. These days we go to the Sands Hotel. They always ring up as soon as the contest finishes and say, 'Let us know where you're going, because if you're coming here we need to know early so we can put on more staff.' So I got their phone call straight after the final, and I told them, 'Yeah, we'll be round there. Get ready, because it's going to be a big one.' They're all local bar staff, and they really look after us. But first you have to go up to the 'office', which is the Rainbow Bay Surf Club, and see the managers, Ray and Robin, and their crew, because they put up with everyone for the whole week of the event. They're super-nice people, and you don't want to get too loose and messy there because they've already had a massive week. So you pick up and move on to the Sands and make an idiot of yourself there.

In 2005, I actually went home pretty early because I was so flogged. But I'd given it a good nudge. The next day I was woken by the Harrington twins, Shaun and Dean, or the Hazzas as they're known, and a few other mates. They brought a blow-up pool, so we filled it with water and sat in it drinking beers all day. I reckon the second day of celebrations is actually more fun, because you're a bit more relaxed and everyone sits around telling stories and being idiots.

MARGS WITH MARGO

That win gave me a lot of confidence going into 2005, and I was really focused on having a strong year on tour and cementing my comeback. But I also found time for some fun side trips. Jon Frank and I were still working on our movie, and we'd hatched a plan to only go on surf trips to places we actually wanted to go, with people we really wanted to spend time with. So, high on our list was a trip to WA's south-west, with one of my favourite surfers and humans, Brendan 'Margo' Margieson. Just from watching Margo in movies like *Green Iguana*, I really wanted to go and surf with him. I knew he was someone who would push my surfing in those sorts of waves. Plus, he's a legend of a bloke. I invited him along one night when I was drunk, and he thought I was joking, but later when I was sober I convinced him I was serious.

In that part of WA you can surf so many different spots it's hard for a group to all agree on where to go. And from the first day it wasn't working, so we all decided that each day of the trip some-one different made the call. We got some really fun waves at the Box and Gas Bay and all those spots. There was no pressure to do anything but go surfing and hang out. We had one big night at the Tavern to see Wolfmother. Big Ted Grambeau took over the dance floor and we all rocked out. I like doing trips like that – not too many people and they all get along. It's not the full photo mission with a huge cast.

Ted and Jon Frank are definitely two of my favourite photographers to work with. Ted is so onto it and always makes good calls; a lot of other photographers really look up to him. Ted's like a mentor to Franky and always has answers to his questions – there's a lot of mutual respect there. At times when Jon could have been shooting stills himself he chose to act as Ted's assistant, being the light meter guy or whatever, just to learn from him. It was really good to watch, and there was no weird competitiveness between them like some photographers.

All in all, I was feeling pretty stoked to be back on tour and able to surf at a level I was happy with. I had another win at the Rip Curl Search event at Reunion Island, on this beautiful left called St Leu. I'd been there about six years earlier and, as soon as I found out the event's location, I started watching the old videos like *Pump* and others featuring Reunion. I visualised that wave a lot. When I got there, I was really enjoying the wave and felt like I was figuring it out. Then I saw Trent Munro surf it, and he was attacking it so well. He has a great backhand, and I thought to myself, *That is how I am going to try and surf it* – with the grab-rail bottom turns to really project into the lip. I felt it was the best backhand surfing I had done to date – and it seemed like I could pick the good waves, like I was at Snapper. Everything came together nicely.

But Kelly and Andy had been going at it for the title, and it was hard for anyone else to get a look-in. Kelly had sewn up the title in Brazil, so I just wanted to put in a good showing in Hawaii to finish the year strongly and as high up the ratings as possible.

I went into Hawaii feeling really confident, just from having spent that time there at the start of the year. The surf was huge for the first event at Haleiwa and then gradually dropped to a really fun four to six foot. It was pretty classic because after spending that time in Hawaii with Pancho at the start of the year we both ended up making the final. He won – I still couldn't quite match his carves with my skinny legs, but I was stoked with a second. I didn't do too well at Sunset; I've never really had great results out there. But going into Pipe it was Andy Irons and me pushing for the Triple Crown. For some reason, the guys in contention for the Triple Crown always seem to be waiting for someone else to lose to decide it. But I remember thinking, *Stuff this, I just want to go as far as I can regardless of what anyone else does.* The biggest thing for me was trying to overtake people in the ratings. I had a tough run through the event. I lost my first-round heat when the waves weren't great and had to surf in the second round against a couple of the heaviest local guys: Sunny Garcia and Dustin Barca. I wasn't doing too well and only had a 6, but no-one else had a really killer score either. I stroked into a big left, knowing I needed a score. It was weird because I could remember catching a wave just like it at Pipe at the start of the year, and it spat so hard it blew me off my board in the barrel. As I paddled into this wave

I thought, *Don't get blown off*, and I held on as hard as possible. I was spat out and scored a high 9, and that one ride set me on my roll for the event. I drew a couple more of the best locals, Jamie O'Brien and Freddy Pattachia, but managed to make it all the way to the final.

Before the final, the Triple Crown director, Randy Rarick, told Andy and me that whoever finished higher would win the Triple Crown. I was psyched and scored a 7 on the first wave. Then the onshore came up, and suddenly that was looking like a pretty solid score. Everyone was thinking there wouldn't be any more good waves. And then Andy stroked into this thing and scored a 10 – and that was pretty much it. Andy won Pipe and the Triple Crown again, but I was stoked to get myself in that position.

I still haven't won an event in Hawaii, and that is one of my biggest goals. I've had three seconds, a third and a fourth, so I've had my chances, but I really want to win one. The Triple Crown is a huge goal as well.

For me, '05 was a year of learning to get back in the game, but I won two events and finished third overall. Kelly and Andy dominated the year again, winning seven of the twelve events between them. But I'd still climbed one place from my ratings the year before the injury, so I felt like my career was back on track. My improved fitness really came to the fore on the final day of events, when we'd sometimes surf four times in a day, from round four through to the final. There were times I was in a final and I could see my opponent was struggling, and I felt like I still had plenty in reserve. The leg felt stronger than it ever had. Sometimes it would tighten up a little, but I'd just stretch it out and it would be back to normal.

Having that time off really put things in perspective. Up to that point I had taken things for granted, but I knew I never would again. That injury was another wake-up call about how quickly things could be snatched from your life, and I was determined not to waste a moment. I'd learnt a lot over the previous twelve months and felt like I'd finally had a chance to evaluate everything I'd been doing. I knew I wanted to go out and do my best, but if my best wasn't good enough, I'd still be happy. I'd also evaluated the previous couple of years and gained an understanding of why I lost when I lost and how I achieved my best. Sometimes I tried too hard, other times I didn't try hard enough, but I was letting too many outside distractions influence how I'd compete – who I was staying with, where I was staying, peripheral things. And I'd learnt something about the ruthlessness of competition. I think that's where Andy and Kelly had an edge on everyone – they didn't let anything distract them from the job at hand. Darren Handley used to tell me, when we'd go to negotiate a new contract, 'There are no friends in business.' We'd look at each other as friends before we negotiated, but as soon as we walked through that door and sat down it was business. I applied that approach to putting on a contest shirt. Now, when it was time to surf a heat, I decided there were no friends – it was down to business.

DR DAVID WOOD – THE SURGEON

A surgical blade slices through fleshy upper thigh and buttock. A power tool drills into bone. A metal hook is screwed into the cavity thus created. The surgeon loops a finger inside the hook and lifts the unconscious body of Mick Fanning a few inches off the operating table, just to make sure it is anchored securely. Then he meticulously attaches the flaccid hamstring muscle to the hook with needle and thread. It seems almost quaint. Dammit! We can sew the boy back together! And so they did.

Dr David Wood was the man charged with reattaching Mick's hamstring muscle. As a surfer himself, and with teenage sons who surf, Dr Wood was acutely aware how much was riding on Mick's recovery. 'I knew if I screwed up I was in big trouble,' he jokes, though that was never likely to happen. Dr Wood has performed this procedure more than any other surgeon in Australia, around 160 times at last count.

'Mick sustained an avulsion of the hamstring origin from the ischial tuberosity,' explains Dr Wood. Pardon? 'In simple terms, Mick pulled his whole hamstring muscle from his pelvic bone. This is a severe injury that is extremely painful at the time of the injury, associated with extensive bruising down the back of the leg. There can be involvement of the major leg nerve, the sciatic nerve, if the injury is untreated. Fortunately, we were able to operate soon enough before any sciatic nerve involvement occurred.'

Though it is a rare injury, requiring lengthy and delicate surgery, Dr Wood says the prospects of full recovery are usually good. 'The success rate of the surgery is now very good and, as long as the surgery is performed within a month to two months of the injury, the huge majority [of athletes with the injury] have got back to their elite level of sport. Even with the delayed repairs we can get a very pleasing result, but the surgery is much more complex at that time.'

Mick's operation, however, was textbook stuff. 'A small incision is made at the top of the back of the thigh. The ischial tuberosity, or bony prominence of the pelvis, is identified and scar tissue scraped away. Three anchors are then placed in the bone with large stitches attached, and the tendon is stitched back onto the bone,' Dr Wood explains. 'The anchors are literally like a Dynabolt, which expands inside the bone to hold it fixed very strongly. The procedure is variable depending on its complexity, but Mick's took about an hour and a half. The sewing process is pretty much as simple as a needle and thread, just a very expensive *needle and thread, as the stitch that strong costs about $80 per stitch. The tendon is just like sewing into the tendon of a tough bit of steak.'*

Keeping the leg as immobile as possible during the early recovery period is vital. 'It takes about six weeks for the tendon to scar back to the bone but six months for it to become as strong a connection as it ever will be,' he says. 'This is a reasonably rare injury but has been much more recognised lately by doctors and physiotherapists. The most common cause of the injury is water-skiing, when people are pulled out of the water and they get flicked forward with the knee straight and the pelvis bent, and it rips the hamstring off the pelvis.'

Of course, even the most skilled surgeon can only do so much, and Dr Wood says it was Mick's commitment to rehab work that guaranteed his full recovery. 'He was a model patient,' says Dr Wood. 'He came down for all his follow-ups. He even came and saw me when we were on holidays in Mooloolaba. He arrived in his red Porsche. The kids were very impressed, and he signed all their caps and T-shirts . . . He's done his rehab really conscientiously; he's done exactly what I've said. He was fantastic. He didn't jump the gun too early.'

And when Mick eventually secured his 2007 world title, Dr Wood was one of the first people he wanted to speak with. 'I have followed his career very closely ever since and have been delighted at how well he has performed,' says Dr Wood. 'I was ecstatic to hear of his world title win. His mother actually rang from Queensland while I was consulting in my rooms in Sydney the morning of his title win. She told me that Mick wanted to speak to me from South America and gave me his number. I telephoned this number, and a voice answered and I said, "Congratulations, Mick – it's David Wood ringing from Australia." The voice then said, "Oh, that's great. How's it been received in Australia?" And I said, "It's been front-page news and leading every bulletin in the news this morning." The voice then said, "Who is it?" and I replied, "It's David Wood, the guy who operated on your hamstring." The voice suddenly said, "Oh, are you the doc who put Mick's butt back together? Look, I'm really sorry. It's Joel Parkinson. I've been vetting all Mick's phone calls, and he really wants to speak to you." Mick then broke a television interview to come and have a chat, which was fabulous.'

Were his teenage sons impressed by his role in returning the world surfing title to Australia? 'It is certainly kudos at home but actually much more amongst my similarly balding, grey-haired, middle-aged surfing mates who have illusions of grandeur out on their longboards,' says Dr Wood.

JAN CARTON – THE TRAINER

The grandly titled CHEK Institute doesn't look too remarkable from the outside, just another large warehouse complex alongside mechanics and DIY Beer Brewers in the West Burleigh industrial area. Even inside there's not a whole lot to indicate the kind of personal and physical metamorphosis this facility inspired in its best-known client. At a glance, it looks like a rather sparsely equipped gym, with a couple of banks of weightlifting apparatus, a few inflatable Fitballs and other scattered bits of equipment.

CHEK training is a holistic approach to fitness, devised by Californian health practitioner Paul Chek. On the morning I visit CHEK's Gold Coast branch, Mick is arched backwards over a Fitball as trainer Jan Carton stretches him diagonally, with a hand on one shoulder and the opposite hip, leaning downwards with most of her weight. Mick's dog, Taylor, lies at his feet obediently, apparently unconcerned by the physical exertions her owner is being put through.

'I didn't know who he was when he first came in,' remembers Jan, a youthful blonde grandmother with twenty-seven years' experience as a personal trainer.

'Chris [Prosser, Mick's chiropractor] brought him in just after the stitches were out. It was a serious injury, but I'd worked on a lot of serious injuries. So much of it depends on the person. The human body is such an amazing piece of machinery – if people want to do it they can.'

Because the surgery was so recent, at first they couldn't do anything that would put a strain on the newly attached hamstring muscle.

'We rebuilt him from the ground up. We were working hard on a lot of other areas while his leg healed,' says Jan. 'It was pretty awesome for a young person who hasn't been exposed to it. His work ethic was amazing.'

At the time, the CHEK Institute was in Ashmore, and Mick dutifully made the ninety-minute return journey – the length of the Gold Coast – every day from his home in Tweed Heads. Mick underwent a thorough assessment that took in not just his physical condition, but diet, attitude and sleep patterns, to arrive at a personally tailored regime. One part of the assessment involves putting the client in earmuffs and a blindfold and asking them to march on the spot for a minute. Without sound and vision to orient themselves, any imbalances in the body will show up by how far they move off the spot. While most people will be convinced they are marching in one place, when they remove the blindfold they find they have moved halfway across the gym. In Mick's case, he was very nearly marching in circles, because of his scoliosis and lopsided musculature in his back.

'I told him, "It's lucky you're not paddling in circles."' Jan grins.

While the leg healed, Jan began working on straightening Mick's spine. 'We did a lot of work on his upper-body mechanics,' she says. 'The scoliosis was really bad. It was functional scoliosis – he wasn't born with it, but created it with overuse patterns.'

CHEK training places as much emphasis on the emotional aspect of the athlete as the physical, and Jan saw Mick battling with depression in the early stages of the injury.

'He did get quite low in the early bit, but I think he was seeing that he was doing stuff, moving forward,' says Jan. 'We had a lot of talks. Once he could see that things were changing within himself, physically there was a bit of hope for him.'

And gradually, Jan began to get a sense that her new client had rather more at stake than just wanting to be able to go for a surf again. 'I was starting to get the picture that he was more than just your weekend surfer, because he was so committed,' says Jan. 'With the work he was putting in, I said, "Mick, you'll not only get back to surfing, you'll be bigger and better than you ever were, because you've probably never known this stuff about your body and how to eat right." I said to him, "Sometimes these things happen for a reason." It's been a really great journey with him, like watching one of your children grow up.'

They were told to expect a two-year turnaround to get back to peak performance, but neither of them were going to accept that time frame. 'If they tell you you can't, you definitely can,' says Jan. 'I've seen it with so many people, people with brain injuries, and they've been told they're never going to do this or that. I said, "This is just a hamstring. I know it's a big issue, but it's just a hamstring, Mick." So we never ever had an attitude that, Hopefully we'll get you back. It was just a matter of when. Let's do the work. And as soon as the surgeon told us he was able to surf again and he had a few surfs, it was all good. I said, "All right, is there anything that's coming up that you want to go for?" And he said, "The Quikkie Pro. I'd like to be able to enter it." And that's when we said, "Well, why don't you want to win it?" And he goes, "Oh yeah, that would be good." Right, that's what we're doing. You're not just going there to make up the numbers. He's low-key – he never gets excited and jumps up and down – but you could see he was lighting up.'

Jan says teaching Mick's body that the hamstring muscle was reattached, and helping him let go of the injury emotionally were major challenges. 'There's a lot that has to happen on the emotional side with injury,' she says. 'Most people that have had something significant don't realise that they are still looking for it. What happens if my hamstring goes again? They don't realise they do it, and you have to emotionally make them aware of letting go of it too. And I think he got halfway through the year and that same thing came up. He said, "I realised what I'm doing. I'm surfing safe. I'm surfing in case I hurt my hamstring." I said, "Mick, I will guarantee you that hamstring is there to stay. From my point of view and the area I work in, you don't have an issue with your hamstring." Even in the early days, after testing it and it was all okay, we said, "Mick, we're not going to talk about the hamstring. It's just as good as the other one." We consider the injury, make sure we do all the right steps, but we don't baby the injury.'

When Mick competed at the Quiksilver Pro after a nine-month lay-off, Jan was stunned to discover just how famous her client was, mobbed on the beach and pressed for autographs everywhere he went. 'We went, "Mick, we had no idea you were this famous." We just laughed, walking behind him going, "Wow, Mick's a rock star."'

And when, true to his word and Jan's prompting, Mick won the event, all the emotion and hard work that had gone into his recovery finally spilled over. 'We were pretty teary about the whole thing. One, it meant so much to us, and he was our little Mick who had been injured. And we got to know his history about his family and Sean, and so it was more about what Mick had been through than just winning a comp. As his mum said, "At one point he just gave up. What else can happen?" She said, "I just can't thank you guys enough, because Mick had given up. He'd lost his brother; this [injury] had happened to him; they told him he wouldn't surf again. I can see this fire in his belly, and I haven't seen that for years – he's got his life back."'

MATT GRIGGS – THE PIT BOSS

Matt Griggs was surfing's first official 'pit boss'.

Surf companies have had team managers before, sure. But Griggs wasn't quite a team manager. In fact, at first no-one was sure quite what to call the fluid, far-reaching role of 'athletic support' Matt had fashioned for himself. (Clearly, that title wouldn't work.) Eventually, they settled on 'pit boss'. The former professional surfer turned magazine journalist had re-invented himself once more as travelling companion and support crew for Rip Curl's A-team of sponsored surfers.

'I was working for Tracks at the time and had a really keen interest in coaching/training,' says Matt. 'I was super-interested in improving and what it took to be the best at something.'

Rip Curl's head of marketing, Neil Ridgway, a former Tracks editor himself, recognised Matt's special talents and offered him a job. 'It was a bit of a swing in the dark, the pit boss concept,' says Matt. 'The only part of it that was understood was, I was there to help.'

Ridgway had dreamed up the position of pit boss after watching a Premier League soccer match between West Ham and Leeds in the UK and marvelling at how much the clubs spent on players. 'Then, musing over a pint, I was amazed at how much money we spent on surfers,' he recalls. 'The difference was that West Ham had coaching and support staff which benefitted their players and helped to maximise the investment in them, while Rip Curl had a bunch of individuals running around the globe trying to do it all on their own.'

Matt had known Mick's older brother Ed when they both did the Junior Series but hadn't had a lot to do with Mick when he landed the Rip Curl gig. 'With Mick it was a baptism of fire. I felt it was best for me to observe in the initial days. So I watched very closely in the first events at Bells in 2004. Hog [Rip Curl surfer Nathan Hedge] and others had taken to me straightaway, because they needed someone. Mick was different – he knew who he was and he knew what he needed from people. Once I worked him out and he worked me out, we got really close and brought the best out in each other. He helped me as a person and a coach.'

But Neil says the role started out much simpler and more pragmatic than that of coach. 'The pit boss was not originally a coach. He was there to be pit crew: pick up the singlets, tell the surfer which bank was most consistent, video the heat for them, caddy in the channel, talk to the head judge about what is important, plonk the cap on the head after each heat, get the food and water, sort the transport for the team signing so it was easy, arrange media interviews at times that suited surfers, and give feedback and communication with the team to Torquay. Griggsy, being who he is, developed the role over three years to include technique coaching, training, nutrition, mental support, medical support and a level of sports science along with the other pit boss stuff too. It didn't set out that way, but he evolved it to that, and I think it worked fantastically well – and Mick really took from it what worked for him as an individual.'

Matt was able to feed Mick's insatiable appetite for improvement when away from his regular coach. 'My role on tour with him evolved a lot. I provided tools to help him evolve,' says Matt. 'I videoed most surfs so he could try boards. We looked at his technique, we worked on strategies, on diet and training. Anything that could help him evolve, he was open to. The best thing about Mick was he came to me as much as I came to him. He was constantly looking for that next level – and able to process any ideas put to him and understand their value, or lack of.'

Matt joined the team not long before Mick injured his hamstring, so he played a pivotal role in Mick's recovery. 'He got injured early in the piece. I stayed with him all the way through it, stayed at his house for a week after and drove him up to Brisbane, all around the Gold Coast looking for answers,' says Matt. 'We learnt a lot about the human body and mind after that experience . . . and a lot about each other. He felt like family after that – and I felt a part of his.'

And Matt saw benefits for Mick in the enforced lay-off. 'Mick Fanning the professional surfer had come on first, so it was a good time for Mick Fanning the person to get to know himself *when he got injured. This gave him time to look within and have a bit of fun being himself while the tour went about its thing. After a few months of this, Mick knew who he wanted to be and set about building his body into a world-title machine after this, getting the right people around him and putting in everything it took. Mick hates uncertainty. Once he knew what he had wrong and how to fix it, the tough times in the gym were easier for him than any uncertainty preceding it.'*

chapter 6.
READY TO WIN

At the start of 2006 I thought, *This is the year that I'm going to challenge for the title.* I was fit and strong, my leg was right, my surfing felt sharp, and I'd learnt a lot about myself and how to compete. But amid all this new knowledge, I'd forgotten one important ingredient – enjoyment. I was so driven to succeed in 2006 that I started taking things way too seriously. I felt a lot of tension and my surfing suffered as a result. I started off with a seventeenth at home, losing to Pancho Sullivan at small D-bah – conditions that should have suited me against a big bloke like Pancho. I managed a fifth at Bells, but followed it with a thirty-third in Tahiti and a ninth in Fiji. I was feeling pretty anxious by the time we turned up in Mexico for the Rip Curl Search event. We didn't have much of an idea where we were going, but when I first saw the wave it was so perfect. I thought, *This is where I can get a result and turn things around.* That wave was ideal for my surfing, but it just didn't happen – I went home with another seventeenth. I was staring down the barrel of my worst season on tour. So much for challenging for the title.

Someone gave me a copy of Kostya Tszyu's biography, *Kostya*. I was reading it on a plane and was really struck by this part where he says, 'You've got to know your opponent, but you've also got to know yourself and know your strengths to beat them.' It made me feel strangely emotional. I wasn't using my strengths. I'd become almost like a robot, doing the exact same thing every wave, every heat, not even enjoying my surfing. I thought I'd recovered from my leg injury, but on some level I don't think I had completely moved past it and, even subconsciously, I was still nursing the leg, surfing in a way that wouldn't put any extra strain on it. I decided I was already out of the title race, so I may as well try and enjoy myself and my surfing again, free things up and see what happens.

When I first came back from the injury, I was putting a lot of emphasis on the moves I knew would score. I was really concentrating on my forehand hack off the top, because that was my money move that the judges rewarded. If that didn't feel right before an event, then I didn't feel right. Even in my free surfs I'd just practise that one turn. I was bored, so I decided I really had to change things. I was concentrating on being too perfect on waves. I lost to Chris Ward in Mexico, and I realised he didn't try and surf every wave perfectly. There were one or two turns where he gagged, but at least he was trying different things, and the judges seemed to appreciate that. I wasn't doing anything different. There were times I could have gone for a massive air, but I did a floater instead because I knew I could make it. I sat there on a flight out of Mexico and asked myself, *How are you going to change all this?*

NEW YORK, NEW YORK

Karissa and I went to Jeffreys Bay via New York and stopped over for a week's holiday. It was the best thing I could have done. It was great to get away from surfing for a while and lose myself in the big city. We had an awesome time, and stayed right on Times Square. I'm not usually into cities, but New York was all-time. I loved the whole atmosphere. When you first walk out into Times Square the energy just hits you, BOOM, like walking into a football stadium. Everyone is going so fast. It was the first time I'd ever done a trip without surfboards, and it was really cool. We were the biggest tourists. We went to the Statue of Liberty, the Empire State Building, Ground Zero, which was this eerie, vacant city block. It was all fenced off and went down about ten storeys into this big dark hole. It was heavy, and everyone standing around it was really quiet, just staring into it. It spun me out, actually. We were looking through all the names of the victims, and I was looking to see if there were any Fannings. And there was my dad's name, exactly the same: John Joseph Fanning.

New York really left an impression on me and was just what I needed to completely get away from the world of surf contests. Even so, I'd catch myself thinking about Jeffreys Bay and all these new things I wanted to try with my surfing when we got there. It was like I'd had a huge holiday, and I couldn't wait to get back to work.

J-BAY LAYBACKS

I went to J-Bay with that magical feeling that I was going to win. It's a really elusive mindset, and I don't think you can manufacture it or conjure it up. Maybe it's just an accumulation of all the work and energy you've put in beforehand, and it always feels like a validation that you are on the right path. The time away had given me some fresh insights. I no longer felt stale – more than anything I just wanted to enjoy my surfing more. On the flight to South Africa I wrote down all the things I could change about my surfing and what I should be doing. And I came up with the idea that if I see a big section, I don't care what comes after it, I've just got to belt it as hard as I can. And that's how I surfed from then on. Every time I surfed J-Bay I was trying big laybacks and all kinds of different stuff. My free surfs became so enjoyable, and that carried over into my heats.

The waves weren't great through most of the event, but it finished in really good four- to six-foot waves. We had to surf four times on the final day. That's where I felt like my fitness gave me an edge and I took out Kelly in the semis and Taj in the final, so I really earnt it. And that started a roll that carried right through to the next year. I felt like I'd found my consistency and a routine that worked, but I'd also found ways to keep my surfing fresh and enjoyable, and that was the magic combination. A world title campaign really begins halfway through the previous season. You can't just come into a new season and throw yourself at it and expect to get results straightaway. You have to build some momentum, and that's how I saw the second half of 2006.

But Kelly was on a roll of his own, and there seemed to be nothing any of us could do to stop him. Bede Durbidge, a largely unsung and unsponsored surfer from North Stradbroke Island off the Queensland coast, showed us all the way when he beat Kelly in the final at Trestles. No-one in America really knew who Bede was, and he was competing in front of a huge, pro-Kelly Californian crowd. He took the champ down with his cool, calm, no-fuss approach. It was an inspiration to all of us. Joel and I actually made a pact after the event that we were going to do whatever we could to climb the ratings and bring the title back to Australia – if not that year then the next. We were seventh and eighth in the ratings, and we said, 'Let's get ourselves back up as far as we can.' We really helped each other out during the next couple of events, giving each other pointers before heats, and it seemed to work. We both made the final in France, and Joel got me again. But it was cool. It sort of felt like what Mick Campbell and Danny Wills had going on when they challenged for the title in 1998. In Mundaka we again gave each other a lot of advice too, but it was only for those couple of events. It wasn't necessarily about trying to stop Kelly, because that particular horse had already bolted, but we just wanted to take out whoever was above us. It really worked for both of us – we had a string of good results and surged up the ratings, even though Kelly still had the title wrapped up. From that point on, everything just fell into place for me.

TAKING THE PLUNGE

It was while we were in France that I decided I was going to propose to Karissa. Meeting Karissa was the other piece in the puzzle that really helped me feel happy, settled and content. We couldn't get a flight home from France for a few days, so we had a bit of a night out. After a few drinks I told Kelly that I was going to go home and propose to my girlfriend. He was stoked for me and said, 'Awesome, congratulations.' It was strange because I think he almost seemed envious, like it was the only thing in life he didn't have. I said, 'Don't worry, yours will show up one day. The moment you don't look for it is the moment it shows up.' He told me later that meant a lot to him, and he actually publicly thanked me for it at the ASP banquet in 2009.

All the way home from France I was thinking about the proposal. I couldn't sleep the whole way. I ran into Danny Wills and his wife, Kirsty, at Singapore airport. They could see I had this weird grin on my face and something on my mind. Call it women's intuition, but Kirsty asked, 'What are you up to?' I told her I was going to propose when I got home, and they were really excited. Willsy asked, 'Have you got a ring?'

'No,' I said. 'I was going to get one in Brisbane when we got there.'

He went, 'Do you know anything about rings?'

'Nah.'

Willsy reckoned he had a mate who was a jeweller, so he knew a bit about them. He walked me around Sinagpore airport looking at rings until I found one I liked. When he gave his stamp of approval I just thought, *right*, and bought it.

When I finally got home Karissa was looking at me funnily, as if she could tell there was something on my mind. We went and got a juice, and she asked, 'Why are you staring at me?'

'Oh, no reason.'

She had a few errands to run, so I went and bought some flowers, hid them in the back of the car and picked her up.

'Let's go up to Kirra Hill and check the surf,' I suggested as casually as possible. I'm sure she was thinking this was all a bit weird because I don't generally invite her to come and check the surf. Maybe she thought I just wanted to go visit the trees we planted for the boys, where their plaques are on top of the hill. We went up and there were a few people around. I didn't want to propose with an audience, so I was waiting for them to move on. When we were finally alone, I said, 'Come on, let's go over and check the waves.'

It must have been getting weirder by the minute for her. It was a pretty nice day, and there was a bit of surf. I got down on one knee and pulled out the ring. She just went, '*Aaaah*,' and started crying. I asked her to marry me and she said, yes. And then I gave her the flowers out of the car. She still had to go to work, so I went to the house to catch up on the sleep I missed on the way home. That night we had some friends and family over and told them our news.

It really felt like everything was right in my world at that point. I finished the year strongly in third place on the ratings, had a win in Brazil and didn't finish worse than the quarterfinals in the second half of the year. That gave me so much confidence going into 2007. Consistency had always been my biggest problem and, once I'd attained that, it felt like there were no more obstacles in my way. Kelly won the title again by a big margin, and the rest of us were starting to get fed up with his continued domination.

That was also the point at which I felt like all my training had really paid off. I could afford to back off a bit and do enough to keep my edge sharp but give myself a bit of time off and just surf more. As I was flying home from Hawaii I realised I'd climbed one spot each year I'd been on the WCT – from fifth to fourth and then, after the injury, third. Seeing I'd come third again, I decided I was going to skip second altogether and go straight to first. For some reason, I had that self-belief – and I just went for it.

It was uncanny during the back half of 2006 and 2007. It didn't matter what happened to me before I got to the beach, once I put on my headphones and started stretching, I went into this zone where I knew everything was right: my boards and everything else around me. Once you manage to generate that self-belief, it's self-perpetuating. You know you can paddle out and find the waves and get the scores, and that's exactly what happens. I had no doubts about anything. I knew I had a couple of things to work on, like the events in heavy lefts – Teahupo'o and Pipe – but I had plans to tackle that too.

Before every heat I'd put my headphones on and listen to the first eight songs of Tool's album *10,000 Days* for my warm-up routine. The first two songs were amp-up music. Then I'd stretch through songs three and four, get my boards ready during song five, skip song six, then look at the waves and warm-up during tracks seven and eight. If I started two heats before I was due to surf, that would take me to about thirteen minutes before my heat started. Then it was time to pull on my contest singlet, walk down the beach, sit and have a final moment of meditation . . . and then go to work. This whole routine got me in the Zone. I felt like I had a little force field around me, and people would just leave me alone.

The biggest thing for me is that I surf best when I'm really clear-headed. So that's what I always try and maintain. I sit there between heats, go within and don't worry too much about what other people are doing. I make sure I'm doing what's right for me. A lot of it has to do with confidence. When you're not feeling confident you end up looking around to see what other people are doing, trying to get inspiration or direction from them, when it really has to come from within.

The other thing that was really working for me was visualisation. I found I could sit, watch the waves and visualise myself surfing them – it almost felt like I'd already surfed the heat. Then I just had to go out and act it out. Your muscles are already turned on and warmed up and seem to know exactly what to do. Studies have found that muscles respond during visualisation almost as if you are doing the action you are visualising. It's amazing how powerful the mind is. And there are no rules to visualisation – you can make everything perfect, exactly the way you want it. You can visualise yourself surfing a wave at Snapper 1000 times, and you never fall off or put a foot wrong. That pattern is embedded in your mind, and then you simply go out and perform it. They say if you can see it, you can do it. That's how skaters, snowboarders and surfers come up with new tricks.

Visualisation is a really valuable tool to have. Even if you haven't surfed for a week, but you've been visualising it, you still feel like you're surfing well. It actually feels like you've been surfing. Sure enough, when you next paddle out it all comes together.

2OO7 WORLD TITLE CAMPAIGN — SNAPPER

I had all this working for me going into the first event of 2007. The final ingredient is the surf itself, and when that came to the party I had a feeling that things were going to happen for me. We had incredible waves for the Quiksilver Pro at Snapper that year, and there were some epic heats. I had an amazing quarterfinal with Josh Kerr in six-foot waves, barrelling from behind the rock, and we both had multiple 9-plus rides. He had me comboed early on, and in the space of two minutes I scored two high 9s and had *him* comboed. At the time, I knew he had one 9, not two, but I knew I needed a big score. I knew those waves were going to come, so I just sat and waited. He had priority for a lot of the time but let me have my second 9, so it worked out all right. I told myself, *Relax and they will come*. And they did.

But I didn't expend any emotion on winning that heat. Once I came in, I got ready for my semi. There was a lot of excitement and noise going on around me, but I blocked it all out. I knew each heat was just one small step in a much bigger marathon. I watched the next heat, which Taj won.

I went in with a straightforward mentality: win every heat and then win the final. There was no point getting excited about the fact that I won that quarter. I've done that in the past, and it dissipates the energy you've generated. The key is to contain that energy until you need it again. I just kept my workman's head on, kept pushing forward. That quarter was over; it was time to move on.

The other thing about that first event was that I got my board the day before the event started, and it was a magic one. Every time I rode it I grew more confident, and it was just one less thing to worry about. I rode it out at D-bah the day it arrived – it felt great right away.

Bede Durbidge and I met in the final, and I think we'd both peaked in our quarters and semis. It was a bit of an anticlimax, but I still won it and felt on top of the world. I was the first of the Cooly Kids to win our home event twice, and I knew it was going to be a big celebration. 'I think it might be dangerous out in the pubs tonight,' I warned reporters after my win.

BELLS

I felt great going into Bells. I had some really good heats where I was at the top of my game. I had a close heat with Joel, and up until then I'd never beaten him in a WCT. Every time I drew him in a heat I'd start stressing out. I think it's a hangover from when we were kids and he'd usually get the better of me. I knew I could beat him, but I never really told myself I could. I'd always try too hard and make mistakes. But the day before our heat I realised if I was going to win the title I'd have to start beating Joel too. So it was a big thing to get past him, and it put one more piece into place for me. I lost to Andy in the semis, but I was pretty happy with a third. Taj beat Andy in the final, and you could tell he was serious about the title this year too. But a third and a first put me into a good position going into Tahiti, which I knew was one of my biggest challenges for the year.

TAHITI

Tahiti was definitely a place where I knew I needed to do some work. I felt comfortable out in the waves, but for some reason I was never as comfortable during the actual event. I felt like I was holding back during heats. But I knew if I could get a good result there, then the rest of the year would come together.

So I decided to go over a few weeks early to surf before the contest crowds descended. I went with Jon Frank, and we stayed at my friend Alain's house. We had the use of Alain's ski, and we went surfing whenever we felt like it. We didn't have any obligations or pressure and just cruised, went surfing and got a few shots. It was all-time. I really learnt to surf the wave and found my way around the line-up during that time. I was happy with my tube riding out there and tried some different things. There were a few locals and some Hawaiians who gave me some helpful pointers. It's hard to get waves when the contest is on, so it was really important I got to know the place.

Surfing Teahupo'o is such an adrenalised experience, like no other wave in the world. You're deep-breathing as the wave approaches, people are screaming from the channel – it can all be a bit over-whelming. I learnt to relax into it a bit more, slow things down in the middle of all that madness. Sometimes when you're really frantic out there it feels like your vision is really narrow, and I learnt to be more aware of what was going on in the present rather than trying to get in and get out. It's all about being comfortable in your surroundings, making clear-headed decisions under pressure. Just from spending that additional time there, you know which waves are going to do what. I'd take off and have an intuitive sense of what the wave was going to do. I tucked into a couple of barrels where I almost disappeared in the foamball, but I had the confidence to hang on to the death – luckily they let me out. You learn when to press the button and go, and when to slow things down a bit.

It all paid off when I made the final at Teahupo'o, my best result there ever. I lost to Damien Hobgood in the final, and probably peaked in my semi with the highest heat score of the event, but I was stoked. Everything felt good. I had a good lead in the points race, but I knew I had to keep working. I couldn't rest. You need eight results to win a world title. I only had three at that stage. The other top guys only had two strong results. Joel was probably the most consistent at that stage, with three quarterfinals, but it was still wide open.

THE COOLY KIDS REUNION TRIP

After Tahiti we had a Cooly Kids reunion trip to the Mentawais, and it was the perfect thing for me at that point. Joel, Dean and I hadn't travelled together on a surf trip, outside of contests, for years, and we were all pumped. Photographer Simon Williams organised the excursion, and it took a bit of juggling to find a time frame that suited everyone. Swilly rang me and said, 'I've booked the boat. Joel says he's in if you're in.' And I'm like, 'I'll go if he goes, but only if Dingo goes too.' Eventually, we all committed. Then Swilly wanted to know who else we wanted to bring, because there were spare berths on the boat. We didn't want to make it a full-on photo trip with all pro surfers, so someone came up with the idea to make it a mates' trip. We all would choose a mate to bring along. So Dingo brought pro surfing buddy Paul Fisher, and Joel brought his wife's brother-in-law, Matty Skeen. I invited Dan Holt from North Straddy, who used to stay with my family when we were kids. And because we only wanted mates on board, we invited our favourite cameramen, Jonny Frank and Shagga, and journo Sean Doherty to write a story.

From the moment we met up at the airport it was comedy. Holty was really scared of flying and sort of embarrassed: 'I'm going to be the biggest kook on the trip and look like the biggest idiot the whole time.' I just told him, 'You're kidding yourself, mate. No-one's judging. It's just a fun trip.' So he got over that and we settled in with a few brews on the plane.

Deano had just been really sick in Tahiti with a bug you can get from eating fish, which puts too much iron into your system. The symptoms are freaky – when you touch cold things they feel like they're burning, and if you touch hot things they feel like they're frozen. So he was on the full health program, trying to shake this thing. Shagga was just being a maniac and providing plenty of entertainment. It was one of those trips where everyone just gelled.

We got to Padang in West Sumatra, and we were all sweating like pigs. Joel asked, 'Who wants some moped fuel?' We were all like, 'Moped fuel?' And he goes, 'Yeah. *Bin, bin, bin, bin, tang, tang, tang,*' imitating the sound of a motorbike starting up. We all agreed, yes, in fact, we would like some moped fuel, or rather a few cold cans of the local brew, Bintang. So that became the call of the trip, 'Who's on the moped fuel? *Bin, bin, bin, bin, tang, tang, tang!*'

We surfed all day, and every afternoon we'd adjourn to the top deck for a couple of cool ones and talk story. Deano wasn't drinking, so he'd come up and start doing yoga in front of us, which wasn't such a pretty sight. I don't think any of us stopped laughing the whole trip. It was so good to be in cruise mode after those first three events in a row and forget all about the tour and the title. I wasn't that pumped to surf every minute of every day. They'd hassle me to go surfing and I was like, 'I'm on holidays. I'll surf when it's good.' Dingo would be out there from sun up to sun down, as he does. We were on the *Mangalui*, which is a classic, local-style timber yacht and the ideal vessel. The phones were off and no-one had a thing to worry about. We talked about what we used to get up to as kids, how much ruckus we used to cause.

Towards the end of the trip we had a couple of flat days and everyone started to devolve a bit, as you do on boats. The cook on the boat, Wal, had been making all this special food for Deano because he was on this really clean detox diet, gluten-free or whatever. Wal had put a lot of time and effort into going to the supermarket and getting all the right things for him, which is hard in Indo. Shagga, on the other hand, would eat anything that was left over. So those two were Wal's best mates, and Wal really looked after them. Which made what happened next all the crueller. We got pretty drunk one night, and everyone eventually stumbled off to bed one by one. I was about the third or fourth one up in the morning, and when I saw Wal he wasn't looking too good. I thought he must have had a big night, which was odd because I could have sworn he'd gone to bed early. Turns out he'd had a big night all right, but not in the usual way. Then I saw Joel and Skeeney, and they said, 'What did you do last night?'

'What do you mean?'

'Go and look at Wal's foot.'

I had a look and it was covered in the biggest blisters. 'What happened to you?' I asked.

And Joel and Skeeney said, 'We were thinking maybe *you* could tell *us*.' Sure, I've got a bit of a reputation for getting loose when I've had a few, but I was innocent.

I told them, 'No, mate, I didn't do anything. How did it happen?'

Wal reckoned someone had put tissues in between his toes and set them on fire while he was asleep. He'd woken up in the middle of the night with his whole foot alight. It didn't take Sherlock Holmes to work out who the culprits were. Everyone else started getting up one by one and denying any involvement, until there were only two people left asleep: Dingo and Shagga. When they finally woke we were all onto them. 'What did you do, you pricks?' Wal was devastated, the poor bloke. He was on this trip, having the time of his life, living the dream, and then his foot is set on fire. We were sure we had our men, but Shagga and Dean kept denying it.

We ended up loosening their tongues with a few drinks that night, and Deano finally cracked over dinner. You've never seen someone so remorseful. 'I'm so sorry,' he kept saying. We had a rule: if you fell asleep anywhere but your bed, you could get hot-heeled. But if you were in bed you were off limits. A hot heel is where you put a cigarette lighter under the back of someone's heel while they're asleep. They normally wake up straightaway. It turns out Wal's only crime was falling asleep on the couch.

'We tried to do it to Wal, but he wouldn't wake up,' Deano claimed. So they packed a whole roll of toilet paper between his toes, set it on fire and bolted. They expected him to wake up immediately. But when they hadn't heard anything after about ten seconds, they came back and his whole foot was on fire. I heard later that Wal's foot took about two and a half months to heal, because he was always on the boat and getting it wet. And he couldn't surf, poor bugger.

On the *Mangalui*, everyone sleeps in the same cabin in bunk beds. A few of the boys would sit up and watch movies most nights, but this night I went to bed early. There was some 'adult entertain-ment' on TV – you know how it is when you've been on a boat for ten days. Fisher was already in bed when he got wind of the programming and announced he was just getting up to brush his teeth. I knew he'd already brushed his teeth, so I couldn't stop laughing – I knew the real reason he was getting out of bed. When he came back about ten minutes later, I slipped out, got my camera and snapped a photo of him with the flash: I caught him literally mid-stroke. He had tissues all laid out and everything. Everyone was losing it. That's the stuff that happens with a bunch of blokes on a boat.

CHILE

Chile was a really different venue for an event. Everyone I'd spoken to about the waves said it was really tricky. I went about five days early, again to acclimatise, and it was pretty nuts: a radical peak breaking over a shallow rock ledge right in front of the gnarliest rocks, surrounded by the dry desert coast. You could only surf it in the morning because the onshore would come up by lunchtime. But coming off that second in Tahiti really gave me a lot of confidence riding backhand barrels, and I had a pretty solid event. I lost to Andy in the semis and he went on to win, but another third was a keeper. I was building up a pretty nice little lead in the overall ratings. There was a bit of a fuss in the media after that about Kelly supposedly retiring after he'd gone out in round four to Deano, but there was nothing in it. I didn't take any notice anyway and wasn't going to let it distract me. I've heard it so many times; Kelly's always carrying on that he's going to retire. I think he says it to take pressure off himself. But I just stayed concentrated on what I was doing.

J-BAY

One of the goals I'd set myself for the year was not to get sucked into playing 'the game' – surfing conservatively just to get through heats. If I was going to push for the world title, I wanted to do it by surfing in a way I could be proud of. But somehow at J-Bay I fell into that trap. I was trying to get a couple of 7-point rides, surfing safely, and it didn't feel right. It worked in a competitive, strategic sense, but it's not the way I like to win. I placed third, but I didn't feel like I deserved it. I was starting to feel the pressure of having the lead. I was watching everyone else's heats and worrying about what they were doing.

Taj won and Kelly got a second, so they were staying in touch. Taj was the first surfer to score two wins for the year, so there was no room for complacency. I came home from J-Bay feeling disappointed, and I made a pact with myself: if I'm going to go for it, then I want to go full-throttle. If I was holding back and didn't win the title, I knew my head would be full of what-ifs. And that was one thing I really didn't want - regrets about the way I'd surfed the year.

PRESSING THE REFRESH BUTTON

We had some time at home after that and enjoyed the memorial contest for Sean and Joel. I relaxed, let myself have a few nights out and a couple of weeks off to refresh and reset the brain.

The boys' memorial contest is always fun. Over time it has become more about celebrating their lives than mourning their loss. It's incredible - every year, on either the Saturday or Sunday morning, the whales swim by and put on a show for us. And every year, without fail, during the final day there are always dolphins surfing through the line-up. That year, in 2007, during the final there was a dolphin and a turtle hanging around the line-up. I've never seen a turtle in the water at Snapper before in my life. That was a really cool sign. I was sitting out in the water with the other finalists - Joel, Occy and a young guy, James Wood - saying, 'How awesome is this? It really feels like the boys are with us, letting us know they're watching.'

I try and go to the boys' memorial site on the top of Kirra Hill before I catch a plane to leave on tour. It's nice to go up there and grab a leaf from each tree and put them in my wallet, like I'm taking them with me when I go on tour. I always feel a bit safer with those couple of leaves in my wallet. The trees have only flowered two or three times in the ten years they've been there, but it always feels like a special event when they start to bud up. This year they were full of buds.

TRESTLES

After that month off, I was ready to head to Trestles for the next event. I was still feeling the pressure, but it wasn't so much from other people. After such a good run of results – I hadn't finished worse than the quarterfinals for almost a year – I was starting to wonder when that bad result was going to come. I almost wanted to get it out of the way.

I didn't do much wrong at Trestles, but I came up against young Californian Dane Reynolds when he was on fire. Everyone knows he's one of the most amazing surfers on tour, but he doesn't really have a great head for competition. When he gets going, though, he's hard to stop. The waves were small and he got the best wave of the heat by a mile. He went to town on it and got a 9, and there wasn't a whole lot I could do. Another wave like that didn't come through the whole heat, and I had a seventeenth to my name.

I wasn't worried about it – I felt like I surfed well and was almost relieved to have that bad result out of the way. I felt like I could move on and refocus for the final stretch. I told the media afterwards, 'When someone comes out and starts with a 9.93 it's pretty difficult to catch up. Congratulations to him, though, he surfed insane out there. I'm looking forward to having him on tour. He's smartened up a lot in the last year. It's great. People like that push the sport of surfing. It's great to have those guys on tour.'

As soon as I went out of the contest, I just knew Kelly was going to win – and sure enough he did. He made up some solid ground on my lead, so the race for the title was definitely intensifying.

FRANCE

I was really lucky to have a tight crew around me as the pressure built. That was one thing that even Kelly commented on later.

Rip Curl pit boss Matt Griggs was a huge asset, someone to bounce ideas off and reinforce little things for me. He was also great at dealing with all the other shit that goes on around events – all I had to do was surf.

I've heard someone comment that I called for reinforcements after Trestles, going into the European leg, but it wasn't really like that. Karissa spontaneously decided the day before she was due to fly home from California that she wanted to come with me to France for a bit more support, and I really appreciated that. Coach Phil McNamara was always going to come to Europe, because I knew that would be the crucial leg going into the home stretch. That was where the title could be won or lost, and I wanted Phil there. One of my best mates, Tony Cohen, was heading off on a round-the-world trip, and France happened to be his first stop, so it was great having him there too. He kept things light and fun, and helped me cruise a bit when the events weren't on, rather than stressing.

Phil's been my coach for a long time now and we really understand each other. He looks at things differently to a lot of people and gives me a fresh perspective and lots of information to work with. He doesn't get caught up in all the hype and really tells it how it is. There're times when I feel like I'm surfing as well as I can, and he'll add something: 'Why don't you try and throw in this turn there?' He's always raising the bar for me a little bit more, which is valuable when heats and world titles can be decided by such tiny increments.

I wanted to treat it like every other event. The other contenders – Kelly, Taj and Joel – were all within range, and I knew I had to just keep getting through heats. Kelly was in the heat before me in round three, and when he lost to Michel Bourez my head started spinning. I really got ahead of myself . . . for about twenty seconds. I was out in the water at the time and thought, *This is where you can really put him out of the picture.* I was matched up against Mickey Picon, a really good French surfer who knows those waves as well as anyone, and I had to get back in the moment and set my focus. All through that event I felt really centred, made good decisions and everything seemed to go my way. And a lot of that had to do with Phil.

For a long time I'd always had shockers in France. It wasn't until 2006 that I started feeling confident. I went there and surfed the WQS events that year just to practise in those French beach breaks; it really helped and I started surfing smarter heats. The tides fluctuate so dramatically that you really have to read what the ocean's doing and how the banks are affected – they can change completely in the space of an hour.

Our whole time in France we had this little routine going called the 'crystal ball'. I'd be sitting on the couch, taking it easy, and Phil would say, 'Let's go check the bank.' We were checking the banks all through the day, forecasting ahead, and that worked in my favour. Whenever I paddled out for a heat I knew exactly what the bank was going to do because I'd thought about it and sat and watched the bank for hours, at all times of the day and all stages of the tide. I'd check the bank the day before at the time I thought I'd surf my heat to see the way the waves were affected.

I had a semifinal with Troy Brooks, and I surfed the heat I was most proud of during that event. The heat before, Joel and Greg Emslie had been surfing these little lefts that were coming through out the back. But the tide was pushing in, and I knew these little inside rights were going to start breaking. I went straight to the spot, waited for them and, sure enough, they turned on and I got a little headstart on Brooko. It's one of the best heats I've seen Troy surf; he posted some big scores and got himself in front. I needed another big score and nailed it – it was one of those heats that go back and forth a few times. I felt like I managed to keep my composure and got the win.

Going into the final against Greg Emslie, I was prepared to sit and wait for my two waves. After my first two rides I had him comboed. But at no stage did I feel like I had it won. I kept my head the whole heat. I felt good about the way I'd dealt with it and came away with a first and a bit more breathing space. But with three events left, there was still plenty of time for someone to make up ground.

MUNDAKA

People were trying to tell me I could sew up the title in Mundaka if I won, but I tried to put all that out of my head - as far as I was concerned, the job wasn't done.

A lot of people have said how hard the Mundaka event is, because you're always driving to the backup site at Bakio, about half an hour away, if Mundaka isn't breaking. But it wasn't hard for me because I was staying at Bakio. It's hard to run an entire event at Mundaka because of the tides, and I knew there was a good chance a fair amount of heats would be at Bakio. And it was nice just to be a bit removed from the whole contest scene. I had a scare in round three when I came up against a local wildcard, Hodei Collazo. He had a 7 and an 8, and I couldn't find a wave out there. I thought it was going to be one of those heats where I just sat there waiting for set waves that never came, and I was starting to freak out. Bakio is a pretty fickle beach break with a lot of close-outs, so it's easy to get caught out being too choosey. But my patience paid off, and all of a sudden I had a high 8 and a 9, and the heat had swung. It was hard work, but I got through and made it as far as the semifinals, when they moved the event back to small Mundaka for the final day.

I don't know what it was but, as I paddled out for my semi-final against Bobby Martinez, I started feeling really emotional. I was thinking about Sean and how much I missed him, and I was nearly in tears. I still have no idea why the sadness came over me. I tried to get myself together, but I felt like I couldn't surf. My legs had no power in them and I fell a lot. There didn't seem to be any trigger for these feelings, no dreams or anything. All I can put it down to is the fact that I'd changed the energy bars I was eating before my heat, and I think they had a lot of sugar in them. I've learnt that things like that, how what you eat and what they contain can really influence your emotions, especially sugar. Just look at the average three-year-old after a sugar hit. Also, I'd been so focused and blinkered in my pursuit of the title for so long, a bit of emotion just has to seep out somewhere, I guess, but right before a crucial semifinal was a tricky time to have a little meltdown. Kelly and Taj were in the other semifinal, so the three contenders were all right there. Bobby was the only one not going for the title, and he was really apologetic when he beat me: 'I'm so sorry, I hope I didn't ruin your title campaign.' But I said, 'No worries, it's sweet. Just go on and win the thing.' Whoever won the other semi out of Kelly and Taj, I didn't want them winning the event. Sure enough, Taj beat Kelly in the semi and Bobby beat Taj in a really close final, so it was all good and no-one had eaten into my lead too much.

Kelly was really gracious about my efforts during the year when asked about my title prospects at Mundaka. 'Mick is a workhorse – he's working harder than any of us out here,' Kelly told the media. 'He's definitely more focused, definitely more prepared before his heats. He's just got this whole scene around him supporting him too, great support from his girlfriend, his team manager and team sponsor, family and friends. He's created a great atmosphere for himself, and it's really working out for him.'

Mundaka was also where Joel dropped out of the world title race when Phil MacDonald beat him in round four. There were times when the pressure of the title race affected my friendship with Joel. We weren't really hanging out together or talking much, and it didn't feel right. I didn't like it at all. But I knew I had to keep pushing on, focusing on what I had to do, trusting that we'd end up mates and everything would go back to normal afterwards. As soon as Joel dropped out of the race, we were fine again, which was a relief.

BRAZIL

Coming home from Europe, everything felt good. I went to Brazil really confident and just knew it was going to happen at that event.

At the same the time, I wasn't about to slow down. I hadn't actually achieved anything yet – mathematically I could still be beaten – and I just wanted to go for it and actually win the title myself, rather than relying on other people losing.

I had a really good mental exercise I was using in Brazil to deal with all the tension. I'd been speaking to Matty Elliott, the coach of the Penrith Panthers rugby league team, and he told me how before a game he would sit quietly in a room for ten minutes and go through all the possible scenarios for the game ahead. And then he thinks about what he wants to happen and holds that thought. At the end, he stands up, walks out of the room and closes the door, and it's like he leaves all those other possibilities behind. I thought I'd try it and see how it worked, and I'm stoked I did because it really helped settle my nerves and clear my head. I had a pretty small room in Brazil, so I'd sit on the toilet and run through all the what-ifs, get all those doubts and rubbish out of the way, and then just walk out and leave all that bullshit behind.

The night before the event, I was thinking I was going to have the worst sleep and toss and turn all night, but I fell asleep straight-away. I woke up a couple of times, wondering what the time was, wanting to get ready. When I woke up in the morning I had some nervous energy. I went down and had breakfast like every other day, and then after brekky I walked upstairs and sat down by myself for five minutes and thought about everything. *It could happen, it could not – I've just got to go out there and keep my focus.* So I got every-thing ready, went through my stretching routine, went down to the beach, and from then on I didn't have any nerves. I knew what I had to do. I was feeling untouchable. The waves were exactly the same as they had been for the two years before when I'd finished second and first in those two events. I knew I could make it happen that day.

It was a public holiday and it seemed like there were a million people on the beach, all drinking and carrying on. By the time all the world title contenders surfed their heats, everyone was really drunk and going crazy.

It was wild running the gauntlet through the crowd. One girl kept jumping in front of me trying to take my photo; security would grab her and throw her out of the way. She was a young, pretty girl and wouldn't take no for an answer – she kept charging back into the throng. One guy tried to put his arm around me and they belted him. Another guy stole my hat and the bouncers went after him and basi-cally said, 'You can keep the hat and die, or give it back.' I never really felt in any danger – I was more scared of the security guards than the crowds. They try really hard to do a good job, but sometimes I feel like they could mellow out a bit and everyone would be cool. It's the closest thing I've ever experienced to being a rock star. There was a dance party, like a big *doof* tent next to the contest, and people were coming out of there and going wild.

Kelly went out for his heat after me and he was absolutely mobbed. It was so funny. I was sitting up there pissing myself while he was besieged. And then he lost his heat to Kai Otton, and suddenly he was out of the title race. It was always my goal to see Kelly out of contention before Pipe. We all know from experience that if he is in with any chance going into Pipe, anything can happen. With Kelly out of the race, I felt a big weight off my shoulders. That just left Taj and me, and I was confident that if it went down to Pipe against Taj I could come out on top. And, one way or another, it was going to be an Aussie world champ.

I had a tight heat with Brazilian surfer Neco Padarataz in the quarterfinals. Neco is such a good competitor and really wears his heart on his sleeve, and I love that about him. I couldn't find my rhythm and I couldn't score over a 5. There was a lot of hometown support for Neco and, with a world title on the line, it was intense. I kept catching these lefts and was only getting 4s and 5s, so I decided I had to find a right. As soon as I did that I got a couple of good scores and put him in a combo situation. So, from that point on, I decided I was just going to go right all day.

And then it came down to Taj and Tom Whittaker in the fourth quarterfinal. I was in the first semifinal, against Joel, straight after, so I couldn't really watch the whole heat, because I was getting ready for my own. Everyone was going wild in the stands, but I knew I had to go out and surf against Joel regardless, so I just focused on the task at hand. I couldn't hear any scores running down the beach, but the last thing I heard was that Taj needed a score. As we were paddling out Joel went, 'Who's winning? I think Tommy's winning.'

'Are you sure?' I asked. Then the hooter went and I asked Tom what happened. It was hard for Tom because Taj is his good mate, and we're mates too – he was caught in the middle. I wouldn't want to be in that position. I guess the best thing is to just go and give it your all, because you don't want people giving you heats. But you wouldn't enjoy beating your mate when he's going for a world title. It was a weird moment. Tommy had just jumped off the back of the ski and given me a thumbs-up, and I thought, *What does that mean?* We were all sitting in the line-up looking at each other, not sure what to do or say or what had just happened. Taj was looking at me, and he looked confident as well. Then the hooter sounded, and I heard something like, 'Congratulations, Tom Whittaker,' and then, 'Congratulations, Mick.'

'Did you win, Tom?' I asked. And he started paddling towards me. I'm thinking, *Did he win or not?*

'I won!' he said.

And Joel's asked, 'What does that mean?'

'It's done and dusted,' I said.

It was mayhem out in the water. I freaked out and jumped on Joel. To be out in the water with one of my oldest friends when I actually won the world title was unbelievable. Then Tom and Taj came over and congratulated me. Taj was really cool about it. It would have been disappointing for him. You can be a bad loser but you can also be a bad winner, so I didn't want to say anything stupid to make him feel worse. I just said congratulations to him too.

Tom handled a difficult situation really well. You could tell he was feeling the pressure. He said afterwards: 'I'm really close with both of those guys. I gave Mick a big hug out there. Him and Joel are best mates and they were super-stoked. I looked around and there's one of my best mates paddling over, who I'd effectively knocked out of the world title race. I just had to go out there and do what I could do and surf it like a normal heat and not think of all that, but I did think about it and it got me pretty nervous.'

Taj handled it well also – and I'm not sure I could have done the same. 'It took me a little while to kind of smile. I was kind of in shock, but I'm obviously really stoked for Mick. It's an Aussie world champ, and if it's not going to be me I'm glad it's Mick. He's showed that much determination and focus that he earnt it. I'm really stoked for him and I'm stoked with my year,' he told the media.

I wanted to go in to the beach and celebrate, but we still had a semifinal to surf. I was saying to Joel, 'What do I do? What do I do?' And he goes, 'Just take off on your first wave switchfoot.' I thought, *Oh, okay, that sounds like the right thing to do.* So I took off switchfoot and Joel dropped in on me regular stance, and I'm thinking, *Hold on, I thought you were going switchfoot too. I'm stinking it up here and you're ripping.* And after that ill-conceived wave I had one of those surfs where everything seemed perfect. It was one of the magical little windows in life when everything clicks together. I was riding these waves and every time I'd think about doing a turn the perfect section just seemed to pop up. The title was already decided and I didn't really want to beat Joel, but then he looked like he was trying, so I thought, *Stuff it*, and started going for it. It was so right to have that heat with Joel, because he was the guy who had pushed me more than anyone throughout my career. I was just having fun surfing – I wasn't even thinking about scores or anything. I was screaming and high-fiving with the ski drivers and Joel, and the crowd was going mental. Joel didn't even have to go to Brazil. He couldn't move up or down in the ratings, but he told me, 'The only reason I'm coming is I want to see you win.'

I was pretty emotional when I came in from that semi, and when someone stuck a microphone in front of me and asked about my injury back in 2004, it all came spilling out: 'That's what life is. It goes up and down. You've got to take the good with the bad, and even though I was injured it was probably the best six months of my life. I didn't have to worry about surfing. I had fun with my friends, and at the end of it I found the girl that I love and want to marry. So even though it was bad for my body, it was a million more times better for my mind and my heart.'

When I paddled in to the beach everything was a blur. The Aussie boys were all there and they just erupted. The two guys who knocked out my rivals – Kai and Tommy – were paddling out for the other semifinal, and they were both surfing amazingly. I almost wished that was the final. I was skolling beer and champagne, and by the time I had to surf against Kai Otton, I was pretty tipsy. It was Kai's first-ever final, and I didn't want to get in his face too much.

I said to him, 'I'm that dizzy, ay.' I believe he thought he had it sewn up. And then on my first wave I scored an 8, and it sort of rattled him. I didn't really care about the result, I was having a ball. I caught this left and, after three or four turns in a row on my backhand, I started feeling really dizzy so I had to jump off. After that, I didn't want to go left again, so I let him take all the lefts.

It was pandemonium on the beach after the final, and I don't remember a whole lot about it. The strange thing was, I remembered this recurring vision I had throughout the whole year of myself holding up the world title trophy. This vision would come to me before events or right before heats. I was free surfing out at Snapper during the year and nothing was working. I was really pissed off and couldn't get anything going. Then all of a sudden I started picturing myself holding up the world title trophy, and my whole surf changed in an instant. I swear, the wind turned offshore, I started getting barrelled and this overwhelming feeling of happiness came over me. Throughout the year I kept seeing that picture in my mind: me holding up the trophy. Afterwards, I saw a Rip Curl ad with a photo of me that day holding the trophy, and it was exactly the picture I'd had in my head all year. It was really weird. I think a lot of my confidence came from visualising that moment.

The other strange thing that happened was this dolphin kept hanging around in the water during my heats. I'd received an email from Dave Rastovich during the event, about his trip to Japan to try and save these dolphins from slaughter. There were some really disturbing photos and all these links telling you what you could do to help stop it. Dave's a professional free surfer and puts a lot of energy into campaigning to save whales and dolphins. It really affected me, and I found myself getting really emotional about it, so I forwarded his email to all my contacts to help spread the message. When this dolphin popped up the next day, I thought, *Maybe it's just saying thanks for helping out.* It was there whenever I free surfed, and it was there during all my heats, this one dolphin in the line-up, just a few metres from me. It would pop up and swim around, then flick its tale and disappear again. It was really cool. I sometimes feel Sean's presence during events, but I hadn't felt him in Brazil up until then. I had a dream about him the night before, so I don't know if it was Sean's spirit letting me know he was around or what. But it felt pretty special.

I feel like Sean has been with me a lot throughout my time on tour. There'll be times when you know he's there, and there'll be other times when you know he's somewhere else. It's weird – you get this extra energy. You feel a little bit bigger. It's pretty wild. I'll sit there and ask him for help in tight heats, and I can feel his presence.

Kelly was really cool after the final. I'm sure it would have been disappointing for him, but he came up and congratulated me. Normally, he would go home as soon as he lost, but he actually hung out, sat with the boys and watched it all go down. At the end, he said some really nice things to me: 'Well done. You smoked us all, so you deserve it.' He gave me one of his boards, the one he'd ridden all year, so I gave him one of my boards. It was a nice sign of mutual respect, like footy players exchanging jumpers at the end of a match. I'm really stoked that I won the title while Kelly was still on tour, because he's the all-time greatest, so that made my win all the sweeter.

That night I had to do a media conference and a few interviews. Then we had to drive back to Florianopolis and there was a bit of a party at a local nightclub. The whole world title win and celebrations have been pretty well documented. But one thing no-one else saw was when I got back to Florianoplois: I walked into the bar of our hotel and every single Australian surfer on tour was there waiting for me – that was the best feeling of all. I really appreciated that. I think I hugged and kissed every single person at least twice. Rip Curl sectioned off the VIP area of this nightclub for us and we all went pretty crazy that night.

The next day I was woken by Bede Durbidge and Tommy Whits, demanding that I join them at the pool bar to drink bloody marys. We had a day to kill before we flew home, so it seemed like the appropriate thing to do given the circumstances. The pool bar got fairly messy, and I think we scared away the rest of the patrons and had it to ourselves: a bunch of Aussie blokes, lolling about in the sun, drinking bloody marys and telling stories. At one point I decided, being in Brazil and all, that I should head off on a little shopping spree for some Brazilian bikinis for Karissa. I managed to persuade Joel and Occy to join me in this dubious endeavour. Somehow, by the time I'd chosen and purchased the bikinis I'd lost my accomplices, so I headed back to the bar on my own. En route, I realised I needed a trip to the men's room and was hit by a bolt of inspiration. *How hilarious would it be to slip into one of the G-string bikini bottoms and walk back into the bar?* I quickly changed in the cubicle and strutted back into the bar, anticipating the howls of laughter I'd be greeted with. Instead, there was a lone barman cleaning up dozens of empty glasses, staring at me with a puzzled expression. He just said, 'Ah, your friends have just left.' I stood there in my G-string, little white legs on show to shocking effect, nodding seriously. 'Ah yes, I see.' It would have made a great photo and tabloid newspaper headline: 'New world champ's cross-dressing fetish!' I walked upstairs, found the boys and told them what had just happened – and they lost it. One of my more embarrassing moments.

BRINGING IT BACK HOME

We all flew home together and it was an epic journey: Florianopolis –São Paulo, São Paulo–Santiago, Santiago–Auckland, Auckland–Sydney, Sydney–Coolangatta. About forty hours, nearly two days of travel. Occ was our spiritual leader. It was his last year on tour, and he was the last Australian world champ, so it was really cool to have him there. I didn't want to make too much of a fuss about it, but he was going, 'You hold that bloody trophy high and be proud.' I was lucky just to make it to the airport. I'd pretty thoroughly overdone it the night before, so I was spewing in my hotel room beforehand and couldn't keep anything down. I was lucky Griggsy was there to get me on the plane. I slept most of the way home, and there wasn't any more fanfare, so it was a good chance to rest and recharge. Once we got to Sydney, though, everyone had had a bit of sleep, and we were back on Australian soil, so we had a few more beers. We were all pretty excited getting on the flight to Coolangatta. It was a mad rush in Sydney to get from the international to the domestic terminal, and we just made it through customs and got on our flight in time. Then they made an announcement on the plane about the world title, and everyone clapped and cheered – it felt really nice to be heading home. We ordered Crown Lagers all round, and I had my face pressed up to the window, waiting for the first glimpse of home. I spotted D-bah out the window and there were little waves breaking, right where I'd put in so many hours developing my surfing. And now here I was, flying home as world champion. It seemed incredible. I didn't know anything about the party waiting for me when I got home, but all the Sydney boys – Phil Macca, Tommy Whits and Griggsy – were hiding up the back of the plane hoping I didn't notice them.

I knew there'd be a bit of media at Cooly airport, but I had no idea what was ahead of me. There was almost a riot. There were so many people there: little kids holding up signs, my friends and family, all the people who'd supported me through my whole career. The police had to shepherd me through the crowd, and then I had a limo waiting to take us home. Paul Fisher hid behind a bush and jumped out fully nude as we drove away. 'Give us a lift,' he said, and he fully fruit-bowled my mum. It was hilarious. The only weird thing was my best friend, Beau, wasn't there. I asked Karissa where he was and she said, 'Oh, he's down the pub looking after a few of your family and friends until we get there.' I got home and had to do another interview – it seemed like they were never-ending.

I thought we were just going to cruise down to the Kirra pub and see a few family and friends – when I got there the whole car park was fenced off. I thought they must be renovating the pub or something. Then I saw a couple of Tooheys tents erected in the car park and thought, *Hang on, what's going on here?* Then I saw Beau.

We walked in and almost everything single person I knew was there, most of them wearing special world title T-shirts and caps that Rip Curl had done up. I couldn't believe it. Just being there in front of all the people who have supported me through my whole career, it really hit home. I shed a few tears of joy.

There was a full stage and a band set up, and I saw the guitar tech from Grinspoon, Cole, a classic character with long hair and a big beard. I thought one of the local bands like Rollerball must be playing, which would have been awesome. And then Grinspoon came out and just went off. I was blown away. I didn't have a clue about any of it. Karissa and Beau had organised the whole thing, and Grinspoon had flown up from Sydney specially for the occasion. Karissa had spoken to their manager, and he'd said they were starting a national tour and didn't know if they could do it. A couple of guys in the band saw the emails and they just said, 'We're doing it no matter what.'

Grinspoon always had really cool sections in surf movies when I was growing up, and I always loved watching them play live. The song 'Champion' that they opened with was in a Rip Curl video for this Bells section, and I used to watch it every time before I went for a surf because I'd get so amped. And it seemed fairly appropriate for the circumstances:

> *Man you're gonna go far*
> *You're world champion now*
> *You're world champion now*
> *You're world champion, champion*
> *You wanna champion or be a homeboy*
> *I'm a macho fucking number-one champion*

They went mad that day. I don't know if they were planning on me getting up and joining them on stage, but I did anyway and screeched along to a few lyrics. At one stage my mum was fully crowd-surfing, at which point I knew the party had really started. Talking to the guys from the band afterwards, they said it was the first gig they had ever played where every single person had a smile on their face the whole time.

From there the party kicked on at the Sands Hotel, while we slipped off and got some dinner, and then a whole lot of people ended up back at our place – including a few of the guys from Grinspoon. I was running on adrenalin by that point. I hadn't had a full night's sleep in several days, and I don't know what time we got to bed, but it didn't seem like I got drunk all night. I knew exactly what was going on the whole time. We woke up the next day and the party just continued.

There were a few really special things about the celebrations. Australia's greatest surfer and four-time world champ Mark Richards was there. It was awesome he made the effort to travel up from Newcastle to celebrate the title coming back to Australia. I'd had a few really good chats with MR through the year, and he'd given me some really good advice at different times. It was the sort of stuff I guess I already knew, but it was important having someone like him to reinforce it at the right moments: just concentrate on yourself; you can't control what others do. He told me how to deal with pressure and take my mind off things, how to deal with the media, that sort of thing. MR did a lot for me. One time I was picking up a board, and we sat down and chatted for over an hour. He was so cool and incredibly humble, one of those people you feel like you can ask anything.

Rabbit Bartholomew was there too, and he got up and announced that it had been the most dominant season in pro surfing history, at that time, which was a bit of a blow-out. To have people like that there really put it in perspective and made me feel a part of a proud lineage of Australian surfers. My achievement really hit home. When I won in Brazil, it felt like I'd won a contest, with a bit of extra excitement thrown in. And then on the flight I had a chance to reflect on it a bit. But coming home to that welcome made me realise how much it meant to so many people. Even walking down the street today, I still get people saying, 'Well done on your world title, thanks for bringing it back to Australia.' It's a really special feeling.

CHRIS PROSSER – THE CHIROPRACTOR

A surfboard rests in the corner of Chris Prosser's chiropractic clinic, signed by many of the world's best surfers.

Mick's dedication is simple and heartfelt: 'Thanks Chris. Without you I'd be a pretzel!! Cheers for your friendship. Mick Fanning.'

He's not alone. Many of the top pros express similar sentiments. 'Feeling a million bucks thanks to you,' writes Taj Burrow.

Chris Prosser has been manipulating the bodies of professional surfers since 1994, along with PGA golfers, Uncle Toby's ironmen and beach volleyballers. As well as maintaining the physical wellbeing of large numbers of elite athletes, Chris has also waged his own battle with bowel cancer, and four years on is well on his way to beating the disease. When Mick was learning to manage his scoliosis and repaired hamstring, struggling with injuries to hips, ankles and wrists, Chris was the person he placed his trust in.

In Chris, Mick found a therapist, friend and confidant who knew a thing or two himself about overcoming adversity, who understood how suddenly your life could be turned on its head. Yet, like many of those in Mick's trusted inner circle, Chris reckons he's learnt more from his young client than he's imparted.

'He's taught me a lot about finding the balance in life,' says Chris. 'If you look at the hamstring injury particularly and the good things that came out of that, that's taught me a lot about life. When I had my challenges with health he was definitely there for me. He's incredibly loyal, strong, compassionate as a friend, and he doesn't judge, so that's a beautiful thing. They're the things I appreciate in Mick more than what he does on a wave.'

Chris recalls being in hospital in 2005 at his lowest ebb after cancer surgery to remove his bowel and subsequent chemotherapy. While a lot of people tended to keep their distance, Mick was right by his side, emptying buckets of vomit and returning some of the nurturing he's received from Chris over the years. 'When I was in hospital sick he was there, and I remember I had a really bad time and needed a bucket all the time, and he was emptying the bucket. I was going, "Fuck, sorry," and he said, "Nah, it's all good,"' Chris recalls. 'His mum came in the next day and I said, "Your son is just an incredible human being."'

When Chris was first diagnosed with cancer, it had spread throughout the bowel lining and into all four lymph nodes, a stage of the disease with only a ten per cent survival rate. He had been ill for some time but says he avoided seeking medical help out of a kind of denial. 'I kind of knew that I had it deep down, in hindsight, and I think for me the fear of what would have to happen was paralysing. It stopped me from doing anything, allowed me to be neglectful and ignore it to the point where it nearly cost me everything.'

When he was forced to face his illness, he says attitude was everything. 'The survivors are the positive ones. I would go in for my chemotherapy and, as harsh as it sounds, just by listening to the people and interacting with them, I'd put money on the people who were going to survive, for sure.'

They're the same qualities he's appreciated in Mick as he's overcome his own adversities. 'Because of what he went through with his family and Sean, people feel like they want to protect him, and that was part of the role I took on. But a lot of the time I'd realise he's stronger than what I was, and I was getting more out of that conversation that we just had than maybe he took away.'

Still, there's no doubting the role Chris has played in keeping Mick fit, in the water and able to compete successfully at the highest level. Chris describes Mick's scoliosis as 'moderate to severe' when he first came to see him in 2001. 'He couldn't surf to his potential, was in a fair bit of pain, couldn't move real well at all. He was unstable; his glutes didn't work; his hip rotation wasn't good.' When Chris prescribed a treatment and exercise regime to remedy the condition, Mick took to it with gusto. 'It was about re-teaching him to paddle, getting his mid-back moving again, turning on his core. It didn't take that long. He actually recovered surprisingly quick. That lower back has maybe recurred once or twice to a minor degree. He's kept on top of that. He's had a lot of other things going on, from shoulders to hips, to obviously the hamstring, to ankles and feet, so there's been constant management, but that first time when we taught him to activate those muscles and got him on a program, he recovered really well. I think he's probably been, out of all my patients, the most consistent in getting care. When he's here, it's probably twice a week for most of the year.'

The challenge of rehabilitating Mick's leg after the hamstring injury in 2004 required a whole new level of care and attention. 'I was doing a lot of unfortunately very painful acupuncture work and release work and adjustments. We developed some techniques, one called "the Mick Fanning technique", based on the different things I learnt out of that, which I apply to everyday practice now, just to get that range of movement back again and get strength, make the scar tissue as flexible as possible.'

Having seen firsthand the work Mick put into his rehabilitation, his win in his first event back from injury at the 2005 Quiksilver Pro came as no surprise to Chris. 'Most people close to him felt like he was going to do that. I should have put some serious money on it.'

Chris reckons it's Mick's ability to assemble a trusted team around him, his willingness to seek help, and his judgement in trusting the right people and following the right advice at the right time, that has given him the edge in competition.

'The reason why it was such a revelation to everyone was because a lot of guys in surfing didn't have those sort of teams. On the PGA Tour there're multiple guys who travel with their chiropractor and their trainer and their nutritionist and their psychologist,' says Chris. 'He had a lot of the guys rattled about how strong and fit and confident he is in his own ability, and how routine he is. You could see guys looking in from the outside going, Shit, that's working. I need to do that. And there was a scramble after '07 for everyone to find that same ingredient.'

Even so, Chris is adamant, only one person deserves the credit for Mick's achievements. 'There's only one person out there surfing and all the credit goes to him. I don't take any of that, because if anyone fails then I have to accept that too.'

PHIL McNAMARA – THE COACH

*Who would have imagined that what started as a program to help
tackle surfer truancy at Palm Beach-Currumbin High would launch
numerous pro surfing careers, deliver at least one world title and
create a boom in overseas student enrolments?*

*When surf coach Phil McNamara was brought in to
head the surfing component of PBC's sports excellence program,
there was still plenty of official scepticism about surfing as
serious sport.*

*'Sports excellence was really rugby league excellence, and
they had a killer rugby league team,' recalls Phil. 'We could see
they had a massive talent pool of surfers who were all wagging,
maybe not Mick because he was always a good lad about doing
the right thing, but there was a lot of wagging. So we pitched it to
the principal: "Look, if they're doing at least two or three lessons
with surfing, they'll be at school for those days . . ." We looked at
it as attacking truancy, and so the headmaster was big on that.'*

That first group of surfers to come through PBC's surfing program included Mick, his brother Sean, Joel Parkinson, Dean Morrison and Luke Munro. 'It was a little bit of serendipity that so many of those surfers went on to pro junior careers so quickly. It was something the school could hang its hat on – we've got these athletes now with semi-professional outcomes,' says Phil. 'They were getting pretty good contracts as sixteen-, seventeen-year-olds, so we rode on the back of their success for a while.'

Hit the PBC website these days and surfing features prominently. The school actively markets its surfing program and attracts overseas students from Brazil, Japan and Indonesia, eager to hone their skills under Phil's tutelage and on the same famous point breaks that gave rise to the all-conquering Cooly Kids. 'They sell their whole school program almost on the surfing, particularly with the international intakes they get now. They get massive international student intakes . . . sixty or eighty international students each semester. They come and do one or two semesters. It's obviously a significant cash injection into the school.'

Phil was already working with Gold Coast and Queensland teams when he started the school program. 'I was following Sean mostly as far as the Fannings were concerned. Because he was older he was surfing way better then, and Mick was always there with Sean.' But it wasn't long before the younger brother began to distinguish himself. 'Just his cutback. At thirteen, he had the most perfect, consistent roundhouse cutback, and I don't even know where he got it. He's almost a self-made athlete. I get so much credit for things I never did. I was just there.'

But it was Mick's willingness to learn that most impressed his coach. 'He'd always try a suggestion. Whether it was technique or psychological preparation, he'd always try it, and then he'd decline or take a piece of it and adapt it in his own way. He's analytical but he's also creative. There's a creativity in the way he applies ideas.'

Mick's outstanding physical fitness soon revealed itself too. 'He'd end up winning school cross-countries because he was a tremendous athlete with incredible cardiovascular capacity, but he'd never train for that. He'd just go in it and beat all the runners. We were really big on heart-rate monitoring then – I'd been classically trained in conditioning and had all these target ranges of heart rate. Traditionally, for those age students it was up to 160, 170 beats per minute we were trying to get them to work at to improve their cardiovascular. Mick would never get there, and I thought he was slacking. I'd drill him but he'd never get above 110. He was just such a brilliant athlete that his capacity to produce power was at a low heart rate.'

Even so, Mick was never the most spectacular natural talent under Phil's charge. 'I wasn't so much excited that he was a freakish talent, I was excited that if determination counted for anything he'd win the world title. I thought, All he needs is someone in his corner who will never change, and if there's one thing I'll pat myself on the back about, that's what my job was and I followed through. I never left his corner . . . It was ten years, a ten-year program to be an overnight sensation.'

When Sean passed away, Phil says the change in Mick was abrupt and profound. 'Before Sean's death Mick was always trying to prove himself to Sean but also to his peers. Once Sean died, surfing was so trivial, and winning or losing, What's it matter? I lost my brother. To a certain extent, after Sean died he could approach a competition like, If I win I win, if I don't I don't. And he surfed so much better because he didn't have that burden of expectation from himself and others.

'He draws on that to calm him down – with the stress of competition, the stress of expectation – like when he was going for the world title. When that starts catching up, he can just take a deep breath and go, Hang on, it's just surfing. If I have to go through the disappointment of losing a world title or losing a heat, it's nothing compared to the disappointment I've been through already.'

Even so, there were some self-destructive elements to Mick's make-up that concerned his coach. 'There was no doubt that he drank to distraction after a loss for a lot of years, even when he was in the top five. He was going on week-long benders after a loss and couldn't break that cycle. I don't drink and I'd always push that side of things on him, that his drinking was affecting his performance, but it didn't really have much of an effect.'

It was a trait that nearly brought Mick undone as he wrestled with the prospect of having his career torn apart, along with his hamstring muscle, in 2004. 'It was a turning point because it was a career-threatening injury, and it's easy to say, Oh, you do *the work and get back out there. But when you're sitting alone by yourself depression is a really scary animal. You don't want it to get a foothold. He did some stupid things when he was straight out of his operation. I've never been the kind of person to get in someone's face and say, Don't do that. But that was the time because a part of him was self-harming. He was doing things that he knew were jeopardising his recovery. He did the bicycle pub crawl they do on the Queen's Birthday weekend, and he did that pretty much fresh out of his operation. He rang me in the middle of the night saying, "I've fallen off my bike four times," and I just figured, that's a cry for attention. That's somebody saying, I'm not really sure where I'm going now. I probably didn't have the skills to deal with it as well as I should have. It was a tricky time.'*

Some unhealthy romantic entanglements around the same time weren't helping either. 'There was this cult of death following Mick a little bit since Sean, and it's something I've noticed, not just with Mick's situation, but with other young people who have lost someone. They attract members of the opposite sex – it must be a nurturing or protective thing, a signal they're sending out. He had a lot of mixed messages coming at him from females, and all that was a bit confusing as well.'

Out of that low point, faced with his demons, Mick forged a new resolve. 'He changed that around and decided, I'm going to be really professional with training, with my approach to alcohol. All these things changed around the time of his hamstring injury. I reckon he reached a fork in the road where he went, Do I want to be known as Eugene, or do I want to be known as a great surfer in Australian surfing history? And I think he made a conscious decision. He'd got all he could out of being in party mode, and it wasn't that much.'

No-one knows better than Phil how hard Mick worked, how deep he had to dig, to rebuild his body and his career. 'It's glibly talked about as a great comeback, but it really was great strength of human endeavour that saw him come back better than ever.'

At the core of their relationship there has always been a common understanding of the value of hard work. 'That's a little favourite saying we've got, "Wishing doesn't work,"' he says. 'Positivity will only get you so far, and that's where the New-Age stuff, like The Secret, doesn't really match reality. You still have to do the work.'

And with such a broad support crew – from coach, to fitness trainer, to tour pit boss, to shaper, to manager – Mick's world title campaign required that all the players knew their roles in what was a well-functioning team. 'We liaised with everyone really closely. It was like a war room. We knew we had to stay in our roles and plan things as a group. There was a general lack of ego among all the people. You've got to realise that Mick's the focus, and he doesn't have that big an ego. But if anyone's going to have an ego it's got to be Mick. That's the only way it can work at an elite level.'

And there's no questioning the level of dedication Mick inspires in those around him. 'Every day I think about what we can do to make Mick a better surfer, so there is a lot of energy spent on it.'

Phil says Mick creates this kind of team support for himself wherever he goes. 'His attention to detail goes beyond just surfing and physical preparation. He's set up accommodation and tour support that's more sophisticated than most other sportspeople. Most individuals I know are going to a pristine hotel environment so they can have their own space. Mick's sort of gone the other way, where he gets down and dirty with a family – if the family's poor, he lives poor that week. And if they eat food that doesn't really agree with him, he'll eat with them and then go and find some other food as well, rather than upset the apple cart and be a diva. He'll fit in.'

That attention to detail extends to making sure he is giving back in some way in all the communities he visits. 'He's got someone in every country that he's kind of helping in really creative ways. He doesn't do it because it helps his competitive act, but it helps.'

For Phil, it was never enough to simply try and help Mick win a world title. 'You've got to be really good to be not only a world champion but also a quality human being. You won't find too many people that Mick burnt a long the way,' says Phil. 'MR [Mark Richards] was my all-time hero in surfing. When I was young, he was untouchable, like Kelly is now. And he was such a different kind of world champion. There were so many qualities I saw in him that were admirable. I talked to Mick about MR and what I saw in his performance. He never gave up. He seemed to win so easily, but there were a lot of times when he wasn't winning but never gave up and won in the last few seconds. And I said, "Being a world champion is one thing, but being a world champion who is a really decent human being is a very rare thing." Most world champions, they have some pretty prickly sides to them. Mick took that on board and saw MR's qualities.'

Phil continues to work with Mick to this day, drilling him in concentrated bursts of practice heats at home, or summoned as support crew through a critical leg of the tour. He'll identify areas to work on, give feedback on what the judges are looking for, video surf sessions then review the footage and provide detailed assessments. It's a rigorous process that continually offers Mick ways to refine his surfing.

But more than the improved discipline, fitness and competitive success, Phil has witnessed a new depth in his young charge. 'That's another jump he made in personal development, being able to contemplate his own navel a little bit,' says Phil. 'That Coolangatta grommet squad, they're pretty hardcore. No-one's sitting around trying to analyse life and be a philosopher. And Mick probably wanted to but never allowed himself because his brothers or his mates would have paid him out. I think it's important for any out and out champion. It's a very lonely place to be, number one. You have to be comfortable by yourself. I think he learnt that in '06 and '07, that he could be totally comfortable with himself. He's very widely read, but as I said to him last year, he can stop reading self-help books now. I think it's time to write one. And I was pretty serious.'

MICK'S TIPS – COMPETITION: GETTING IN THE ZONE

Competing is a funny thing. Some people are born to it and others aren't. I've always enjoyed competing and I started young. Being the youngest of five children, I was always the underdog in everything, from getting the last piece of chocolate cake to trying to tackle my brothers in backyard footy. I always strive to better myself in every situation, learn from both my mistakes and what I did right to try and improve. People always tend to learn from mistakes, but rarely do people try and learn from what they did right and break down how they did it. In competing, this can be such a huge tool to help you succeed.

In surfing, there are no written scripts on how to prepare for a contest or heat, and not too many coaches direct this sort of preparation. I'm sure it will start to come in as surfing becomes more and more professional. The best time to experiment is when you're competing in club contests or junior titles and so on. When you have a good heat and everything feels like it worked to perfection, think back on how you prepared for that particular heat. Try and see what you did body-wise, like stretching or a warm-up surf. Were you sitting by yourself or listening to your favourite song? Were you super-amped or very relaxed? Try and identify these things for when you did well and when you didn't do well. Write them down in two columns, and go through and note what you did differently each time. It might only be one or two things, but that's usually what makes the difference. These are the little things that get you in the Zone. The Zone is the place where you feel like everything is right. This changes from person to person, but the key is knowing how to reproduce that feeling with the flick of a switch or with what some people call 'triggers'. People have triggers that can allow them to change their state of mind in a heartbeat: it can be a song, or a mantra – a few keywords you say to yourself or an entire warm-up routine. Whatever gets you into the Zone. Some surfers' routines start before they even get to the beach, and others are so quick you probably wouldn't notice them.

As a kid I never had a routine – my thoughts were random and unfocused. I was at the O&E Pro Junior in 2000, and they had this new format where you had five minutes to catch one or two waves, one guy after another, for five rounds. After two rounds of this I was not doing well. I said to my best friend, Beau Campi, 'I suck. This is shit. I can't surf.' I was looking for sympathy, but Beau wasn't buying into it. He looked at me and said, 'What do you do and feel when you're winning?' I was almost shocked at the simplicity of the idea. I thought back to the 1999 event when I won, and other events I'd done well in, and realised I'd listened to music to clear my head. So, on went the headphones. I sat by myself for a little while and cleared my head. I started thinking about my surfing. I went on to place second behind Deano after a really bad start, but that moment when Beau pointed out such a simple thing changed my heat preparation from then on. That is why I always have headphones on listening to music before my heats.

I don't talk to anyone – I just concentrate on myself and what I'm going to do. I like to be calm before my heats. If I get too amped, I try too hard and think I can do things that are way too difficult and start falling off a lot. I learnt this early on, too, at the 1997 Australian Titles. Phil thought it would be good to give me a strong pep talk before my heat. I was so amped afterwards that I was like a runaway train. I couldn't control anything. I thought I could pull off every move. How wrong I was. Phil still remembers it as the worst heat I ever surfed. From then on, I would have a warm-up surf just before my heats to get all that excess adrenaline out. Now I control it by breathing through the stretching routine and warm-ups I do. As I run down for my heat, I'm pretty pumped and like to shake out all the nervous energy before I sit down and close my eyes. People always ask why I do this. I take some deep breaths as I visualise a few waves at the venue I am surfing at that day. Then I use my trigger words: 'Let's do it.' Then it's heat time. When I have done my routine I know there is nothing else to do but surf my heats to the best of my ability. I have been doing this routine for about six years, and I know that it gets me in the Zone. But it took a lot of trial and error before I got to that point. We're all different. The point is to identify the things that do work for *you* and develop *your* own routine based on *your* experiences.

In the lead-up to events I like to go out and have thirty-minute surfs. This is the regular length of time we usually have in heats, so I keep the intensity up for that short span. I find after a few of these surfs I start to feel like my heats are just free surfs, and I feel switched-on from the very first minute. It also allows me to realise that I have a lot of time to score, instead of freaking out and making poor wave selections. I actually heard that's what Tom Curren did when he won his world title from the trials in 1990.

These short, sharp surfs rarely last longer than an hour. I find this keeps me fresh and excited to surf. If I surf a lot before an event, my motivation levels go down slightly. I feel a little stale and my boards don't feel so electric. A couple of times each year, I'll close my garage door, where all my boards are kept, for a week or however long it takes to get motivated again. I just forget about surfing – completely shut it out.

MATT ELLIOTT - THE NRL COACH

It's a measure of Mick's abiding sense of loyalty that he remains a staunch New South Welshman, especially at State of Origin time, even while surrounded by Queensland parochialism. He chooses to live just south of the Queensland-New South Wales border in Tweed Heads, and still follows the Penrith Panthers in the NRL.

It's a loyalty appreciated by Penrith coach Matt Elliott, who's become a good mate and close follower of Mick's career. Elliot was first commissioned by Rip Curl marketing manager, Neil Ridgway, an old university friend, to speak to his team of sponsored surfers in 2004 at Bells Beach. 'Neil asked me to talk to their team,' says Matt, 'and twice a year I'd speak to each of the surfers, not about specific performance issues, obviously, but more about approaches to preparation and maybe giving an insight into what other sports people do in different areas.'

Matt and Mick hit it off straightaway and have remained close.

'The first time I met him I was blissfully unaware of his status in surfing, but I said, That bloke over there has got a bit of presence – and he did. He did have a bit of an impact on me. He's not outgoing or gregarious, but he had a bit of inner confidence or aura,' explains Matt.

Like many who have watched Mick's career evolve, Elliott now feels like the master–student relationship has been reversed. 'He's made a good transformation from being that laid-back, whacky guy to having serious ambitions, and he knows what he wants to achieve in the sport. We keep in fairly regular contact. We went through some in-depth processes on physical preparation techniques and ways of thinking about performance, and I think over a period of time maybe the shoes changed feet. I was kidding myself for a few years that it was me providing Mick with insights, but I've finally realised he's the one giving me insights. And now he's gone to texting me and emailing me with tips about the team and, even scarier, I'm listening. I'm smart enough, if someone has that approach to things I certainly pay attention.'

It was Elliott who introduced Mick to some of the meditation and relaxation techniques he used so effectively to diffuse the stress of his world title campaign. 'It's quite hard to talk about it as an Australian male, so I'll use a scientific term. It's called autogenic training, but in reality it's a 3000- to 4000-year-old art,' says Matt. 'I encourage my players to do it – sit down for ten minutes and think about what you have to do, your performance, so when you finish that ten-minute period you don't need to think about it again. Mick's taken that training to another level. If you can do that leading into an event, maybe for two five-minute stints over a twenty-four-hour period, in between you can relax because you don't need to think about it.'

He's also been impressed by, and learnt more than a little from, Mick's own training and preparation. 'It's elite. It's comprehensive. He's very measured in what he does. He knows how to take good advice and he knows how to ignore bad advice,' says Matt. 'Quite often I've tossed up ideas and been quietly disappointed when he goes, "That's not for me." His approach to preparation is a little alternative, the CHEK training and the submerged-breathing training – it's cutting edge. I'm impressed with the support that he's got from his coach and Rip Curl. He's very clear on what's best for him and has an absolute belief in what he does. His coach, Phil McNamara – I sat with him on the beach and watched him while Mick surfed practice heats. He's getting good advice.'

Matt reckons Mick's the sort of athlete he likes his players to be around. 'He's had contact with the players, and it's quite interesting how athletes from different sports gravitate to each other. There's a real mutual respect and admiration. It's something I've been able to sit back and admire. They've clicked at once.'

Matt makes a point of watching Mick compete whenever he can, live or via webcast, but as a relative latecomer to riding waves himself, is happy to remain on the beach when the swell's up. 'It's fucking frightening, let's be honest. Being on the beach is a good place to be sometimes.'

chapter 7.
HERE AND NOW

I've had a lot of time to reflect on the world title and what it means to me. I honestly think if I hadn't had that injury in 2004 I might never have won. I learnt so much from that whole experience – about my body, health, fitness, diet, motivation. I was pretty loose before the accident, partying, and I might never have grown out of it. It makes you realise that what seems like a setback can prove to be a blessing in the long term. Things happen for a reason.

But a world title campaign really takes a toll on you and the people around you. You have to be so selfish – it's all about you and being in the right space for your next heat. I felt like I had to back off a bit and give back to the people close to me in 2008, like Karissa, Mum and my mates, and I guess it showed in my ratings. It's hard to maintain that level of intensity. You look at someone like Ian Thorpe. He trains so hard, for so many years, and then suddenly he realises there's a big, wide world out there. He wants to go and enjoy it – and who can blame him? I think that happens to a lot of sportspeople.

If you try to keep going at that level of intensity, you can really burn out. 2008 was about trying to get the balance right, and it's been a good learning curve. There's a time to be intense and there's a time to switch off and enjoy your life and your relationships with the people closest to you. I think I'm a lot more relaxed within myself now and close to getting that balance right.

I was also sick of that strenuous routine I'd been on. I wasn't really comfortable with all the media commitments that come with being a world champion, and that was a big adjustment too. I wanted to stop, shut it all down and not deal with any of it. I wasn't having fun around events. I felt like I couldn't do what I wanted to do, like I was always on someone else's clock. I had a lot of advice from a lot of people about how to deal with it all, but I wanted to figure it out for myself.

In 2008 I didn't seem to have any motivation going into events. I spoke to MR and said, 'I feel really relaxed about it.' And he said, 'You feel relaxed because you know you can do it.' But then I realised I felt relaxed because I didn't really care. When I started losing, I realised, Well, I don't like losing either. It's challenging some-times, when you achieve a life goal, to set new goals and move on. I had some guidance from people like my good friend Taylor Knox. It all came to a head in Hawaii – that's when I decided I really didn't like the direction I was heading. I was trying to work on myself and work out what was really good in my life, what I really enjoyed about my career.

In 2009 I feel a lot more relaxed, but I've definitely got that desire to go for the title again. I've realised there's more to life than surfing contests, but my motivation is to get the best out of myself. I gain fulfilment out of doing my best – and being fit, healthy and clear-minded. I feel like I can put myself back in position to be a contender again. But I also want to make sure I'm enjoying the journey. If an opportunity comes along to have some fun, I don't want to pass it up. My biggest goal is to be a good husband, a good friend, a good brother and a good son.

Goal-setting is important, even in everyday life. I find sometimes when I'm just working around the house that it helps if I set myself a picture of what I want my surroundings to look like when I'm finished and work towards that. Otherwise, it's too easy to start fluffing around and get lost along the way. I think that's what happened to me in 2008.

At the time of writing, Joel's really setting the pace on tour, and I'm stoked for him, but I'm not about to make it easy for him. There's no way I'd lay down in a contest for a mate. I always knew Joel had it in him – he just never worked for it. It's good to see him making a run. If I can't win then I'd like him to. And I know we'll still be mates when it's all over.

You leave the competitive stuff out in the water. You go out and surf your heats, but then you should be able to go about your life like normal. The tour's not everything.

THE FAME GAME

The attention from the media and the public can sometimes get a bit much, and that was definitely something I struggled with in 2008.

I'm lucky that I have a great bunch of friends and family at home who keep me grounded. My mates treat me exactly the same. Sometimes we go out, and someone random will start saying, 'Oh, Mick Fanning . . .' My mates will say, 'Who cares? It's only Mick. Beat it.' They're so funny. They also keep me focused because if I have a bad result they pay me out.

Sometimes all the attention does get a bit much, when you're out and all you want to do is hang with your friends and you have people coming up and asking for photos. It's cool to give them a bit of time, and you can't be a dick about it. When I first started being approached, I really didn't like it all. Phil said to me one day, 'Just from people seeing you or having one interaction with you, for some reason it makes their day better. It might not be anything to you, but you've just got to be polite.' And I always try and remember that. My mates will ask how I handle getting so heckled at the pub. Why don't I just snap? But I can't – that's part of my job. It's awesome, though, to go somewhere where you can be anonymous and act like an idiot.

But we don't get nearly as much attention as a lot of other sportspeople and celebrities. I think it's because we do our thing, surfing, in the public realm. We're always in the pubic eye, so people don't see us and go, *aaaahhh*, like they would with a movie star. They see that we're just normal people.

Dealing with the media is a whole other world. The media can be your best friend or your worst enemy. They can present you any way they want, and you've got to be very careful what you say to them. If you give an inch, they'll take a mile – that's their job, so you can't hate them for it. There are times when it gets difficult, when you're trying to concentrate on surfing or all you want to do is disappear, but it feels like someone is tracking your every move. You can't just zip off to Indo without someone finding out and wanting to get photos. It's a very small world, especially these days.

I can't complain though. There are plenty of nice trappings to being in this position, and I decided last year that I really wanted to make the most of the opportunities that came up and enjoy it.

FUN AND GAMES

Joel and I were invited to play in the Victorian bushfire appeal cricket match at the SCG in 2009 with a lot of other sportspeople, and that was a blast. It was a great chance to help out people who'd lost everything in such devastating circumstances. I was so nervous walking out onto the SCG – in fact, I've never been so scared in my life. And Joel was making me even more nervous because he can't play cricket to save his life. We were always going to be in trouble. There were a bunch of past and present Australian cricketers matched with the other sports stars, and it was an amazing day with 20,000 people in attendance. We had Michael Slater and Mark Taylor on our team. They had Glenn McGrath, Steve Waugh, Matty Hayden, Dave Warner and Shannon Noll, who was claiming to be some crazy cricketer. Their team was pretty sick and our team was pretty much a joke. Joel was hopeless and Sydney Swans forward Barry Hall was hilarious. Most of us had no idea about cricket.

I got to bowl two overs, of fairly gentle medium pace, and Matty Hayden was on strike. First ball he's gone for the big swing.

I don't know what happened but he lost hold of his bat, got all flustered and started running. We ended up running him out, so I was pretty stoked. Then my next over Dave Warner belted me for two sixes in a row, so that was fairly humbling. I can't imagine what it's like when the SCG is a packed house. I ended up batting at number eight, and we lost our wickets so quickly that I was still putting on my pads when they said, 'You're out there.' I was so nervous walking out, trying to put on my gloves and dropping my helmet. I must have looked like a bit of a goose. But I got nine or ten runs, so I did okay.

All the different sportspeople seemed to get on really well. They all understand how hard it is to reach the top in your field, so there's a lot of mutual respect. The first time I met Andrew Johns, through his mate Matt Hoy, Hoyo was saying, 'He's really stoked to meet you.' I'm like, 'What do you mean? He's *Andrew Johns*.' For some reason a lot of those guys really froth on surfing, but I get starstruck meeting them.

In 2008, Andrew Johns rang up and said, 'We want you to come and hang out with the New South Wales team and talk to them before the next State of Origin game.' I said, 'You're kidding, aren't you?' I didn't think it would be that hard to get up and talk in front of them, but I had the whole team there – all my favourite footy players – and I was lost. I wish I could have turned it around and listened to them talk instead, asking them all the questions. I was so overawed and intimidated.

A couple of days before the game, I went and had dinner with the team. I'd met a few of them in the past, and a few of them surf, too, like Kurt Gidley and Craig Fitzgibbon. I was sitting next to Steve 'Blocker' Roach at dinner, and thought, *This could be interesting*. The players went home early, and I ended up staying there with Blocker and Joey, laughing at their stories.

Then, when it was game time, I was so in awe of them. I went to get on the bus, and I didn't want to get in their space or start talking to someone if that's not acceptable before games. I accidentally sat in the coach's seat, and they were all yelling, 'Get out of there!' Then I didn't know where to sit. It was crazy, and there's so much tension before a game. Being a surfer, it's an individual effort and as serious or relaxed as you want to make it. But when you have eighteen blokes who are that primed and ready to go, it's heavy. Being in the dressing sheds before the game, it was interesting to see how the different guys worked. Danny Buderus had his little area and he'd stretch by himself. Other guys would go and get massages. Some guys were cruising around cracking jokes. Matt Cooper looked like he wanted to sleep. But when the clock went for them to start their pre-game warm-ups, and the coach, Craig Bellamy, came in and took them through it, they were all so united. The atmosphere in that little room was electric. It was game two, and they got flogged 30–6, so Johnsy was like, 'Great motivational speaker you turned out to be!' I'm not sure if I'll be invited back again.

When you're an individual athlete, you've got no-one else to rely on and there's nowhere to hide, no-one to cover for you if you have an off day. Sometimes I miss that team spirit. We go on tour and, even though you're travelling with forty other blokes, you're all on your own. You might all be travelling to the same place, but you always check in solo. With a footy team, they're all together with the same schedule, working towards the same goal.

I'm pretty good mates with Matty Elliott who coaches Penrith, and he invited me up to Brisbane to watch a game from the coach's box. I thought, *Wow, this will be fun.* But when the game started, holy shit, I've never been so sworn at in my whole life. Matt got so worked up, and I copped it all because I happened to be sitting next to him. For eighty minutes, I was torn to strips. Never again am I going anywhere near a coach's box. I don't care who it is. I told Matt after the game, that was the first and last time.

I've always thought it must be amazing running into a packed footy stadium. It's such a coliseum. We get some big crowds on the beach, but it's different. You can't see everyone, and they're not all in a circle around you. If you face out towards the ocean, you can almost pretend they're not even there. It would be a crazy experience to have a wave pool with 50,000 people sitting around watching you surf. That would take surfing to another level.

Joel and I had a great semifinal at Kirra for the Quiksilver Pro at the start of 2009, and that was one of the best atmospheres I've experienced at a surf contest. It was amazing to have a heat with one of my best friends out at pumping Kirra in front of a huge crowd. It wasn't proper Kirra, because it's still choked up with sand from all the sand pumping, but there were some bombs and the crowd was going wild. I didn't realise how many people were there until I broke my board and had to come into the beach – they were lined up all along the point.

There were a bunch of high scores. Joel got off to an early lead with a couple of 7s, and that's when I broke my board. At that point I knew I was really behind the eight ball. If that happened to me at the start of my career, I wouldn't have been able to pull myself back. But with experience you learn to relax and stay confident: the waves will come and you can get the scores. Sure enough, I went back out and comboed him with an 8 and a 9, but then Joel put up a 9 and a 10 – it was all over. Still, I was happy with the way I kept my head and fought back. The reception I received when I came in was like I won anyway. It was really cool and I still felt like I'd achieved something.

There were so many days as grommets when we'd fantasise about getting to surf our local break by ourselves, but it rarely happened because the waves on the Goldy are usually so crowded. So to surf that day at Kirra with just Joel, and thousands of people lined up along the point, was like a dream come true. But I don't know if we would have even dreamed that one up as kids.

A GLIMPSE INTO THE FUTURE

Mid-2009, I did another Mentawai trip with the Red Bull team, but this one was a little different to your typical Indo boat trip. Red Bull created the excursion to bring together their top WCT surfers, a couple of the best women and a bunch of hot young groms to inspire and push each other in quality waves. We also had three coaches on board, equipped with the latest GPS equipment, computers, exercise bikes, lactate tests, hydration tests and basically every bit of hi-tech sports science to measure and monitor every aspect of our surfing. It was pretty wild.

Red Bull's high-performance manager, Andy Walshe, was until recently the sports science director for the US Ski Team and took them from fifth in the world to first. He has a PhD in Applied Biomechanics, so he knows what he's talking about. Andy has dealt with many high-end athletes and has so much knowledge – I learnt a lot from him. Red Bull also has Andy King and Dan Ross on the coaching team, so we were in good hands.

Surfing with the GPS equipment was amazing. Dan Ross and I used it during one surf at Rags Rights. It shows exactly where you paddle in the line-up, when you accelerate on a wave and how fast you're going. We were only surfing three-foot waves and we hit 42 kilometres per hour. It also shows your heart rate, so it was really interesting to see how that fluctuates during a surf session, and even a ride. You have a sense of when you're working hardest on a wave, but to have that backup data to show exactly what was going on was fascinating. I'd love to try it again at a couple different spots. We had exercise bikes on the boat, so there was lots of fitness testing, monitoring how quickly we recovered after exercise.

And the surfing itself was mind-blowing. Everyone has probably seen Jordy Smith's rodeo flip, but all the surfers were doing incredible things. Everyone lifted their game just by frothing off everyone else.

That day at Macaronis, Julian Wilson went out and made one of his sushi rolls, and all the cameramen came in freaking out. That got Jordy excited to go out and try some airs. It was cool to see how Jordy and Julian were feeding off each other, talking each other through the different flips. I even got inspired to try a couple of airs, but after watching those guys I think I'll stick to the water. They took that aerial game to a whole new level. Jordy was sacrificing manoeuvres just to attempt one big air, and when he landed that crazy rodeo flip everyone just went, *Are you kidding me?* That was the best manoeuvre of the trip, hands down.

The two girls on the trip, Sally Fitzgibbon and Sofia Mulanovich, were charging. We were all calling them into waves, and they had a real good dig. And there were a bunch of groms onboard going crazy. We were on the *Indies Trader IV*, which is pretty much the fanciest surf charter boat in the business so, unlike myself, those kids were starting at the top when it came to boat trips. I loved surfing with the kids and they all fully ripped – it's amazing how developed their surfing is for how young they are.

I got a lot out of the experience. I tried a bunch of new fins, and watching all the different surfers and the way they approached the waves was inspiring. The sports science data and research was really helpful. I'd been getting a bit bored with my contest preparation, and I asked a few questions and tried a few new things that felt pretty good, so hopefully that will give me some new momentum going into heats.

It's radical to think what kind of surfing these kids might be doing in the future and where this sophisticated sports science approach could take surfing. It's an exciting time in surfing, and I was stoked to be a part of it.

LIFE AFTER THE TOUR

I don't honestly know how long I'll stay on tour. I can't imagine going for as long as someone like Occy or Kelly. I think that's why I'm going so hard now. It could be only another four or five years. I want to raise a family, do more surf trips and enjoy my free surfing while I'm still fit and able to do so at a high level. The tour's fun and has provided me with a dream career, but I think there's so much more to life as well. I've spoken to a lot of ex-pro surfers about retirement and they all say that the tour's so addictive – it's really hard to adapt to life afterwards. I've spoken to footy players after they've retired, and it's like their whole world stops. They don't even get to play footy anymore. You don't have your mates constantly around you, no reason to keep professionally fit. A few of them told me they actually fell into depression. I think that's why Occ's been on the tour for so many years. He just loves it, loves watching competition and being at the beach and the whole atmosphere. It must be difficult to leave that behind. At least surfers get to keep surfing even after we retire from the tour. The ocean's not going anywhere.

The biggest thing is just to enjoy the journey. A lot of people don't, and if you're not enjoying it, it usually shows in your results. Really appreciate why you are where you are. You've got a gift, so enjoy it.

LOVE AND MARRIAGE

To be honest, 2008 was about a few other things more important than surf contests. I got married for a start, and that's a big enough deal in itself. I let Karrisa handle the details. It's really the girl's big day, and she knew exactly the way she wanted it. We had an 1800s theme, so everyone was dressed up in period costume. We wanted to do something different and everything Karissa does is fancy dress. People seem to loosen up and enjoy themselves more when they're in costume. We had a photo booth where people could go have their portraits taken and printed out in sepia tone so they looked really old. Everyone had a great time and it was a really special day. So, after all the pressure of my world title year, I really wanted to take it easy and enjoy married life.

2008 was also the tenth anniversary of Sean and Joel's passing, and that memorial contest was the last one. It was really special to have that event for the past ten years, but it had to come to an end eventually. Otherwise, I think people start to lose sight of what we're celebrating. I didn't want it to become one of those contests where people would come down to try and get a result. I didn't want competitors blowing up about the judging. The whole point of it was to celebrate the lives of Sean and Joel, and it's a great way of bringing the community back together, not just my generation but all the old locals. It's about everyone coming together with no ego and simply hanging out. Every year I try to catch up with everyone and go from table to table for a chat. It's cool to hear all the different stories over the years about Sean and Joel from everyone who knew and loved them.

THE FANNING FAMILY CREST

People sometimes ask me what that little crest is on all my boards, my website and tattooed on my arm. It's the Fanning family crest, and it's just my little way of saying that nothing's more important than family. We've always had the family crest hanging in the house. I've always liked it, and when we were looking for a little logo I thought, *What could be better than the family shield*? The yellow stands for courage and the V-shaped strip represents a chevron, or the rafters of a roof, which is supposed to signify shelter and protection for your family. Karissa and I are keen to start a family of our own one day, but I want to wait until I've finished with the tour. I'd rather be a home dad and do all the fun things, like take the kids to soccer. I'd find it pretty hard to concentrate on surfing on tour and the kids as well.

My main priority since I started making a living from surfing was to try and set myself up for the future. You only have ten or fifteen years as a professional athlete earning an income, and you need to be smart. I've always tried to invest in property, because you can't really lose. I've learnt a lot from Luke Egan, who's been really smart managing his finances and set himself up for retirement. If you can buy a few properties and get them paid off, then you can just live off the rent, so that's my goal. If I need to work one day, then I'll do whatever I need to do to support my family. But I'm really lucky to be among the first generation of pro surfers who have the opportunity to set themselves up for life. A lot of great surfers have done the tour for years and walked away with nothing to show for it, so I'm really aware of how lucky I am.

Pro surfing looks like a dream job, and a lot of the time it is, but it can also be a pretty cutthroat business. Many surfers have gone on tour with all the talent in the world and haven't achieved the results or have injured themselves or lost the plot, and all of a sudden they're not sponsored anymore. There have been a lot of casualties. Sure, the top guys make good money today, but you have to earn it. If you aren't selling product for your sponsors, you won't stay on the team for long. Companies want you to win world titles, get photos and do media. It's easy for someone sitting behind a desk to look at your schedule and go, Well, he's got a month off after Bells. Let's send him somewhere on the other side of the world. Sometimes it's like, What do you want me to concentrate on? If you want photos, I'll be a free surfer. If you want contest results and world titles, I'll do contests. You pick. You need to have a life at home too, and you need to be able to work on your boards and maintain your close relationships with family and friends.

I've always stood up for what I believe in. I see people who cave in to sponsors, whereas if I don't want to do something, I'm not doing it and that's final. I've had arguments with my sponsors about it and arguments with Mum about it – and it all works out in the end. You've got to stand up for what you believe in, but you've also got to compromise. It's a fine line between getting taken advantage of and trying to do what's right for you.

People sometimes ask me what my motivation has been to work so hard at my surfing to achieve my goals. My drive has always been really personal. It's not about doing it for anyone else or because someone says I *can't* do it. I never really did anything for anyone but myself. If someone says I can't do it, I don't really take any notice. I just concentrate on myself. If I get too hot-headed about trying to prove something to someone, I can't really control my energy and I don't do my best. My main motivation is that I love trying to better myself in everything I do. It's not just sport, it's been like that since I was a kid. I've always been out there practising and figuring out new ways to do things. I get enjoyment out of knowing I'm improving.

It's like anything, if you don't believe or feel you want to do it, then you won't do it. Whatever your goals, you aren't going to find the answers looking to others to make it happen – it has to come from within.

MICK BAKER – THE INDIGENOUS ARTIST

Mick Baker, or Dhinawan as he's known in his native language, is an Indigenous artist and dancer, descended from the Gamillaroi Bigambul people of southern Queensland. He and his dance troop have performed the opening ceremony for the Cooly Kids Memorial Contest every year since it started. He saw first-hand the devastation wrought by the loss of the two young friends, Sean Fanning and Joel Green, on the Coolangatta surfing community.

'We heard there was a lot of bad shit going on, drinking and stuff,' says Dhinawan. 'We said, "We've got to release these fellas' spirits properly."' As part of their ceremony, they threw two boomerangs into the ocean, representing the two boys' spirits. 'We said if anyone found them to give them to the parents.' Joel's boomerang was found and returned to his father, but Sean's boomerang was never found. 'I told Mick, "Sean's spirit lives in the ocean now, and you can visit him whenever you like. Any

time you're out there in the ocean, your brother's spirit is out there. Take that time to be with him." You could see it helped.'

He explained to Mick that in their culture whales and dolphins represent ancestors coming to visit. 'Just as the final started two whales popped up. Everybody went, Yes! You could hear it running through the crowd, "Look, look, see the whales." We knew the boys had come to visit.'

When Mick built his dream home on Kirra Hill, he invited Dhinawan to conduct a blessing. 'We did a smoking ceremony for his house, a blessing, to scare away the negative and bad energy. It's going to be a place of love,' Dhinawan explains.

'They came and did a welcome dance for the house and scared off all the spirits that were lurking around. They blessed the house so that if we created a family, we'd always be safe here. That was really cool,' says Mick.

Dhinawan also painted a mural by Mick's front door and consulted with the architects to create a special pond and cave-like alcove to accommodate the painting.

'I said, "I can see the spirit within you." I didn't know how he would take it. I said, "You're like that water goanna, the way you move through the water."' Dhinawan indicates with one hand a rapid waving motion. 'The water goanna just waves his tail and takes off. Mick's surfing reminded me of that . . . When he behaves like the water goanna, that is his medicine.'

Dhinawan explains the painting is a creation story, with elements that will take on special meaning at different points in Mick's life. 'Within that, there are strong symbols for strength, *wisdom, family,' he explains. 'I wanted to represent Mick with the water goanna. The water goanna has no self-doubt. If he's hungry, he gets what he needs to eat.'*

The mural also depicts a pelican and a crocodile. 'The crocodile has patience and knows when is the right time to snap. That's what the crocodile does – it can not eat for two months and just watches everything around it, and then knows when to act. It teaches Mick to relax, teaches him about respect.'

The waterways around Mick's home, he says, are the playgrounds of the pelican, and the ridge line he lives on, known locally as Razorback, is an important 'old story place'.

'I wanted him to realise that this is his environment. Respect country. It's special that he knows the story of the land. There's so much native bush and medicine on that hill.'

When Mick returned from Brazil in 2007 after clinching the world title, Dhinawan sensed there was something on Mick's mind. He didn't know then that a dolphin had shadowed Mick in the water throughout the final day of competition in Brazil. 'When he came back he was trying to tell me something, but there were so many people there. When I watched the movie and saw the dolphin I knew what that was all about.'

Dhinawan and Mick's family have become close, helping bring the local Indigenous and surfing communities closer too. 'The relationship's really grown. A lot of the Cooly boys have opened up. The family has been very receptive and very open. Mick takes the chance to talk to the media [about Indigenous issues]. For young Aboriginal people to hear that is very rewarding. I've got ninety kids that I train, and if I bump into Mick he gives them the time of day – he poses for pictures, answers questions. They go, "I talked to Mick Fanning!" It's a big thing for them.'

For Mick, Aboriginal culture seems to fit into a kind of open, non-denominational spiritualism that runs through his family.

'From that first memorial contest, we thought we'd love to get them down each year to dance and play the didgeridoo. It puts a really good vibe on what's going on, just to appreciate the culture of the land,' says Mick. 'There's definitely something there, the spiritual side of things. Mum's really spiritual too, and we thought, What more spiritual people than the Aboriginals? And we stayed in contact with them ever since. I don't think you have to be Aboriginal to respect what they do.'

MICK'S TIPS – FIT TO SURF

One of the biggest things in training for surfing is working on your core. Your core is the centre of your body, and that's what is going to control your legs and your arms, and hold everything together. A lot of the training I do in the gym involves trying to mimic the different turns that I do on a wave with applied weight. That way, you are building in the strength required to complete all the manoeuvres with power. Because surfing is so unique and the water is an unstable medium, you want to work on an unstable surface as much as possible. The BOSU is really good – it's like half an exercise ball with a flat table on it that you balance on. All your stabilising muscles in your feet, legs, hips and core get a work-out when you have to balance on an unstable surface. Fitballs, or exercise balls, are really good to practice standing on, too. It's really hard at first – I couldn't do it initially because I had very little core stability. As I kept practising, eventually I could stand on one, have balls thrown to me, catch them and throw them back, all while keeping my balance.

I know some skiers who can jump from one ball to another while keeping their balance, so it's amazing how far you can take it to improve your core stability.

I'm modifying my training all the time. There are different levels to work at depending on when you are competing. If you're a couple of months off competing, in the off-season, then you lift heavy weights to get the endurance in the muscles, and then you start tapering it down to more explosive exercises with less weight as you approach contest time. Because surfing is so explosive, you want to develop that power in all your movements. You decrease the weight, but the motion is really fast and strong.

And then a couple of weeks out from competing, you train the way you surf, and that's when you really concentrate on weight work that mimics the various surfing manoeuvres. Because surfing is pretty fast-twitched, you decrease the weight again and do really quick repetitions - *bang, bang, bang,* - as many as you can. I use weights on pulley systems, medicine balls, tornado balls (medicine balls on a rope) and kettle bells (small weights with a handle on the top). An experienced trainer can help you develop a training regime ideal for your sport and your physical condition, and that's where the CHEK training has been so valuable.

During competition, the idea is to keep your body switched on. You don't have to go to the gym every single day – in fact, it's really important not to overdo it at this point. You need to have already put in the hard work by then, and cramming on the eve of a competition is actually going to work against you. You compete best when you're fresh and have heaps of energy, so you want to do only a little bit, just to keep the muscles firing. In most sports you know exactly when you are going to compete, but it's tricky on the WCT because we don't know from one day to the next if the event is going to be on, so you are in a holding pattern. For me, I won't train the day before we are likely to compete. There are light exercises you can do with no weight involved just to keep everything fired and activated, like riding an exercise bike, but by that point you should have done all the bodybuilding and strength work you need.

It's important to mix up your training because it can get pretty boring and repetitive. It's like anything, if you eat ham and eggs every day, you're going to get bored of it. You have to keep evolving the training as your body evolves. You don't want to do things that are too easy or too hard. And don't be afraid to try new techniques. I'll try anything once.

I've started doing this breath-enhancement training in a swimming pool that Joel's been doing for a while, and I am loving it. So now I do a combination of CHEK training, breath training and surfing. Another important thing I learnt from experience: don't put training ahead of surfing. There's no training for surfing like surfing itself. It took me a while to figure that out because you get so addicted to training and you feel really good and strong. I wanted to do it more and more. But then I learnt as I went on that surfing has to come first and training is mainly a way to prevent injuries when you're surfing, by building strength in your body. Swimmers can go up and down the pool all day long, but eventually they have to go into the gym to balance out their body or strengthen up their shoulders, otherwise they're just going to blow something out. It's the same in surfing. You develop over-use patterns and you start blowing things left, right and centre.

You've got to have a really good relationship with your trainer, someone who can see your dream and motivate you to achieve it. You can work with the best trainer in the world, but if he doesn't motivate you to do the work, it's not going to do you much good. Sometimes you just need a kick in the bum at the right time to actually do the work – and keep coming back for more.

The breath-enhancement training is really good for surfing, because it increases your ability to hold your breath and helps mentally with pushing your own limits. A lot of big-wave surfers have been doing it for years, and a lot of the cyclists in the Tour de France use it to prepare for the long rides up into the Alps or Pyrenees where they can get short of oxygen at high altitude.

I've been working in the pool with Nam Baldwin. It's a 12.5 metre pool, and you start out swimming intervals of one lap under water, then one lap above water. Then, as you get into it, you start swimming every lap underwater and just come up for two breaths at the end of each lap. It teaches your body to use the oxygen in your muscles instead of just using what's in your lungs. You've got to work pretty hard kicking underwater to get to the other end, so it's important that your body uses that oxygen more efficiently.

When Nam first told me to swim eight lengths of the pool underwater, with just two breaths at each end, I thought there was no way I could. As you get into it you've got to keep pushing yourself, so it helps make you mentally stronger, too. It is a really hard, strenuous work-out, but that's just the first half of it.

From there, you go into eight minutes of just slowing down the heart rate and your entire body. You hang off the lane ropes and concentrate on breathing through the body, almost like a yogic breathing exercise. You start at the top of your body and work your way down, relaxing your muscle groups and breathing right into your stomach. And as you focus on your breathing you can feel your legs rise up in the water and then fall back down. It's a really good way to recover for the next stage, which is more mental.

You breathe out all your oxygen and sit underwater for extended periods. You start off at fifteen or thirty seconds - I was getting up to fifty seconds by the end of it. You just lay there, keeping everything still. If your mind starts wandering, you start using more oxygen and you've got to come up. So it's another good way of learning to focus on the breath and still the mind. It's not something you want to try without proper instruction, because it could be dangerous if you don't know exactly what you are doing. It leaves you really exhausted, but also calm and clear-minded. It almost feels like you float home afterwards, but your mind is really sharp.

In 2008, I was having trouble keeping my mind still. I knew what to do, but I just needed to retrain it. For me, I can't just sit in a room for half an hour and meditate, so this was a really good way for me to learn how to still the mind. I was pretty busy a lot of the time, but after doing that breath training I felt like I could focus on one thing at a time. It's almost as though time slows down. I had time to do everything I needed to do, even though I was busy. And in the surf I could pick my turns properly and nothing was a stress. That's a great asset in whatever you're doing, and it's probably the same thing people get from meditation, but this works well for me.

TAYLOR KNOX – THE TOUR VET

At 38, Taylor Knox, a strong natural-footer from Carlsbad, southern California, is the oldest surfer still competing on the WCT. As friend, mentor and Rip Curl stable mate, he has also become one of Mick's closest confidants on tour.

'It's weird because I always knew there would be a day when we'd hang out more but never knew when,' says Taylor. 'We're similar in a lot of ways – training and surfing are the obvious ones – but it's our humour and values on friendship that I feel we see eye to eye on. I think there is also a connection with going through some injuries and hardships in life that we can relate to, because there's a lot more to an injury than just the physical.'

At fifteen, Taylor was told he would never surf again. Already a promising junior destined for the US national team, Taylor was diagnosed with a rare spinal condition and told he would end up paralysed from the waist down unless he underwent immediate spinal surgery. Even with the surgery, doctors told him he would be in a body cast for nine months and never surf again. He was out of the cast in six months and has gone on to a long and celebrated surfing career, clocking up sixteen years on the WCT. He attributes his recovery and longevity to yoga, and has produced his own yoga DVD specifically for surfers.

With his handlebar moustache and sometimes mohawked hairdo, Knox is the last surviving member still on tour from Kelly Slater's highly touted 'new school' or 'Momentum' crew of the early 90s, apart from Kelly himself. And Knox, variously known as 'Fort Knox' (for his strength) or 'Bonehead' (for his sometimes questionable competitive strategies) is still schooling much younger surfers on the virtues of good, clean, on-rail carving. He is also one of Mick's favourite surfers.

'When I first saw Knox surf in Taylor Steele's earliest surf vids he became an instant favourite. I honestly believe he has one of the best forehand carves in surfing history,' says Mick. 'He's also overcome a serious back injury that threatened his career, and I respect him for that.'

It's a respect that's returned liberally, and the pair have formed a tight bond, despite hailing from different eras and countries. Taylor's someone Mick has turned to repeatedly for guidance at crucial points in his career, particularly during his return from injury. Did Taylor always believe Mick would make it back?

'Yeah, I had no doubt he was going to come back, because of his personality. I know that was a bad injury, but it's not the end-all. I think the way he trains is pretty much spot-on. I've been training with a lot of the same stuff for the last year, and I'm loving the results. Mick has put together a great team of people around him, which I know has helped him a lot through different aspects of his life.'

And Taylor reckons he's one old dog still learning a few tricks from his younger buddy. 'Man, I'm learning a lot from surfing with him. I mean, what's there not to like? Fast, on-rail and radical with precision. People that surf a lot know that's a hard combination to put together. I watch the way he gets lift going through his speed turns.'

And Taylor says he's never seen Mick's well-documented fondness for the occasional good time as getting in the way of his competitive success. 'I didn't ever consider him a party boy. I know he can party, and when he does, he does it well. I love Eugene, for the record. I never saw that side of him getting in the way. Maybe he was different when I really started to hang out with him, but I heard the stories and experienced it myself. It's just a good human grounding on down with friends and strangers – and anyone else who wants to have a good time.'

But Taylor also understands, as elder, friend and Rip Curl teammate, it is his role to make sure Eugene makes it home safely when they are away together. 'All I can say is that we laugh a lot and have similar humour,' says Knox. 'Being on the [US] East Coast promo tour was super-funny because we got to connect with people that don't get to see him very much but are big fans. One night in Virginia we ended up in a cab with people we didn't know, going to a club that didn't exist, but we always make sure that we *get home in one piece. Liz would kill me if I let something happen to her boy under my watch!'*

He also observes a more serious side to Mick, with the quiet, unobtrusive concern of a true friend. 'I didn't know Sean, but there are times I see his tattoo and I know that his thoughts must be with him in certain situations. I mean, I have a feeling sometimes, but I don't ask because his thoughts are his and if he wants to share them he knows he can any time.'

LIZ'S STORY, PART 4

'People say, "You must be so proud of Mick," and I say, "I'm proud
of all my children because they've all done really well,"' says Liz.
'I've always tried to be as fair as possible with all the kids and not
favour anyone.'

It's clear that Mick's family provides a grounding base
back home, where ASP rankings and world titles count for little,
where he is still just a little brother. 'My kids don't buy into the
fame and fortune,' says Liz. 'They don't ask for anything. A lot
of people ask for things, like, "Can I have a signature? Can I have
a T-shirt?" They never ask because he's their little brother and
he deserves everything he gets – we're not going to be the ones to
take things off him. There's too many people around taking things
from Mick. We're just there to love him.'

Even so, it's difficult for Liz to hide the pride she has for
Mick's accomplishments. 'The thing I'm most proud of about Mick
is not that he's the world champion, it's just that he's fulfilling

his dreams and he's happy and he's free. And that's the gift I hope every one of my kids has. He's always been determined. He's always put 100 per cent into everything he's ever done. He's always been that kind of a kid, where if it was worth doing it was worth doing properly. He always wanted to do his best. And he always respects people along the way.'

Was there anything to indicate early on the reserves of resilience and determination Mick would reveal later in life? 'I have to say that Edward, Rachel and Mick have been extraordinary long-distance runners. They've always shown that endurance. I don't know where he got this endurance, tenacity and determination. I hope I've contributed to that. When I was separating from John, some of the things that helped me along, that I said to the kids as well, were inspirational things like, You never give up and you never give in. I've always tried to say, Have the courage to confront things, and have the courage to go on. You can do anything – you can face anything. Because if you face it, it's not as bad. It's the thought of facing it that's hard.'

Even so, her maternal instincts command a healthy protective streak for her son. Mick still texts his mum every time he gets off a plane to let her know he's arrived safely. 'He used to ring me at work in the middle of a meeting with the Minister for Health or something.' Liz recalls a terrified, seventeen-year-old Mick calling from Jakarta airport at the height of the 1998 riots that toppled President Suharto. Or in agony with stomach pains in the middle of the night in France.

'I don't care who's in the room with me – the Minister for Health – that boy is more important to me than anything, because I've already lost one and nothing is going to come in between me and my kids. I was happy to do it because I wanted him to succeed, and I could see that he was capable. I wanted to give him every opportunity because you've got to give 100 per cent, take the risk and do it. If it doesn't work then at least you've tried. You've got to focus on things and put your heart into it. That's the only place to come from.'

To keep coming from the heart, with all the Fanning family has been through – this, more than world titles or real-estate portfolios, might be their greatest achievement.

'I was talking to this guy not so long ago about life, and he was asking me questions. I don't know him very well, but he wrote me a message that said, "You've done a great job – it must be very difficult to bring all those little hearts through separation, fame and losing a brother, and you haven't hardened your hearts." All of us, really, we haven't hardened our hearts.'

We have been talking for over two hours, and Liz has been in turn candid, emotional and always scrupulously measured in discussing her children. Finally, a mother's simple pride is too great to contain. 'He's just such a lovely guy. Proud isn't even good enough. How my heart swells at what he's done and how he's come through it, for such a young man to face so many dif-ficulties,' she releases in a torrent. 'He's got such courage to go on, and have that loyalty in his heart for Sean. He's held that for ten years – they all have. Sean is still living in this house, talked about every day and loved as if he was still here by all of us. In the past, I've always rung everyone on Sean's birthday and said, "Happy birthday, Sean." This year, Mick sent a text to me, to all of us. "Happy birthday, Sean. Have a good day everybody."'

Liz admits she was worried about how Mick would have coped if he hadn't won the world title in 2007, having devoted himself to that goal so completely. 'I talked to the kids actually and my fear, just in case he didn't become the world champ, was, "Well guys, we've got to think how we can support Mick if he doesn't win this title, because that's what he's going to need: our support." I was worried about him if he didn't win, because he's lost so much.'

There have also been times she's felt defensive about the constant media scrutiny he now attracts. 'It hasn't been easy, this career. They've all got something to say about Mick Fanning. The year before it was, "Oh, he's far too serious," and all those commentators on the internet, they almost put him down for his training and being serious. And then you find out the next year everybody is doing the training. And the next thing it's, "Eugene, oh, he's always drinking. It's disgraceful." The next year, it's, "Where's Eugene?"'

Mick is much more relaxed now, she observes, less torn between opposite extremes, finding balance and happiness in his new life with Karissa. 'I think Karissa's had a lot to do with that. I think he felt fulfilled that he had this beautiful girl in his life, and he loved her so much. I really think he wanted to win it before he got married. Not that he wanted to prove anything to Karissa, *because he didn't need to, but that was the time because then he wanted to devote his time to the relationship.'*

His challenge now, she says, may be learning to win in different ways, for different reasons. 'I think he's in a much more relaxed space. He doesn't have to prove anything to himself. He knows he can do it. He learnt how to be world champion . . . I think he will go on to be world champion again, with a lot more maturity, by being himself and not having to force himself. Emotionally, it must have been terrible. He gave up everything really to do that, but he never gave up his friends and his family.'

By the time you read this, the 2009 world title will be coming down to the wire, but mid-year Liz was clearly enjoying the spectacle of the two boyhood friends vying for the title and predicting a close finish. 'He is feeling a lot freer and more confident. It will be a big tussle this year between him and Joel – and may the best man win.'

KARRISA – THE LOVE

Fisherman's Wharf, at the northern end of the Gold Coast, is not a venue renowned for giving rise to deep and meaningful relationships. Its rowdy Sunday Sessions on the Broadwater were once legendary, but for rather more fleeting liaisons. So when a funny, confident, slightly drunk bloke approached communications student and part-time model Karissa Dalton and told her she had beautiful eyelashes, she didn't think too much of it. 'He thought it was this amazing pick-up line, but it wasn't really.' She laughs. 'We got along well straightaway – he's a really funny, charismatic person who doesn't take himself too seriously.'

At the time, Karissa knew nothing about surfing or who Mick was. 'Mick's a pretty humble guy; he's definitely not one to brag and never spoke about surfing when we first met,' she says. 'I grew up travelling all around Australia when I was really young, but spent most of my life in Hervey Bay, so I knew nothing about professional surfing. Looking back, I'm really glad because I might have shaped a different opinion or attached a certain stereotype to him that I know a lot of people have when they think of professional surfers. Instead, I got to know the amazing person that Mick is without any of that. There's so much more to him than what he does for a living.'

When their paths crossed on two more occasions, and he invited her over for dinner, Karissa eventually relented. She recalls pulling up at the address and looking at this large, imposing hilltop home and figuring she'd made a mistake. 'I was already a bit nervous as it was and then I was just like, No, that can't be his house. I called him just to make sure that it was the right address.'

His culinary skills were the next thing to make an impression. 'He cooked a pretty mean roast – he still does – it's a bit of a signature dish.'

The proverbial whirlwind romance ensued and, within a few months, Karissa was receiving a crash course in surfing contests and the fluctuating career fortunes of Australia's next great world title hope. When she turned up at the 2005 Quiksilver Pro to watch her new boyfriend compete, she had no idea what was at stake or what he'd been through to get there. 'I'd never really watched a surfing contest or anything like that. I had no idea about the whole format or scoring. Then when he won the event – it was all a bit bizarre and a bit of a blur. Mick had told me a bit about the injury he was recovering from before the contest, but it wasn't until I heard the full story and learnt more about his history that I realised what a huge triumph winning that event was for him.'

A few months later, Karissa found herself travelling overseas for the first time, flying to South Africa with Mick for the Billabong Pro at Jeffreys Bay. 'I didn't even have a passport before I met Mick, and I remember him asking me to come overseas – I think as a twenty-first birthday present,' she recalls. It was at Jeffreys Bay where she learnt a bit more about Mick's family history and the tragic loss they'd endured. 'We spent a lot of time staying up late talking, getting to know each other, and it was heart-breaking to learn about Sean.'

Since then, Karissa has had to get used to life with a public figure, the many demands placed on him and the intense pressure he's put on himself in pursuit of his dreams. 'It doesn't get too intrusive. Mick's really good at keeping our private life separate. Sometimes when he goes out it can be a bit much, but it's not too bad.'

What was more difficult was watching him put it all on the line in 2007 and devote himself entirely to his quest for the world title. 'It was definitely hard. It was amazing to see him working to achieve his dreams. It was inspiring, but you were always careful not to step on his toes, always conscious of what you were saying all the time, giving him space. It was hard especially towards the end, with the pressure and the focus he had to sustain 100 per cent of the time. There wasn't really any down time, but we were all more than willing to make that sacrifice for him. I think the hardest part was afterwards, trying to get that work–life balance back again. It all happened so quickly. The media frenzy consumed a lot of his time, and I don't think he had the chance to really reflect on the achievement until later on.'

Mick's best mate, Beau, and Karissa were determined that his world title party, at least, would be for Mick and those closest to him.

They organised the celebrations in secret as the title race unfolded in Brazil.

'We knew his sponsors would want to do something commercial and more for the public than for Mick, so we wanted to make sure that that party would be really personal with only the people who have had a big impact on his life,' she says. 'Beau and I just wanted to make sure that when Mick arrived and looked around that he knew every single face and it was really meaningful for him. When we were leaving Coolangatta airport I tried to play it down and told him his dad, brothers and a couple of mates were waiting for him at the Kirra Pub to have some private drinks before we went out later on. When he arrived there were over 300 of his closest friends – some who had travelled really far to be there. It was a very special moment for him. We also organised for Mark Richards to say a few words on stage as I know there'd been times throughout the year that he'd said a few things to Mick that had a huge impact on him, and he was more than happy to. I know that really meant a lot to Mick.

'It was hard to try and keep it a secret – we didn't know if he was going to win in Brazil and we had to have it all on stand-by just in case. The night before I remember talking to Beau, and we said, "We don't even know if he is going to win in Brazil and we've got this huge party planned – we've got Grinspoon lined up. I don't know what we're going to do if he doesn't win."'

They needn't have worried – all the hard work, sacrifice and planning paid off when Mick flew home victorious and walked into his world title party with no inkling of what was in store for him. 'That moment when he walked through the door, seeing the look on his face and the satisfaction of everything he'd worked so hard for come together was amazing.'

Still, Karissa's no doting WAG, waiting idly by for her man to return home from his latest campaign to bask in the reflected glory. She's completed a communications degree and launched her own web-based business, promoting wedding services, and is determined to have a life and identity of her own.

'I'm a really independent person. I always have been,' she says. 'There's definitely a stigma attached to being the wife of a professional athlete, and it's hard not be placed in that category. I really believe you have to have your separate interests and ambitions outside of your relationship for it to work. Everyone has different circumstances, but for Mick and me, this is what works. We're both really happy to do our own thing and then spend quality time together when we can. It makes that time more rewarding. Of course I love supporting Mick, but having my own career is just as important. Life for me is about pursuing goals and dreams, about constantly learning and growing . . . I can't do that by following my husband around on tour 24/7.'

Even so, the protracted time apart can be a challenge. In 2009, Mick returned from two weeks in Tahiti, just long enough to collect fresh boards and clean clothes, and within a few hours was back on a plane to Indonesia for a two-week boat trip. 'There are times like that when he's away for long periods at a time and that gets pretty hard, especially on boat trips when we can't call each other. But we just make it work. You have to – it's always been that way so we're used to it. And when he's away it gives me the chance to work hard and do what I need to do so that when he's home we can spend quality time together. Plus, surfing can be a short-lived career, so you have to make the most of it while you can.'

What are the qualities she most admires in Mick?

'He's such a strong, driven, motivated person. The things he's been through could really break someone. It absolutely blows my mind to see how strong he is, and the positive outlook he has on life is really infectious. He's so much fun to be around. We've got fairly similar family backgrounds, growing up with single parents and having to work hard to get where we are. Mick's family is just amazing; they're really grounded and supportive. He's gone through a lot growing up, and I think those experiences have really shaped the person he is.'

chapter **8**.
GIVING BACK

There's no doubt about it – surfing for a living is a pretty amazing gig. We travel to some of the most beautiful places in the world, to many of the greatest waves on earth in prime surf season and surf them with just one other person. A lot of people work and save all year just for a week or two holidaying at one of these destinations. Tahiti, Fiji, Indonesia, France, South Africa, Hawaii – there's a lot to like about the itinerary of the modern pro surfer.

We also see a lot of pretty radical poverty, often butted up hard against the idyllic beach lifestyle we enjoy, places where people live in the most basic tin shacks or lean-tos, where the necessities of life – food, water, shelter – are a daily struggle. In the shanty towns of South Africa or the favelas of Brazil or the remote island villages of Indonesia, children go hungry every day, and have only the slimmest chance at good health and education. It's hard to reconcile this harsh reality with the privileged life we lead.

I do believe this job carries with it a certain amount of responsibility to give something back to the places and communities we visit. A lot of the surfers quietly do what they can to help out in their own ways – giving away boards, clothes and wetsuits to kids who can't afford them, supporting local charities. But there's a lot more we could do. I'd like to see pro surfing contributing in real, practical, tangible ways in all the places we visit. They don't have to be big things, but in lots of small ways, as well-known athletes, we can make differences in the lives of kids who might just want the chance to surf and meet their heroes.

WORLD PROFESSIONAL SURFERS

For a few years now the pro surfers have had their own representative body, World Professional Surfers, lobby for our best interests, almost like a union. While the ASP administers the world tour and has to balance the needs of sponsors, surfers, event organisers and fans, WPS gives us a unified voice to try and do some good things. I've taken on the role as the surfers' rep to liaise between the WPS and the ASP, and I really want to leave the tour in better shape than I found it, and try to make a positive difference along the way.

I came up with the idea of the 'Surf With the Pros' days as a simple way of connecting with local communities, inspiring the local grommets and learning a bit more about the people and places that host us. It's also a way to get more of the top forty-five surfers in the public eye a bit, not just the top handful. Originally, we were going to give free surf lessons at each stop of the tour, but as it evolved it became a bit of a free-for-all. Trying to control grommets is a bit like herding cats, so now we invite them all down to the beach at an appointed time and place. We all charge out for a surf, give them a few tips, have a barbecue on the beach, sign some free posters and generally stoke out the grommets. They are always incredible days. It's a lot more fun and meaningful than just doing a signing at a surf shop, where people turn up looking for free stuff and don't really get to interact with the surfers. Just by giving a couple of hours of our time, we actually forge relationships with the local communities. These grommets become your little mates at each stop on tour and love saying g'day whenever they see you.

Every pro surfer knows what it's like to be a grommet, excited to meet your heroes. Even though we sometimes might grumble about all the different demands on our time, you will never find a surfer who begrudges taking the time to sign an autograph and say hello to some stoked kid. At Bells Beach, people drove a twelve-hours round trip from Lakes Entrance on the other side of Victoria just so their kids could meet the surfers and share a wave with them. It shows how much it means. And the event at Coolangatta was hilarious. Bede Durbidge had kids hanging off both arms like he was Gulliver in Lilliput, and everyone was loving it. The session we had with the kids at Jeffreys Bay, South Africa, was extra special because non-whites used to be prohibited from even setting foot on whites-only beaches. To see a bunch of South African grommets – white, black, whatever – all surfing side by side, all stoked, really made a statement about the unifying power of surfing. Hopefully we can keep hosting more of these events, and they can evolve into other things. It's a really good entry point into learning more about the communities we visit, whether there's a local environmental cause we can promote or worthy charities we can support.

The WPS role also means playing a guiding hand in the future of pro surfing, and that's important to me. I don't want to leave it to other people to decide where my career is heading.

WPS was really started with the help of a guy named Greville Mitchell, who is an amazing person, a businessman who has become a big supporter of the surfers and pro surfing. He could see that we don't always get a fair deal from the powers that be and decided to try and help. Jake Paterson and Sunny Garcia were the two surfers who really stepped up and helped Greville get WPS off the ground as surfer reps on the ASP board. I've always had a good relationship with Jake, and when he retired he left big shoes to fill. It's hard to deal with forty-five different egos and come up with a united position on their behalf. Everyone has got their opinion on where pro surfing should go and what they think is best for the sport, or what's best for them. And that's fine, everyone has the right to an opinion. But I'm hoping I can help all the surfers take the sport where we think it should be. That's why I took over from Jake when he retired, and now Kieren Perrow and Clyde Martin, who works for WPS, have also come on board as surfer reps.

Everyone loves surfing. Everyone loves watching people ride waves – even non-surfers. The ocean is such a beautiful medium and we all know how great surfing makes you feel. I think there are better ways to market the sport, better ways to present it to the general public. Even little things like the 'Surf With the Pros' days can make a difference to how surfing is perceived. And all the little things can add up to big things if the surfers act together to achieve a vision for the sport.

I look at my life, and everything I have is from surfing – my house, my car, my income. I get paid to go surfing and I'll never take that for granted. It's important to find ways to give back, almost as a way of saying thank you. Sometimes it is a massive headache trying to bring about change and sit through meetings and satisfy a whole range of competing interests. At the end of the day, we are all trying to achieve the same thing, to be able to earn a livelihood doing what we love and present surfing in the best possible way. If we can overcome our differences, maybe one day surfing could become the sport we all know it can be.

REDISCOVER THE STOKE

One sure way to rediscover the stoke of surfing is teaching someone else how to surf. I've been teaching people to surf a bit lately and it's always a blast and takes you back to your first days learning. Even if the waves are total crap, you're having a ball because you get the enjoyment of what the other person is feeling and discovering. I took Karissa surfing in Waikiki, on the old longboards, and recently took my sister out. I even took TV personality Fifi Box surfing down at Bells. It was freezing cold and the waves were horrible, but she was so stoked to do it that we had a great time. It's a good reminder of how much fun it can be doing something simple for others.

One recent experience crystallised this idea of sharing the stoke. I first met Barney a few years ago when he turned up at contests in his wheelchair. I'd always try and help him out with good seats and passes. Barney's from Sawtell on the New South Wales North Coast, and he'd always come up to the Goldy for our contest celebrations and we became good mates. You'd think someone in a wheelchair might be a bit reserved or self-conscious, but he's just one of the boys and gets as loose as anyone when there's a party on. We've had some memorable moments together. He was at my world title celebration party and the guys from Grinspoon reckoned it was the first time they'd seen a guy crowd-surfing in a wheelchair.

Barney was a passenger in a car on his way home from work when the driver took a corner at speed and they ended up rolling. The driver was thrown out of the car and broke his collar bone, but Barney was stuck in the wreckage and lost the use of his legs. It's a heavy one but he keeps pushing on, and it doesn't stop him from doing much.

Last Hawaiian season we took Barney surfing one day down near Chuns, a mellow little break on the North Shore between Haleiwa and Waimea. Local surf coach Brian Surratt came along and set us up with a soft beginner's board and we pushed him into these waves – it was incredible. I'd catch the wave after and surf behind Barney, just to be there in case he came off. But he got five of the sickest waves and rode them forever. It was so amazing to see the smile on his face. The crowd parted and let him catch whatever wave he wanted. I saw Brian later, and he said one of the guys that works for him was really quiet after we'd all left. Brian asked him what was up. The guy lifted his head and had tears in his eyes. He just said, 'Thanks for bringing

me along. That was the most amazing thing I've ever done in my life.'
Something that seems so simple to us – going out and catching a few
waves – was made so special by having Barney there and giving him
that opportunity. It was only one or two foot, but it goes down as one
of my most memorable surfs.

People in the 'developed world' get caught up in material
things and feel like they need so much just to be happy. Yet you can
see some kid in a village in Africa who is happy playing soccer with a
plastic bottle or a tin can, and if you gave them a soccer ball it would
be the happiest day of their life. It's a good lesson to try and be happy
with the simple things.

I'd always see those ads for World Vision about sponsoring a
child and think, *That's something I'd like to do*, and finally one day I
got on the internet and did it. Then Mum got a call from World Vision
saying that they'd noticed I was a sponsor and asked if I'd like to get
more involved as a World Vision ambassador. I didn't even have to
think about it. Now, if they have a campaign coming up and want
to try and capture the attention of younger people, they'll ask me
to help out. The last campaign was about stopping child labour and
helping kids who are living on the streets in some of the poorest parts
of the world. It was aimed squarely at the younger generation, and I
was only too happy to help out. If I can get someone to sponsor a child
just by giving an hour or two of my time, how could I not help?

The issue of making a difference became a lot more personal
for me a few years ago in South Africa when I met Primrose. Karissa
and I had only been together a few months when I took her to Jeffreys
Bay, which is one of my favourite places in the world. Mum came too

and we rented a house right on the beach. The maid who worked at the house was a local lady named Primrose. She was pregnant at the time and she would get tired easily, so Mum and Karissa didn't want her to work too hard. They'd make her sit down and fetch her cups of tea, which I don't think she was used to. We started talking and became friends, and we found out she was having trouble affording all the things she needed for her new baby. So Mum went, I'll change that, and bought her a whole lot of stuff, like nappies and clothes. Primrose couldn't believe it and we kept in touch after we left. When she had the baby, Primrose discovered she had AIDS, and the baby had it also. She lost her child at just six months of age. She was completely devastated and doing it really tough. We sent over some money so she could get all the right medical help. When we went back the following year we helped her out a bit more. I said, 'Do whatever you want with it – we just want to see you and your family healthy.' She and her sister used that money to build a little room off the side of their house and start their own hair salon. They could earn a bit more money to buy the medicine Primrose needs, along with better food. They could have done anything with that money, but to see them improve their standard of living by starting their own business – on top of their regular jobs – was really impressive. We've remained great friends and always look forward to seeing each other whenever we go to Jeffreys Bay.

In 2008, Primrose decided that she wanted to study to become an AIDS counsellor and help others who have found themselves in that situation. I feel privileged that I am in a position to help her make that a reality. Now she's qualified and visits others in the township, educating people about AIDS prevention and treatment. She has become like family to us. To go back and see her doing so well, and in good health, brings a tear to my eye. She was a huge inspiration when World Vision rang up and asked me to get involved because, even though I can't help everyone, maybe I can inspire others to help someone.

Primrose and her sister, Timbaland, and their friends all work in the houses where a lot of the surfers stay. When we are competing in the event, they are all out on the balconies watching and cheering and checking the scores. They give us big hugs before we go out and it's amazing to have that support. Primrose is thirty, a couple of years older than me, and we have such different lives, but she feels like family. I hope she can come out to Australia one day to stay with us and visit our world.

I especially love working with kids, and I'd like to think there's something I can do in that area after the tour, whether it's coaching or just giving tips to help other kids fulfil their dreams. If they want to be a pro surfer, I could point them in the right direction and help them avoid some of the pitfalls along the way.

I've always been anti-drugs, and that's another message I would like to promote. I have seen the damage drugs can do at close quarters. When I was growing up, I saw a few of the older guys experimenting, and they were soon bogged down, doing nothing. I'd look at them and think, *Why do you just want to sit around and smoke bongs or go out and do coke?* It's such an unsociable thing, and it really seems to close you off from other people. At least when you sit down and have a beer it's out in the open and people can talk to each other. But people on drugs get all paranoid. They're in the toilets carrying on as if they're in their own cool little club. Or if they're stoned they sit there going, 'Oh, I'm too lazy to do anything.' I don't want to be around that kind of energy. I know people who do it and I wouldn't *not* be their friend because of it, but I don't want to be around them when they're on the gear. People know I'm anti-drugs, so they don't ask me to join in, and that's fine.

When mum worked in a psych unit, she would come home and tell stories about what people do when they've lost it on drugs. I figure you've only got one life, so why waste it? But if people want to do it, that's their choice. There's time when it's been going on all around me, and I've puffed on a joint before, but it doesn't do anything for me. I know guys, when the waves are firing, they're like, 'I've got to have another bong before I paddle out.' That is so lame.

A lot of my attitudes to life have been shaped by the ocean. Every day brings something new, and there's always something to look forward to when you're surfing and around the ocean. The ocean holds a lot of life lessons. It is always changing – no two days of waves are ever exactly the same. It teaches you to accept change and observe the patterns and cycles of nature. There have been times I've felt totally lost in life, and heading back to the ocean and going surfing has always helped me clear my head and regain my bearings. Just diving in the ocean or running your feet through the water really levels you out and calms everything down. The ocean teaches you how to make sense of your own moods and observe and accept the changes in life. You can observe the ocean's flux from moment to moment. I honestly don't know what I would be doing if I hadn't found surfing and the ocean. I don't like to think about it.

It's been a pretty big journey for a kid from Penrith and the son of a couple of ten-pound Poms. I like the idea that it's the world's oceans that link all the countries and continents and people, that there are no borders out in the water. When any kid from any part of the planet paddles into the waves, it begins a journey that could take them anywhere.

PRIMROSE – THE INSPIRATION

It is the second day of the Billabong Pro at Jeffreys Bay, South Africa, and Mick has just been knocked out, courtesy of a remarkable, 10-point ride from his opponent, Michel Bourez from Tahiti. Mick could be bummed. A seventeenth is his worst result for the year and, with the continued dominance of his mate Joel Parkinson, a world title in 2009 is looking increasingly unlikely. But Mick seems philosophical. He surfed an almost perfect heat, collected two high-scoring rides and his 17.17 total (out of a possible 20 points) would have been enough to win almost any other heat during the day. The ocean delivered Bourez a gift from heaven, a perfect barrelling wave that he rode brilliantly – with three separate tube rides – the length of the point. Mick knows the ocean well enough to accept that there wasn't a whole lot he could have done differently. 'I wish I'd made a mistake or something, so I had something to be angry about,' he reflects later, managing a smile.

Mick's local friend Primrose Manyangaza has more immediate concerns. Last night's wind blew a section of roof off her small, one-room home in the nearby black township, known as the Location, letting in the rain and soaking her few belongings. She is heading home after watching Mick's heat to get her brothers to help fix the roof. We ask if we can we help. Primrose says she'll be fine, that she'll stay at her sister's place until it is fixed. 'Can I take a few Red Bulls for the boys?' is all she asks. The fridge is filled with cans of the sweet, red energy drink, courtesy of Mick's sponsorship deal with the company. Primrose stuffs a few cans in her handbag and gets a lift back to the township, and I am left in our rented beachfront mansion at Jeffreys Bay contemplating the duality of life in modern post-apartheid South Africa.

Mick and Primrose have been friends since 2005. If you ask her why, she says, 'This is God's work. Sometimes when you believe in Him good things happen. I just fell in love with [the Fannings] and they fell in love with me. They were trying to look after me, and then we were friends. They were not like the others – they were so nice – and we start to talk and we talk and we go the Location where I stay, in the township, and we go to my house. Then they bought clothes for my baby, but sadly that baby passed away.'

That simple statement hangs heavy in the air, barely hinting at the anguish Primrose went through. The Fannings had kept in touch with Primrose, and when they learnt of her plight, sent funds over to pay for her medical expenses. 'Mick's mum said,

"You know we want to help you however we can. I've been through a lot of things." When I was sick, they were there. They were in Australia, but their hearts were here with me ... And when they come down here they try and do whatever they can to make me happy.'

Primrose's story is not an isolated one. The South African Department of Health estimates that in 2007 twenty-eight per cent of all pregnant women in the country had AIDS. In the same year, the World Health Organisation estimates 350,000 South Africans died from the virus. Health officials have described the AIDS epidemic in South Africa as 'astounding', 'disturbing' and 'alarming.' But there are signs that the spread of the virus may have stabilised or even dropped slightly in recent years due to education and safe-sex practices. Primrose has dedicated herself to this cause by studying nursing and counselling to try and help others.

'I studied last year doing counselling skills and I was helping people in the community, people living with HIV-AIDS,' says Primrose. 'I thought, I must get further training, so I did the nursing course, and Mick and his mum helped me to pay my fees and transport up and down, up and down, to Port Elizabeth and to stay there. I'm not finished yet, I want to do it further, but at the same time I also want to work. There is a clinic that they are opening in the community, and they promise to hire us because I do have skills now. That would be a good job for me.'

Until then, she is working as a volunteer counsellor in her community. 'I can do visiting for voluntary testing. There's this stigma [about testing] so some of the people are afraid. I will go and talk to some of them. They know me, so probably they will come to my house and ask for my help. This year I had two patients die on me. They were getting better but they were drinking and smoking, so I can't help them if they are drinking and smoking. If they drink, they are going to run their immune system down.'

Now, Primrose's own health is good and she is pregnant again, and with the right medical care there is no reason why she can't give birth to a healthy baby. With Mick's help, she can afford the medication that keeps her in good health and prevents her unborn baby from contracting the virus.

'I am fine. Before I was not, but now I am. I have learnt to live my life. Why not? It is not the end of the world. Even now I am pregnant. I didn't plan to be pregnant. I won't say I wanted to have a baby, but sometimes you think, If I'm going to die tomorrow they won't have a picture of me, but if I have a child, that child can live on. I'm on good treatment and everything is fine.'

Having a child has made her more determined to improve her circumstances. 'I have a responsibility to take care of my baby. It's lovely to work for the community and work for free, because these people really need help. Now, it's not like I don't want to help them, but I must also earn money because I have to support my baby. So that's why I want to get this job. I really do. If they don't take, me I will cry – but I won't give up. I will keep on trying.'

Still, there is no avoiding the harsh realities of daily life in the Location – crime, drugs, gang violence. As you head south out of the popular holiday town of Jeffreys Bay, the smart beach houses and holiday apartments, surf shops, restaurants and cafés give way to narrow dusty streets and brightly painted, squat concrete and crude timber homes that form a grid-like pattern throughout the township. A piece of graffiti on a low brick wall reads, 'Thug Life'. And these are the lucky ones. The poorest of the poor live in ramshackle lean-tos cobbled together from scrap timber, corrugated iron and black plastic. Glue-sniffing, among children as young as six or seven, is rampant as it staves off the pangs of hunger and winter cold. Children can be left paralysed or die from the effects of glue-sniffing, yet few understand the risks. The global economic downturn has only worsened the dire poverty of the townships.

'This year here in J-Bay there are no jobs,' Primrose says. 'I can't say only J-Bay, because I think everywhere . . . When there's no work crime goes up, because people are going to steal from your house and sell your things, or you're going to get robbed.'

Primrose's family had yet more hardship to deal with in 2008 when her brother-in-law was killed in a car accident, and his son, Primrose's seven-year-old nephew, Dolla, was injured. 'He died on the scene and Dolla saw everything, so that was difficult, and he was aggressive because he sees his father under the wheel – so he goes up and down,' says Primrose sadly.

Amid this grim environment, the annual surfing contest and the arrival of her friends from Australia is a much-anticipated bright spot. Mick's entire circle of surfing friends dote on Dolla and adore Primrose. Dolla has a problem with his tear ducts as result of the accident, so he looks like he is always weeping, but he visibly lights up when he is around Mick.

'Dolla enjoys being with Mick,' Primrose says, 'and they help us last year, after the accident. That was not easy for me, for my sister, for everyone. But when the boys are here, when I come with Dolla here, he's going to enjoy himself. He didn't want to go to school. After the boys were here, he wanted to go to school again, because Mick gave him a surfboard and also gave me a surfboard, and he was so excited. He's better now. It is exciting when they come. I know they are going to come and pick me up. If they have a chance, they will spoil me. It is nice when they come, and after they leave there's a huge space. But, anyway, it's the way it is, so in life you have to accept. If you accept it's like this, you're going to be fine.'

They all feel the separation, and Karissa says Primrose has had a huge effect on Mick. 'Two years ago when I was here last and we came back and saw Primrose, I remember Mick saying – almost through tears, really – as we were leaving, just how her positive spirit after what she's been through is absolutely amazing and how she is, hands down, his hero.'

Primrose especially misses Mick's mum, who hasn't come to Jeffreys Bay for the last couple of years. Mick and Karissa had hoped to fly Primrose out to Australia for their wedding, but she was unable to get a visa. They all remain hopeful she will come to Australia one day. 'If Liz doesn't come to J-Bay, then I must go because I miss her. I love her. She always phones me and we text each other. She always says, "Primrose, I miss you." She always makes me cry. I can see Mick, but I can't see Liz. Mick is like a brother to me. I don't take him as a professional surfer. I take Mick as person, as a human being, not like he's a professional surfer or whatever, uh-uh.'

Even so, Mick enjoys great local support whenever he competes at J-Bay. 'He has a lot of support – he does – because I have a lot of friends, and they all know Mick loves me, so they all like him. They're like, "Hey, when is your friend surfing?" They say he is my father or my brother. "When is your brother surfing?" He does have a lot of friends around here.'

If karma worked in surfing contests, Mick would have won this event five years running. 'I pray for him in my language. I love to watch Mick. I would love him to win, even if he comes second, but as long as he gets to the final,' says Primrose.

She was disappointed when he was eliminated from the contest but, like Mick, philosophical. She knows she has a far bigger contest on her hands, to strive for good health and a better future for herself and her child.

She is having a girl and she is going to call her Liza, which means 'wave' in her language. 'You know when you are caught in a stormy sea you have to catch a wave. That's why I call her Liza. I'm going to catch her and hold on to her and ride her all the way in,' Primrose tells me.

AFTERWORD – THE LOVE GAME

Mick's changed into his NSW Blues rugby league singlet – always a worrying sign. With his close-cropped blond hair and bare, pale, tattooed arms swinging loosely by his side, you can suddenly see the Irish in him, like some Dublin street fighter with a few Guinnesses under his belt. Trouble written all over him. This is where I get held to my word, I figure, to not try and portray Mick as deeper and more virtuous than he actually is, to give the dreaded Eugene a bit of airtime.

It is the day after the final of the 2009 Billabong Pro at Jeffreys Bay, and Mick has slowly turned a stubborn hangover into a minor, two-day bender. There's been the customary big night out to celebrate Joel Parkinson's win and his runaway world ratings lead. Mick was among the first to congratulate his friend, seeking him out amid the throng in the contest area afterwards and shaking his hand. 'Well done, brother. I'll meet you later for a beer,' Mick tells him, before Parko is whisked away for the official presentation. Joel's win, his third for the season, means that Mick's own hopes for a second world title are looking like more of a long shot by the day.

True to his word, Mick engages in the business of celebrating Parko's victory with perhaps a little too much enthusiasm, requiring that he is carried home later that night by several of his comrades – Bobby Martinez, Bede Durbidge and Chris Prosser.

Today has been a bit of a hazy, lost affair, lazing around watching the Ashes cricket on cable, nursing hangovers and killing time. The ocean's gone flat, and there's almost a sense of melancholy in the air, the buzz and excitement of the event quickly dissipating and not even any waves to replace it. We're the chumps who couldn't change our air tickets and are stuck here while the contest scaffolding, tents and judges' tower are pulled down.

So, a dozen or so bored pro surfers and their significant others have drifted in to Mick's beachfront rental during the course of the day and just, sort of, stayed. Someone goes and buys some beer. Someone else suggests a barbecue, or a *braai* in the local vernacular. A pile of meat is purchased. Soon, it's all on again. Bobby Martinez's wife, Cleo, a hairdresser by trade, gets her hot tongs out and begins alternately transforming those with straight hair into curls, and those with curls to straight. The effect is strangely hilarious. Together with the new hairdos, a few of the boys are comprehensively and theatrically styled by the girls with make-up and extravagant fashion accoutrements. Hawaiian Roy Powers looks like a brooding emo with heavy black mascara and Hitler fringe. Aussie bloodnut Bede Durbidge with straight hair attracts comparisons with everyone from Hawaiian big-wave charger Mark Healy to *Happy Days*' Richie Cunningham to pop artist Andy Warhol. Part-Mexican, Bobby Martinez is dolled up in jewellery and scarves, a beret and skinny jeans, like some Parisian dandy or Bondi metrosexual. His ironic posing is straight from *Zoolander*, or fellow pro surfer and style-master Luke Stedman's book of deliberate vanity, earning him the new nicknames Mexican Steds and Bondi Bob. The normally straight-haired, stocky Hawaiian Kekoa Bacalso, with a head of curls, suddenly metamorphoses into a little old Polynesian lady. It is suggested he could go on the women's pro tour with that do and win the world title. For some unknown reason, the girls all decide to dress in Mick's distinctive yellow-and-black wetsuits. It is turning into a strange evening. The drinks are flowing and witty banter's flying while the meat sizzles, and there's talk of heading into town for karaoke.

You get the impression this crew have become expert at staving off boredom and pangs of homesickness in such circumstances, generating their own cosy, extended family vibe. But Mick, perhaps in response to his own fractured family life, is the master of the art.

'Who wants to play a game?' he asks. *This will be good*, I figure. Animal thumper, the dance of the flaming arseholes perhaps, or one of the myriad other legendary Aussie drinking games, which often seem to result in Mick getting nude and/or wrestling someone. There are nods of agreement.

'It's called the Love Game,' Mick announces like a game show host. 'You have to go around the room and take turns telling every person why you love them. By the end of it, everyone's feeling so good about themselves, you always have the best night.'

There are a few puzzled glances exchanged – this wasn't quite what anyone was expecting – but Mick's on a mission. He works his way around the room, telling each person in turn, in plain, simple terms what he loves about them. It's classic. People are genuinely touched. Despite everyone's surreal appearances, there is suddenly a palpable, heartfelt warmth in the room. Mick loves Karissa because he can make the biggest idiot of himself and she still loves him. He loves Cleo because she is always so happy and positive. He loves Bede because 'he is pretty much the nicest person in the world'. There are lots of touching 'aaaahs' and 'ooooohs'. It is agreed that if each person has a turn we'll be here all night, so in the interests of brevity we are all just going to reciprocate and tell Mick why we love him too and leave it at that. There are lots of mentions of his 'big heart' and his giving nature. When Roy Powers announces boldly, 'I love Mick because no matter what happens, how many contests or world titles he wins, he is still the same person', there is much nodding and babbling of agreement. And with that, this odd assembly traipses off into the night in search of karaoke.

I must be getting old, because two nights on the trot is a bit much for me, and I pull the pin and go to bed. With the house suddenly emptied, I'm left pondering what I've just witnessed. If that was Eugene, he's a whole lot less scary, and more compassionate, than I'd been led to believe.

The next day is Nelson Mandela's ninety-first birthday, the cause for huge national and international celebrations. The Nelson Mandela Foundation requests everyone performs sixty-seven minutes of community service on the day, to mark Mandela's sixty-seven years of political activism. As it happens, Mick has organised to take Primrose; her sister, Timbaland, and Timbaland's son, Dolla, out for their customary dinner that night. Dolla's cousin, Dinga, comes along for the night out, too. Even in 2009 post-apartheid South Africa, Mick has to give some thought to the dinner venue. It's happened before – go to the wrong restaurant and they might be refused service or watch other diners simply stand up and leave. As we enter the smart seafood establishment in Jeffreys Bay's main street I notice a sign in the doorway: 'Right of admission reserved'. I wonder what, exactly, that might mean. The only other black Africans in the place are working in the kitchen. When I go to the bathroom, a pamphlet on the wall promotes guided 'Township Tours', turning Primrose's community into a tourist attraction, almost like one of the surrounding wildlife parks. 'Join local guide Cas on a safe, fun-filled and educational tour of our local community,' it advertises, for 150 rand (about AUD$25).

But I needn't have worried. Our 'mixed' party turns a few heads, but the staff are gracious and attentive. As Dolla and Dinga rip into their soft drinks and the sugar kicks in, like little boys everywhere, they begin to run amok. But the stares of other diners are only charmed and approving. As Mick wrestles them on his knee, encourages them to eat their pizza and fish and chips, chides them about homework and school attendance, few of his fellow diners could be unaware of his identity. The contest here in this bustling holiday town has been big news all week, and as a two-time former winner and 2007 world champion, he is a well-recognised face.

It's only a small thing, taking a few friends out to dinner, on the birthday of a man who spent twenty-eight years in prison before leading his country's rise to representative democracy. But in his own quiet way, it seems to me Mick is doing his little bit to help erase the lingering traces of prejudice here. Surf companies pay him the big bucks, after all, because he influences people, inspires them to want to emulate his deeds, because what he says, does and wears becomes cool and desirable. Most of the time, this means people buying T-shirts or board shorts decorated with his sponsors' logos. If it can also mean striking one small blow for relegating generations of entrenched racism to history, then it's a role Mick seems happy to play – if he's even aware of it.

The next day, we are all packing and there's just time for one more quick trip into the township to say goodbye to Primrose and her family and get a few photos. We pull up outside Dolla's family's small, whitewashed concrete home, and he appears in a flash and climbs into Mick's rental car, as if just waiting to be whisked away to that other parallel universe of plenty. We have to explain that we have just come to say goodbye. Dolla climbs out of the car reluctantly. Mick offers him a legrope to play with as some small consolation. He has already off-loaded a few of his boards, a couple of wetsuits and most of his clothes to a local surfing club in the township.

I wonder if we are just indulging in some self-serving feel-good exercise here. It is all too easy for us to jump on a plane and catch our flights home or, in Mick's case, to California for the US Open of Surfing at Huntington Beach. In a few days, he will be competing for a $100,000 first prize purse, the richest in pro surfing history, in front of tens of thousands of screaming fans in the epicentre of the world surf industry. He'll finish second to local hero

Brett Simpson, and follow it up with three days in Vegas to celebrate a friend's birthday. It is a long way from Tokyo Sexwale Township, named after the former ANC leader Mosima 'Tokyo' Sexwale, who was jailed along with Nelson Mandela on Robben Island for thirteen years. The township only sprung up, almost overnight, in the mid-90s in response to the real estate and building boom, which created jobs for unskilled labourers. Five thousand migrant workers from surrounding districts arrived in the space of a month. The same 'sea change' and beach culture that affords Mick his privileged existence, that feeds the bloated excess of the US Open, also spawned the birth of this township.

A week earlier, before the event started, Mick and the WPS had organised one of their 'Surf With the Pros' days at J-Bay. Of all the places they stage these gatherings, where local kids get to surf alongside their heroes, the one here in South Africa has special significance. Steven Jeggels from the Jeffreys Bay Surf Club arrived with a large contingent of kids from the township. 'They've been at my shop since 7 am,' he reported keenly. Steve and his brother, Paul, were two of the first non-white surfers at Jeffreys Bay. 'We started to surf in the apartheid era. We weren't allowed on certain beaches,' said Steven. 'We had to hide in the bushes because the police would stop you and ask what are you doing in a white area. The local guys supported us, surfers embraced the idea of what we were doing, and it made us more determined to succeed. I'm not talking about becoming pro surfers, but just to surf and experience nature.' Paul is the only black surfboard shaper in South Africa and repairs broken and damaged boards for the local grommets.

'We try and take that experience and positivity and put it back into the kids, try to expose them to what it is to surf, how healthy it is,' Steven said.

Mick spent the entire time helping one young kid out through the surf, pushing him into waves on a battered old board. The kid had cut his hand on a shard of broken fibreglass on the shattered rail of his board while trying to paddle out and was too frightened to try again. Mick spotted his dilemma and patiently coaxed him back into the water, paddling alongside him like an attentive mother duck with her offspring, guiding him out the back and launching him into several successful rides. They came in after an hour with matching broad grins. The photo opportunity of the world champ and the tiny kid from the township in the threadbare wetsuit walking up the beach together proved irresistible and photographers swarmed. The kid looked shy and tongue-tied, shivering from the cold. His name was Stefano Jantjies. 'It was a very good time,' was all he had to say. There was a barbecue underway, and posters being signed and handed out, a gaggle of kids in an eager scrum about the pro surfers, eating sausages and drinking Coke.

'It's very powerful for the kids in the township. We lose a lot of kids to gangs and alcohol. This helps keep the focus on surfing, so this will mean a lot,' said Steven.

In the space of a generation, surfing has gone from the perceived ruination of youth to its salvation. It's a cultural shift Mick has ridden with his life and – from Malin Head to Tokyo Sexwale – the ripples are felt around the world.

EPILOGUE – THE RIGHT THING AT THE RIGHT TIME

When the first edition of this book went to press, Mick had just scored a seventeenth at Jeffreys Bay, his worst result for the season, and was sitting in seventh position on the world ratings. Meanwhile, his boyhood Cooly Kid mate Joel Parkinson had just racked up his third win from five events and held a whopping 1400-point ratings lead from his nearest challenger. The world title race looked done and dusted. I even wrote as much in the afterword. By the time the second edition went to press, Mick had won his first event for the year at Trestles in California, where Joel scored an uncharacteristic seventeenth, dogged by a nagging ankle injury he'd incurred free surfing in Bali. Suddenly, the momentum had shifted.

Over the next few weeks, during the gruelling and decisive European leg of the tour, Mick scored two more event victories, in France and Portugal, and Joel suffered two more seventeenths as he struggled to mend his dodgy ankle while trying to hang on to his rapidly diminishing ratings lead. By Portugal, Joel looked close to 100 per cent and the pair seemed destined for an epic finals clash in the penultimate event of the year before the tour's traditional climax at Pipeline in Hawaii. But Mick's mate Bede Durbidge had other ideas and snatched his semifinal against Parko in the dying minutes, and then succumbed to Mick in the final. By the time the tour headed to Hawaii, Mick held a handy 300-point lead, and Joel had to score at least a third-place finish or better to claim the world title that had looked stitched up just a few months earlier.

The lead-up to the Hawaiian world title showdown was the stuff of a classic sporting fairytale: boyhood friends, now rated one and two in the world, battling it out for the world title at the most famous and dangerous wave on the planet as the entire surfing world watched on. There were whispers of a strained friendship, of mind games in the media and stink eye in the water, while in the public eye at least they maintained cordial, if cool, relations. But those hoping for a bitter grudge match between estranged friends were to be disappointed. In a thrilling finale in perfect six- to eight-foot barrels at Pipe, the pair conducted themselves with the kind of skill and sportsmanship that makes Australian sports fans beam with pride. This is Mick's own blow-by-blow account of an epic sporting rivalry, recorded just day's after he secured the world title, wearied from four days of celebrations and endless rounds of media interviews. Sitting on the porch of the Rip Curl team's palatial beachfront rental right at Backdoor, adjacent to Pipeline, Mick was in a relaxed mood after an early surf and before packing up to escape the madness of the North Shore and the still hovering media pack.

As his co-author, I have to say, I could only look on with profound gratitude and a little awe as he set about mustering one of the greatest rolls and late-season comebacks in pro surfing history. Mick's personal mantra of always endeavouring to do the right thing at the right time has never been better exemplified.

Without further ado then, ladies and gentlemen, your new 2009 – and now two-time – world champion, Mr Mick Fanning.

THE BEGINNING OF A ROLL

I knew I was surfing well in the first half of 2009, despite the lack of results. I still had confidence that I could win events. I was thinking about changing my approach to competition slightly, just to keep things fresh, and after J-Bay it felt like the perfect time to try some new things. So I treated the next event, the US Open at Huntington, a Qualifying Series event, as a chance to experiment with those changes.

I wanted to make my preparation time before heats shorter, because I was finding it wearing maintaining that rigorous pre-heat ritual every time. But mainly I just wanted to have more fun in heats and actually surf the way I wanted to surf in competition. After Huntington, a bunch of us had planned a few days in Vegas to celebrate a friend's birthday, and I was putting more thought into organising the trip than the contest. It wasn't my normal focused, disciplined contest preparation, but during that Huntington event I felt really relaxed. I was talking to people a lot more freely. I just felt more human, almost. But for some reason I could zone in more quickly when it was time to surf a heat. I was excited to surf contests again. There was a great big-crowd atmosphere, and I came second to local hero Brett Simpson, which didn't affect the world-title ratings but did give me boost of confidence going into the second half of the year. It seemed as soon as I implemented those changes I got on a roll.

I had five weeks at home after the US Open, and normally I'd take a few weeks off, but I felt like I'd had my time off in Vegas. I got straight back in the gym and was surfing heaps. I wanted to get the body and mind right for the rest of the year. I was working on a new movie for one of my sponsors, Reef, and we were doing six to eight hours of surfing a day, the most I'd surfed in a long time.

I had a lot of potential distractions in 2009. I was working on this book, shooting the Reef movie, working as a surfer rep in ASP meetings – it was a lot to juggle. But I really enjoy that side of the job. I learnt so much through the year about business and how people react in negotiations. It was cool to work with people on all these different projects. It also stopped me from thinking too much about surfing contests, but I always made sure I put aside plenty of time purely to go surfing.

I went into the next world tour event at Trestles, California, fit and keen to win. But I still thought Joel was going to be unstoppable at that stage – he was surfing great, he already had three wins, and it still felt like he had momentum rolling his way. I knew Joel had injured his ankle surfing in Bali for the new Billabong movie, and he asked me for advice about how to deal with it, I guess because I've had to overcome a few injuries in my time. He rang right before we left for Trestles, and I just said, 'You've got to do what feels right for you. If the body doesn't feel right, maybe you shouldn't do the event. Maybe you should just have an event off. It's amazing how much the body can heal in a week or two.' He was trying to play it down and tell everyone he was fine, but I knew he wasn't fine. He wasn't surfing at his normal level, and he definitely lost a bit of confidence in heats. I didn't want to play on his injury, but at the same time I knew if someone put a good run together there was an opportunity there.

I really wanted to surf well at Trestles. Kelly Slater has won it so many times, and he always steps it up to a new level when the event is there to be won. I had Kelly in the semis and Dane Reynolds in the final; there was a lot of hype about those two potentially meeting in the final, but I just concentrated on myself. My whole strategy was to apply pressure early and see if they could come back. I went on to beat Dane in the final, and Joel copped his first seventeenth of the year – it was clear he was restricted in his surfing. But I still knew Joel could turn it around pretty easily. It was only one result and he was still a long way in front.

It wasn't until I won the next event in France, and Joel suffered another seventeenth, that I thought I was in with a real chance. The waves weren't great through Europe, but I think that's where my preparation and routine help. It's definitely hard sometimes to get yourself up for an event in bad surf, but you've got to accept that that's part of the job. Sometimes you don't get great waves. And that little left we surfed in France, I thought it was fun. That win gave me a slender 40-point lead on unadjusted ratings, but I still felt like I was behind because you discount your two worst results at the end of the year. On adjusted ratings Joel still had the lead.

It's a long leg through the US and Europe. We're away from home for two solid months, and you've got to be able to switch off sometimes. If you're constantly thinking about your next heat, you burn out. We finished France early, so Karrisa and I packed the car and went to a winery. We relaxed, did the winery tour and headed on to Mundaka, Spain, where I was really busy with ASP meetings. There was talk of a so-called 'rebel' or break-away tour being formed, with various surfers being approached to join. I thought it was impor-tant that the surfers stuck together and took a united position. The meetings were intense and I was really busy while we waited for waves for the event to start, but it was good too because it took my mind off surfing and the lack of waves. Everbody else was just bored, sitting in their hotel rooms, waiting for swell. I was so tired from these meetings every day; I slept like a baby. In the end, we listened to all parties involved and tried to present the facts as we understood them to all the surfers. A clear majority wanted to stick with the ASP, and we were able to negotiate some changes to the tour: increased prize money and changes to the structure of the ASP Board so there were more independent board members. I think it was a good result. It was good to see the surfers work together to achieve something positive.

The waves were terrible in Spain and neither Joel nor I got a result, so nothing much changed in the ratings. We were still talking, but we started to give each other a little more space as the world-title tensions grew. He was still trying to recover from his ankle injury and I'd just ask how it was going. We never really talked about surfing contests or the title race. I could feel sympathy for him, because he'd worked so hard to get where he was, but there was no way I was going to back off. I genuinely wanted him to get better and be able to surf freely, but I've dealt with injuries before and no-one ever laid down for me. There are no free tickets when it comes to competition.

As soon as I lost in Spain I headed straight down to Portugal for the next event. I just went, *I'm out of here. I'm going to enjoy my time down there and surf as much as possible*. I was hanging out with local pro Tiago Pieres, and my mates Shagga, Taylor Knox and Kekoa Bacalso – those characters are always going to keep things fun and interesting. I felt like that event was one of my strongest all year. We surfed four different waves in radically different conditions, and you could see people were exhausted from that long leg. I just kept telling myself, *don't worry, there's only a week to go*. Stay focused and do what you have to do at the right time. The second to last day we had huge waves at this radical beachbreak called Supertubes, doing a fair impersonation of Pipeline. That day gave me a lot of confidence going into Hawaii. All my best scores were on lefts, and I was pretty psyched with the challenging conditions. It was wild out there – there were a lot of close outs and the waves people did make were pretty much the only makeable waves. I thought everyone surfed really well that day, and we all took some poundings.

The surf dropped dramatically for the last day, and Joel and I were both through to the semis. Unfortunately, my opponent, Owen Wright, couldn't compete because he'd burst his eardrum and strained his neck in a horrendous wipe-out the day before. He didn't even realise it at the time but he'd also injured his knee. Of course, the conspiracy theorists got online and suggested Owen had laid down for me to help my title campaign, because he's also sponsored by Rip Curl, but nothing could be further from the truth. He was still keen to paddle out, and I was ready to surf against him, but the doctors said he could really do some serious damage if he went back in the surf. He was devastated. He'd had such a huge year, dominating the Junior Series and qualifying for the world tour; I think he almost needed the enforced rest.

I was ready to surf against Joel in the final because he was leading his semi up until the last few minutes. But then he made an uncharacteristic error and let Bede get a wave under his priority. I've never seen him make a mistake like that before; maybe he was thinking too much. So I met Bede in the final and got the win and a little more breathing space in the ratings going into the final event in Hawaii.

The other thing I had going for me through the US and Europe was some drastically shortened equipment. I'd told DH that I wanted a little 5'11" for small waves and asked him to put FCS (detachable fins) on for easier travel. I usually ride a 6'½" with glassed-on fins, so it was a big departure. But it was just as well I ordered that board because we had a lot of small waves to deal with through that leg of the tour.

When we didn't get swell for Trestles, the 5'11" felt like the premier board in my quiver, so the decision was made to ride it unless the waves came up. They never really did and before I knew it the board won me the event plus the $105,000 prize money. From then on the board was called the Money Maker. I took it to Europe and won two more events, adding another $86,300 to its credit – not bad for two months' work. Never in my wildest dreams would I have thought I would be riding a 5'11" board with FCS fins and winning events. It just goes to show, if you have a board you are confident on anything can happen.

I came home from Europe after that long leg away and walked straight into the publicity tour for this book. I knew I had that coming up, and it wasn't a burden, but I did feel like I needed a bit of time at home before Hawaii, just to regroup. The book tour helped me decide to delay going over to Hawaii, and that ended up being a really good decision.

There are three Hawaiian events, known collectively as the Triple Crown, but only the final event at Pipeline counts towards the world title. Still, to win the Triple Crown is a prestigious title in its own right, so I was torn over whether to go over for the first event. As it turned out, the decision was made for me because I forgot to enter the first event at Haleiwa. There's a thirty-day cut-off to enter Qualifying Series events, but because I don't do many of them I forgot all about it. I rang my sponsor Reef, because it was their event, to see if I could get the wildcard, but in the end I didn't feel right about it because I'd be taking someone else's spot. And I simply felt tired, so I had that extra time at home, which really helped. I was going to stay home even longer, but at one stage I felt like I was ready to go. I was monitoring the conditions the whole time and I hadn't missed any surf. Then I saw there was going to be swell, and that's when I jumped on a plane. I was working on my gut feelings rather than what anyone was saying, and I think I made the right decision.

Once I got to Hawaii the tension between Joel and me definitely went up a notch. There were times we were both free surfing and you could feel the tension in the water. It was almost like we were competing right there and then.

But overall I was feeling relaxed in the lead-up to Pipe and enjoying my surfing. I went in the second event of the Triple Crown at Sunset without hardly surfing the break – I was surfing Pipe as much as I could. I wanted that time to get familiar with the reef and the line-up. I had a great event. My quarter and semifinals at Sunset were probably the best surfs I've ever had there, and Joel and I both made the final. He is so good out there – he's won the event twice before – and he went on to win it again. I was happy with my surfing and my third-place finish, but that's when the world title pressure went up another notch. There was a photo of us after that event sitting either side of the world title trophy, and you can see how much we both wanted it. But, of course, only one of us could have it. After that final was the first time I felt like I engaged in any mind games. I commented after Sunset that all the pressure was on Joel. He had to finish at least third at Pipe to win the world title, and the further I went in the event the harder it became for him to win. It was just a way of deflecting some of the pressure away from me and onto him. I'm sure if the roles were reversed he would have said the same thing.

It was tense going into Pipe. We bumped into each other on the beach and in the water a couple of times, because we were staying a few doors away from each other right on the beach-front at Backdoor/Off the Wall. It was always hard to know what to say, so we didn't say much, and that silence seemed to increase the tension.

I feel confident at Pipe. I've made finals there before, so I wasn't stressing. There was a lot of talk about what a factor the local wildcards could be in the draw, because they surf Pipe so well, but I knew man-on-man I could have success. I felt like my preparation coming into Pipe was spot-on.

The nerves really started kicking in two days before the event. I was sitting in my room, stickering up my boards, feeling really anxious. I wanted to give myself a bit of quiet time to process it all. When I'm feeling stressed, I'll go through a process where I'll sit there and these doubts will creep in. I'll start turning them around in my head. *What happens if this happens?* Then I'll think, *well, I can't control that so stop thinking about it.* I went through and systematically diffused all those possible doubts, but that night I was still dreaming about it all. I tossed and turned all night.

The night before my heat I felt like I'd worked through a lot of the nerves, but I still needed a little natural sleeping pill to quiet my mind and get off to sleep. The nerves returned in force the next morning after I went for a free surf because I got absolutely flogged. I rode too short a board and couldn't get any good waves. I thought, *oh no, this isn't good.* I went back to my room and shut the curtains and went through my warm-up routine. Once I'd done that, when I opened the curtains again and saw how good the waves were, I went, *it's on – time to get barrelled.* All the nerves were out of the way and I just went to work. I was in the second heat of the morning, and when I got my first good score I felt like it was all going to be all right. The nerves completely disappeared and I went into contest mode. I won pretty comfortably over local wildcard Torrey Meister, and then the pressure really was on Joel. I could sit back and relax, and he had to surf in the last heat of the round to keep his title hopes alive.

In those pressure situations, having that strict contest routine before a heat is such an asset. Once I start that routine I feel fine. I forget what's going on around me – all the peripheral stuff. I know that it's time for business, and then I go and do it.

I could tell Joel was nervous. I could see it in his face. Other people might not have noticed, but we know each other so well that I could just tell. When Joel's relaxed, the waves seem to come to him, as if by magic, but when he's nervous that magic doesn't seem to be working. Among the top surfers, everyone knows when someone's going to be on. Everyone knows how different people move and different people react – you can see when they have that aura. I just wanted to concentrate on myself, but even when we walked down the beach I could see in his face that he was nervous.

After winning my morning heat, I came back to the house and relaxed. I got a lot of confidence out of that heat. We had some friends over, local surfer Pancho Sullivan and his family, and we simply watched their kids play, laughing along with them, making funny faces at each other. It was perfect because kids don't care what's going on. They just go on feelings, and it was really good to share in that mindset.

Then I went down to the beach with Phil, Karissa and Liz to set up camp and get ready for my next heat. I didn't especially want to watch Joel's heat; I was just down there at the time I normally would be before I had to surf again. But as the draw worked out, Joel was in the water against another local wildcard, Gavin Gillette. I'd drawn another good friend, Dean Morrison, the third Cooly Kid, in my fourth-round heat. Before I went down to the beach for my heat, sitting on the exercise bike, I thought how weird it was. I was imagining how it would be if the world title was decided while Deano was in the water with me, and that thought started ticking around in my head. I told myself not to think like that.

Down on the beach I went through my usual routine while Joel and Gavin battled out in the water. I did my stretches, got my singlet and went down to the water's edge to have my little moment of quiet meditation before I paddled out. While I had my eyes closed all these cameramen swarmed around me, and when I opened my eyes after a few minutes all I could see were all these lenses pointing at me. It was wild.

Then I waded out into the water to get away from all the chaos on the beach and had a little moment to myself, standing in thigh-deep water, watching the waves, nothing but the sound of the ocean in my ears. I felt like that was the last piece in the puzzle, the final stage of pre-heat preparation. My head was clear again, and I was ready to go and do what I had to do. As I was standing there, Joel took off on a wave and fell out of the lip. It was a pretty spectacular wipe-out, but nothing too remarkable at Pipeline, and I started paddling out for my heat.

It's complicated to explain, but at Pipe they use an overlapping heat system, so I was actually in the water while Joel's heat was still going. It was uncanny too, because Joel's opponent, Gavin, is a good friend of mine. And my other good Hawaiian friend, Kekoa Bacalso, was in the heat after me. They were the ones who stayed with me in Australia as grommets and had been there the night I met Karissa. Two of my best and oldest friends, Dean and Joel, just happened to be out in the water with two of my Hawaiian friends. It was all too weird to believe.

As I was paddling out I could hear the crowd starting to roar and knew Gavin must have got a good wave, but I had to duck-dive. When I surfaced I heard the crowd going crazy and saw Gavin doing a cutback, but he didn't even really try to finish it and just fell off his board. I could see how stoked he was and knew that he must have got a good barrel. He only needed a 7 or so to take the lead, and I knew straightaway he'd got the score. They announced his wave score – 9.3 – and suddenly Gavin was in the lead. That meant Joel needed a 6.5 to get back on top with a few minutes left. I knew Joel could do that with his eyes closed, but I also knew if he got knocked out I'd win the world title. I was sitting off to the side, trying to take all this in, and started feeling nervous. I paddled a bit further to stay out of everyone's way. I couldn't even look at Joel or Dean. Then they were counting down the last thirty seconds. A set came and I saw Joel paddling for it. From where I was it definitely looked like a close-out. I couldn't really see it, but Joel fell out of the lip in a carbon copy of the wipe-out I'd witnessed earlier. Kekoa yelled, 'There's no way that's a six.' I thought, *oh my god* and started screaming. It was a wild moment as the reality sunk in that I'd just won the world title. Deano paddled over and hugged me, and then Gavin and Kekoa paddled over as well. Kekoa was in the next heat with Dane Reynolds, but he didn't care. Dane said, 'Have they stopped our heat?' And Kekoa went, 'No, I'm just giving him a hug.'

Then Joel paddled back out from his wipe-out, and that was probably the hardest moment of the whole experience. I didn't want to scream and carry on in his face. He came over to congratulate me, and I thought that was a really brave thing to do. He could have just gone in to deal with the disappointment alone, out of the public eye, but he paddled all the way back to give me a hug. I said, 'Sorry, mate.' He went, 'This fucking ankle.' And we had a laugh to finally break the tension. I still had to surf the end of my heat with Dean, but I didn't even really want to get through. I just wanted to go in and see my wife and friends and celebrate, but you've got to surf your heat. I was going, 'Come on, Deano. Get some scores.' My first wave as world champion was actually a swan dive out of the lip, like those two of Joel's, except I gave a one-finger salute on the way down, going over the falls claiming it. For the rest of the heat I was just having fun getting tubed, and Deano took the win.

By the time we paddled in, Joel had been back to his house to deal with the grief of watching a world title slip by. He reckons he shed a few tears in the shower, but then he was man enough to come back down the beach and wait for me at the water's edge. Two of my best mates, Joel and Deano, carried me up the beach to the podium, and there's no two people I'd rather have do the honours. It was a big thing for Joel to do. I wouldn't have been disappointed if he wasn't there, but I told him later it meant the world to me. He just said, 'Don't worry about it. You'd do the same thing for me.' I was chuffed.

The scene on the beach was bedlam. The media crowded around me for about half an hour. They were all asking questions and sticking cameras and microphones in my face; I could hardly utter a coherent word. I wanted to run away and find Karissa. She thought I'd already gone back to the house, and so she was running back there; but I caught her in the walkway to the beach in front of Pipe. It was that classic, Hawaiian afternoon light, mottled by overhanging branches, and we hugged. She's been so supportive and was the first person I wanted to see. I didn't want to be stuck in that media scrum; I just wanted to give my wife a cuddle.

From there it was back to the house to begin the celebrations. The only trouble was there wasn't one single beer in the place. It just showed how focused I'd been and what a good environment I had working for me. I didn't have a single beer in the whole lead-up to that event, and I didn't have people carrying on around me. So someone went off for a quick beer run and the party got started.

I think the most satisfying thing for me was that I'd learned to win in a new way, just like Mum had predicted, without putting myself and those around me under so much stress. It was definitely a lot more fun than the first world title. I didn't realise how big a toll that title campaign had taken on my loved ones.

We had a big night that first night, and the party carried on, even after Karissa and I went to bed – I was exhausted. In the end, the police came to shut it down and clear the last of the stragglers out. The next night, Karissa had organised a really special celebration at the Turtle Bay Hilton, just north of Sunset Beach, with all my good friends and family. Then Parko won the Triple Crown, which was a pretty good consolation for him because he'd really earnt it, and Taj Burrow won Pipe – there was yet more celebrating to be done.

Stephanie Gilmore had already won the women's world title, so it was a good year for the Aussies.

I have now had time to reflect on what actually happened and how other people perceived the events. And I feel like their perceptions were accurate. I was calm and relaxed, but strong and confident at the same time. I really followed my gut instinct. When I wanted to surf, I surfed. When I wanted to eat, I ate. When I was tired, I rested. One thing that no one probably saw was that I was training hard the whole time, using a program that Jan gave me and one I thought was best for the Hawaiian waves. I also felt fine to be on my own and comfortable with my own thoughts. I wasn't seeking approval or a pump-up from others. It was more the opposite – I would shy away from people who I thought would do that. I spent a lot of time in my room, preparing or reading and relaxing.

After the celebrations died down, I decided to head into Waikiki to get away with Karissa before heading to Whistler for a Christmas of snowboarding. We went with my good friends Shaun Harrington, Jay 'Bottle' and Janey Thompson, and Jenn Kong and her friend Kim. It was a great time to step away from surfing and just be Mick, laughing and enjoying the Christmas spirit. I didn't have to explain myself to anyone or talk surfing. After a week in the snow, it was back to Hawaii for Deano and his beautiful wife Alana's wedding.

Finally, I headed back to Australia, and it was a totally different vibe from 2007. A late-evening flight into Coolangatta meant no one was at the airport and it was very easy to slip into the car and zip home. The first day back was amazing. I surfed D-bah a few times and took my dog to the beach. But the reprieve only lasted one day. I was back on a plane again down to Sydney to see the Penrith Panthers and their coach, Matt Elliott, for their pre-season camp. I addressed the team and explained what was working for me and why. It was nerve-racking for sure, as I am not a great public speaker, but it was great to see how they worked as a team. I stood on the sideline and watched them train all day. I was really impressed by Petro Civoniceva; he was a true leader, but very down-to-earth.

The following day was the media run – up early in the city for the *Today Show* before heading to Red Bull HQ for a full day of interviews. That exhausting day finished, but the job wasn't done yet. I headed back home to spend a few hours at a kids' surfing camp. It was refreshing and the kids were really inquisitive, and on top of that there were some really good surfers. I can't wait to see how they progress.

That evening was my world title party on the 78th floor of the Q1 building for everyone at home. Close friends and family filled the place with good vibes. Karissa once again showed her excellent planning skills in organising it all, even convincing Xavier Rudd to play. I woke up the next day sore from dancing all night.

I am really happy where I am in life right now. The second half of this year happened so fast, I didn't even think I could win the world title and was just using it to build some momentum for next year, so who knows what the next year holds. I do know Parko will be even harder to beat, because now I've got him really fired up. I have already started training with Jan, and I'm really excited about the road ahead. I just want to enjoy my surfing and all the other aspects of my life, and continue to find ways to win while having fun. I'll still do all the work I need to, but I think I've found that balance now. And I feel a lot more comfortable about carrying the title World Champion – I don't feel burnt out by it all.

But you've got to constantly evolve and reinvent yourself, because there is always a new generation of kids coming up, ready to knock you off. The aerials the young guys are doing today are incredible. At the start of the year I'll sit down and look at who's coming on tour and think about how I can keep winning and doing the right things at the right time. You've got to keep up with the times if you want to stay on tour.

The other great thing that happened in the second half of the year is that Primrose had her baby girl and named her Liza, and they are both doing fine. I just got a text message from her the other day, and it will be really special to go back to J-Bay and meet her new daughter.

I think the most important thing I've learnt through the 2009 campaign is to be true to yourself and have fun along the way. If you're having fun, then everything works better. But sometimes it just takes a lot of hard work to figure that out.

ACKNOWLEDGEMENTS

If I tried to thank everyone I need to by name, I would have to write a new book. Career-wise, though, I'd like to thank Rip Curl, Claw Warbrick and Gary Dunne for their belief and guidance in my surfing career; Reef, Red Bull, Dragon and Creatures for long, honest relationships. Even though it has been business, I have made lifelong friends in all of these companies. The Business MAN (ha, ha), Darren Handley, you have been there to support me since we first started. I think of you as a big brother and your friendship will always remain important to me. Wade and Erin Tokoro, thank you for your amazing friendship and support. To all the people who have ever made me a board, thank you for trusting that I could give you honest feedback.

To Occy, you are an amazing human who showed me you can be a champion and still be honest and humane to everyone you meet. I have learned a lot on how to treat people from you. Danny Wills, your professionalism in surfing has inspired me to get where

I am today. From the first day I met you, I respected you, and that respect grows every time we have the opportunity to hang out. You're a great family man with an amazing family! Andy Irons, your drive and determination are qualities I have always respected. You're a great person with a huge heart. Kelly Slater, you are the reason I wanted to win world titles. You have been the Everest that every surfer wants to conquer – huge amounts of respect. To all my Australian tour compatriots and their families – MacDonald, Whitaker, Emerton, Lowe, Campbell, Munro, Durbidge, Paterson and all the rest – thank you for being the down-to-earth Aussies the world has come to know. You are special people who will always remain strongly in my heart.

Huge thanks to my support crew: Phil McNamara, a wise man with a huge heart. Jan Carton, a very patient, understanding person with the most dedication to people I have ever met. Matt Griggs, for putting up with me on tour – many good times, though. Chris Prosser and family: you not only help out with chiro but life lessons, too. Very glad to have met you when I did, and you have such an amazing, beautiful family. And Dr David Wood, for stitching me back together and giving me the chance to resume my career.

To my international surfing family, thanks for your friendship and support. Taylor Knox, you are my favourite surfer and, more importantly, a best friend. Thanks to you and your family. You have helped me out with guidance and good times I will never forget. A wise and true man who follows his heart, with a family full of love. Bobby Martinez, you funny man, I love hanging with you. For some reason we never stop laughing about the dumbest shit that no one gets . . . Yeah, mate! Plus all the families around the world I stay with: the Riou family, the Jose Marie family, the Namotu family and all my Hawaiian friends, who are like family. Pancho Sullivan and family, thanks for guidance and hospitality and the inspiring example you set in Hawaii. Thanks to Primrose, Dolla and Timbaland for your friendship and inspiration.

Dean Morrison and Joel Parkinson, you guys have been huge inspirations to me – and still are. Without you two I wouldn't be where I am today. The rivalries have been great, but to remain such good friends with you guys is the biggest thing in my eyes. Your families are part of mine, too.

To the Campis, you have all been such a huge part of my life. I really appreciate your guidance and love.

To all my friends at home, you guys have kept me grounded throughout my life. You all know who you are – I am lucky I have too many to name. You're all the reason I love coming home.

To Kirra Boardriders Club, thanks for your support and guidance over the years. I am honoured to be part of such a long-standing surfing institution on the Gold Coast.

Tim Baker, thanks for making this project so easy. It has been very enjoyable, and I really respect you as a professional and a friend.

To all my friends who have passed away, I miss you all: Joel Green, Abe Green, Nicholas Holt, Andrew Murphy, Mark Pripic, Malik Joyeux, Peter Whittaker, Denis Callinan, Vaughn Thompson, Greg Hedge and all the others I may have missed. Your memories will last forever.

To Mum, you're an amazing person with a big heart. You have taught me and my friends so much about life, supported us unconditionally and taught me to fight for what I believe in.

Thanks, Dad, for being strong and honest, and teaching me how to be a man. Rachel and Stuart, you are great parents and I hope I can measure up to you when I have a family. Your kids are so funny and delightful.

Peter and Kai, you have taught me so many life lessons, even if you don't know it. Thank you. Your children are beautiful.

Edward, thanks for taking me to the beach as a kid and teaching me about surfing when we were growing up.

Sean, as a kid you taught me so much and you were always there for me, backed me up constantly and always looked out for me. I am forever missing your company, and your memory is with me every day.

To my wife, Karissa, I will treasure your love and compassion forever. Growing with you is an amazing journey – and it has only just begun. I look forward to spending the rest of my life with you, and I enjoy waking up with you every day.

Lastly, thanks to anyone that has made me laugh or made my time on this earth so enjoyable. Never lose sight of your dreams, and follow your heart.

– Mick Fanning

First and foremost, I want to thank Mick, Karissa and Liz, and all their family and friends, for trusting me with their stories. I think they are all wonderful, and the way they have rallied around each other, through good times and bad, is a lesson for us all. Mick was a dream subject and a genuine equal partner in the project, sitting down and writing many sections himself, giving his time generously, editing with a sharp eye for detail and nuance.

Brandon VanOver has, as always, been a sensitive, diligent and supportive editor and, even more, a valued collaborator in the entire process. All this at a time when he was about to become a dad again is a measure of the man. Thanks.

Ted Grambeau, Jon Frank and Matt Kelson have been generous in making their rich archives accessible, and I thank them for their always beautiful work. Alison Urquhart and Jane Burridge are the two coolest chicks in Sydney – their good taste evident in their love of AFL (if not their actual choice of clubs) and their favoured authors, and Jane cooks a killer curry. Thank you, thank you, thank you. I want to also thank Rob Cribb from Xcel wetsuits for hooking me up with a great suit for J-Bay at a very good price – and convincing me that the 3mm would do the job and get more use than a 4mm. Right on both counts. Cathy Robinson from Ucango Travel in Buderim, who specialises in South African travel, got me a great deal on an airfare, and the lovely people at Singapore Airlines did their typically polished and gracious job of transporting me there and back, plus boards, with no excess! Thanks. Also, Salome, Marissa and Winston at the Supertubes Guesthouse took excellent care of us in J-Bay. And an eternal debt of gratitude to Primrose, Timbaland

and Dolla for welcoming us into their world. Special thanks to the other housemates at Khaya Zinza in J-Bay – Bobby, Cleo, Bede and Tarryn – for putting up with my presence while finishing this book. And thanks to Garth and Yvonne Robinson for their hospitality in J-Bay.

And, of course, as always, my deepest gratitude to the lovely Kirst and our amazing children, Vivi and Alex, for keeping the home fires burning. Love you.

It's a bit of a funny old time in the world of media, and books are my place of refuge. The more the so-called 'new' or, as I prefer to think of them, 'infantile' media chase potent 300-word doses of venom – shock, controversy, nastiness – the more I want to head in the opposite direction: long, considered stories that pick us up and carry us along for a while. A love of story has been encoded into our DNA over thousands of years – it's how we learn; it sustains us – and despite some contrary fads, I don't think it's going anywhere. The grand sweep of Mick's family's story, from the life his father led as a child in rural Ireland to the world Mick inhabits today, is as implausible and rich in life lessons as any I've come across. I hope I have done it justice.

I have to admit to a certain initial wariness at even taking on this project, following on as it does from my biographies of surfing champions Rabbit Bartholomew and Mark Occhilupo. When it first came up I commented to my agent, Jane Burridge, that I didn't want to be pigeon-holed as simply a biographer of surf stars. There was an uneasy silence on the other end of the phone as a sudden realisation struck me. 'It's too late, isn't it?' I asked rhetorically. Jane, bless her, murmured soothing agreement as gently as she could. So, if I'm to be pigeon-holed, it must be said it's not an altogether unpleasant pigeon-hole I find myself in, one that can transport me to Hawaii; Fiji; or in this case, Jeffreys Bay, South Africa, in the name of research. Even so, I'd like to consider this the final part in a trilogy of three generations of great Australian and Gold Coast surfers – Rabbit, Occy, Mick – who have each contributed something lasting and unique to our surfing culture. I could not have wished for better or more engaging subjects.

At a time when our oceans and coastlines are in danger on numerous fronts, I also hope this body of work might serve as a reminder that the exquisite waves of the southern Gold Coast have fed and fuelled the rise of all these surfers, and sustained thousands more. And that these surreal, watery, spinning tunnels are a recreational, social and spiritual resource we squander at our peril.

Next for me, the great unfinished surfing novel can wait no longer. You have been warned.

– Tim Baker

ABOUT THE AUTHOR

Tim Baker is the bestselling author of *Bustin' Down the Door*, *High Surf* and *Occy: the Rise and Fall and Rise of Mark Occhilupo*. He also edited the anthology *Waves: Great Stories from the Surf*. He has twice won the Surfing Hall of Fame culture award and has been nominated for the CUB Australian Sports Writing Awards. He is a former editor of *Tracks* and *Surfing Life* magazines, and his work has appeared in *The Sydney Morning Herald*, *The Australian Financial Review*, *Rolling Stone*, *Playboy*, *The Bulletin*, *GQ*, *Inside Sport* and *Alpha*, as well as surfing magazines around the world. He lives in Currumbin, Queensland.

For more information, go to: www.bytimbaker.com

Also by Random House Australia